BY CHRISTOPHER WHITCOMB

Cold Zero: Inside the FBI
Hostage Rescue Team

Black

White

Anonymous Male

Anonymous Male

[A LIFE AMONG SPIES]

Christopher Whitcomb

RANDOM HOUSE
NEW YORK

Random House
An imprint and division of Penguin Random House LLC
1745 Broadway, New York, NY 10019
randomhousebooks.com
penguinrandomhouse.com

The letter from Philip Fracassi is printed with his permission.

Library of Congress Cataloging-in-Publication Data
Names: Whitcomb, Christopher, author.
Title: Anonymous male / by Christopher Whitcomb.
Description: First edition. | New York, NY: Random House, 2025.
Identifiers: LCCN 2025008053 (print) | LCCN 2025008054 (ebook) |
ISBN 9780593597002 (hardcover) | ISBN 9780593597019 (ebook)
Subjects: LCSH: Whitcomb, Christopher | United States. Federal Bureau of
Investigation. Hostage Rescue Team—Officials and employees—Biography. |
Intelligence officers—United States—Biography. | Private security services—
Timor-Leste—History—21st century. | APAC Security (Firm)
Classification: LCC HV7911.W43 A3 2025 (print) | LCC HV7911.W43 (ebook) |
DDC 363.289—dc23/eng/20250502
LC record available at https://lccn.loc.gov/2025008053
LC ebook record available at https://lccn.loc.gov/2025008054

Printed in the United States of America on acid-free paper

2 4 6 8 9 7 5 3 1

BOOK TEAM: Production editor: Robert Siek • Managing editor: Rebecca Berlant •
Production manager: Sandra Sjursen • Copy editor: Jenna Dolan •
Proofreaders: Pam Rehm, Muriel Jorgensen, and Judy Kiviat

FIRST EDITION

Book design by Ralph Fowler

The authorized representative in the EU for product safety and
compliance is Penguin Random House Ireland, Morrison Chambers,
32 Nassau Street, Dublin D02 YH68, Ireland. https://eu-contact.penguin.ie

To my parents, Jon and Linda Whitcomb

Author's Note

Jon Christopher Whitcomb worked as a speechwriter and press secretary for United States representative Silvio O. Conte (R-MA) and as a special agent with the Federal Bureau of Investigation. He has never officially been employed by any other government agency, bureau, office, or entity, either foreign or domestic.

This manuscript has been reviewed by the intelligence community for sensitive sources and methods, edited by the publisher for length and content, and scoured for liability by attorneys. Names of several of the persons discussed in the work have been changed.

What remains is my best attempt at sharing recollections of a life in a world that is complex and often quite difficult to explain. I've done my best. I hope you understand.

Livingston, Montana
September 2024

Anonymous Male

Balochi Province

[NOVEMBER 2001]

The road goes through mountains, a maze of switchbacks and talus that has vexed invaders since the time of Alexander. Today it rolls along crowded with donkey carts and brightly colored buses, scooters weaving among jingle trucks as camels dodge over-stacked lorries. The air is thick with diesel smoke and the smell of overworked clutches. Kids chase moms in rose-blue burkas; old men stand with their hands behind their backs for no apparent reason. The ground is scorched silty, a barren landscape punctuated by old fortresses and the skeletons of cars. There are no shrubs or trees, no grass. It has not rained in years.

"Taliban."

I'm sitting in the back of a Daewoo sedan with a bottle of Johnny Walker from the station in Islamabad and a photographer from GQ magazine. Let's call him Joe. We're racing west against the sun, because it is Ramadan, and the driver is hungry, and this place is dangerous enough when you can see the enemy. At night he is everywhere.

"Taliban."

The driver is a middle-aged man named Rafiullah Orakzai, but we are Americans, so we call him Clark. He is clean-shaven and good-humored, a native Achakzai who speaks passable English and claims to know the road. He says he has a wife and three sons in Spin Bolduc, and he points to photographs taped to the dash, right next to an air freshener that says John Deere. Two separate intelligence services have vouched for him, but he requires almost constant attention. Fixers like Clark are invaluable during times of war, but war is a mercenary trade, and money is always a complication. Clark starts every journey with a price, only to demand more each time we suggest revision—in this case, silence. He loves to chat.

"Bibita, bibita, bibita Taliban."

"No shit," Joe mumbles. "How much longer to Kandahar?"

I hear Clark say something about hours, but time seems skewed because I have contracted some form of dysentery, and fever broils my perceptions. All I know is that we are three days late for a meeting with a Baluchi warlord named Raziq who has agreed to guide us to the fighting. We'd be there by now, but I have spent the past seventy-two hours twitching fetal around the toilet hole in a safe-house floor. The delirium has scrubbed me of short-term recollection, so I do not remember the flight into Quetta, nor the combat landing, nor much of anything else except dill hallucinations and Joe watching soccer on a black-and-white TV. That and lying naked under a blanket, soaked in cold gray water. A concrete floor.

The good news is that Joe has managed to find me a codeine syrup, something called Paregoric, and pills he claims are a local treatment for TB. The bad news is that Joe is starting to look at me with suspicion. He has known me since I was a sniper on the FBI's Hostage Rescue Team, and he wonders if there's more to this story than simply reporting for a magazine. He has not yet asked why I have ten thousand dollars in my boot. He hasn't asked how we were the only Western journalists headed north through Malakand into the Swat Valley to sit with radical clerics recruiting for jihad. He hasn't asked who arranged our fixers or why I take meetings alone at night, hasn't complained about the stern men who rummage through his bags. He hasn't mentioned the trunks full of machine guns or the chance meetings with locals who always seem to know my name. He has not complained about the filth, the days without food, the weeks masquerading in local costume, the nights freezing our asses off on pallets in sheds where villagers keep their wood. But he's starting to wonder.

"No matter what, we're not getting on our knees," Joe has stated on at least two occasions. He is fearless, an excellent photographer.

I roll down my window for some air, and he points his camera at a passing truck. Everyone is racing south, away from the fighting, a piecemeal caravan of bearded men, bandaged heads, splinted limbs. Joe tries to record their faces, but they are a beaten lot, too tired and pained for expression. They chug along, with the healthiest men upright, the dying prone. Their look is common to war and this highway, *ennui.*

"Bibita, bibita, bibita," Clark says. His English falters when he's scared.

Sources tell us the Wesh–Chaman crossing is closed, but that means little here. Pashtun tribesmen have used back roads and mountain trails to defend this ground for millennia, fending off Persians, Macedonians, Greeks, White Huns, Turks, the Mongols. These are a warring people, sinter hard and suited to depravation. They have worked the Great Game as an art form, bankrupting East India merchants, massacring Crusaders, expelling Soviet tanks, and now they are bowed up against George W. Bush, because what makes him any different?

"Taliban."

The N-25 rumbles inchoate with traffic, echoes of arc light to the north. American bombing seems more symbolic than strategic, but anyone who has witnessed an air campaign understands that things have changed. It's not just mullahs talking shit anymore; this affects everyone. Conversations from Kashmir to the sea revolve around the new alliance of northern poppy barons itching for a fight with the strident Mullah Omar. Average people can tell you the CIA are here and what that might mean in terms of dollars and guns. They talk indignantly about al Qaeda and the 1,700-year-old moral code of Pashtunwali, which prohibits all self-respecting locals from denying shelter to a visitor, no matter the cost. They are quick to remind a journalist that bin Laden was a hero to the U.S. Congress during its proxy war with the Soviets in the 1980s, a tiger of the mujahideen. They have never heard of New York.

"Taliban."

"Pay him, Whit," Joe tells me. "Shut him up."

"Bibita, bibita, Taliban."

"That truck says United Nations," I scold our driver. "No Taliban. Don't be a pussy."

I try to give Clark a bunch of rupees, but without warning, he yanks the wheel to his right, somehow avoiding a farm tractor and two trucks overtaking. He downshifts with his left hand; the Daewoo bounces on worthless shocks and skids to a stop in a cloud of dust.

"Must toilet." He nods.

I watch as Clark climbs out of his seat, walks a few steps, hikes up his shalwar kameez, and squats. Seems like a good idea, so I get out, find my own spot, and turn away from traffic. Joe walks to the front of the car and grabs something stuck to one of the wipers. He holds up what appears to be a coaster-size flap of hair.

"Check this out," he tells me. "It's part of his head."

Joe lays the thing on the hood, gauges the light, and snaps a few pics. It's the guy we hit about an hour ago, an old man on a bicycle whom Clark either did not see or did not appreciate getting in our way. There's one law around here: Small yields to large. Penalties can be severe.

"No camera!" Clark objects, squatting over a dark puddle in the dirt.

Then Joe steps back and starts to document our surroundings, clouds drifting over mountains, rocky chasms, life rolling by. He uses a 50 mm lens because he believes in getting close to his subjects, tends to walk right into whatever catches his eye. Traffic swerves past him, but he doesn't care; he's gone local.

I look around, trying to find my bearings. On a clear day, one can look down from the Khojak Pass, across the Sulaiman range to where the Pishin plains meet the horizon. If the wind is right, you can imagine gun battles between tribes of Afghans, indistinguishable in their clothes and their weapons, at least to me. But today is not a clear day, and fever roils through me, a pervasive mirage. Everything is red: the earth, the mood, the sky. My eyes burn with talcum filth, this vestige of the Silk Road to its horizons a sun-faded brochure of despair.

"Taliban."

I look off as far as I can, wondering what time it is in Virginia. Then the light changes, and I imagine this view during other campaigns, perhaps a Spetsnaz trooper stopping for a smoke the last time white men passed on their way to war. The Mongols, the Huns.

"Bush no good!" someone yells from a bus. Apparently, I suck at disguise.

An old Bedford Rocket rattles past us painted psychedelic patterns like the hippie buses I grew up around in New Hampshire. Yellows, blues, greens. It lolls along, top-heavy with cargo, the windows open and full of faces: the dark eyes of children, the scowls of indignant men, all traces of women obscured by dupattas.

I remember the sound of the bumper hitting that old man on the bicycle, his face cracking the windshield, tumbling fabric and the wind stealing his hat, the corpse changing shape as it flew. I can see the bike coming apart in pieces, all glimmer and glint, watching the old man land in the road behind us, the flail and the skid. The first couple of trucks lurched as they gathered him up in their tandems, but everything settled down as he flattened. Roadkill is a rare sight here, where there are no animals, nor bushes to spring from. We must have been doing sixty.

"Please do not worry, of course," Clark had said.

I remember him pulling a CD from the sleeve and popping it into the player. I remember the blare erupting from a three-inch speaker right behind my ear, some bootleg version of Celine Dion's "All by Myself." The song starting and stopping completely out of meter, an effect that might have been potholes, or Mumbai reproduction, or the migraine in my head.

"All by my . . . self. I don't wan . . ."

"Pay him, Whit," Joe says. "Jesus Christ, just pay the guy."

"Taliban."

"Clark, how much to turn this shit off?"

". . . na be . . . all by myself."

"Taliban."

Back and forth, for miles.

"Fucking guy."

But now the piss break is over, and we're back in the car. Back in traffic. Driving north. Joe points his Nikon at a passing Hilux full of men with beards, then at me. I try to ignore him.

"Is dark, soon," Clark warns. The moon rising, a sliver, the long last light of November. "We go faster."

I think about that old man dying in the slow motion of my codeine dreams. About squatting at the side of the road while Joe lay the scalp on the hood of the car. The obtuse angle of that shattered leg. What had been a bicycle. The way the wind took his hat and then his loose-draped clothes, and then all that I could see of his humanity as he disappeared beneath the trucks full of rice. The cold gray water of that ass-wipe hose.

Today is Thanksgiving. My oldest son's birthday.

"Please do not worry, of course."

That's exactly what Clark said as he hit the gas and drove on, pretending nothing had happened. Nothing at all.

My earliest memory is winter. Standing in snow. I am not in school yet, so maybe four years old. I know I'm in a dream. I know the dream is colored by fever, hallucination.

"Whit."

We live at my grandfather's house, my teenage parents, my little sister and me. The house is a gabled Victorian near a cellar hole that had previously been the Maplewood Hotel, one of those grand destination resorts that burned mysteriously following the advent of cars. A town called Bethlehem. There is a movie theater, a promenade lined with boarded-up stores. I remember the summer population of Hasidim parading down Main Street in long black coats, sideburns curled to their shoulders. Tall hats for the men, plain dresses for their wives. A community pool.

"Whit." It's Joe's voice. "Wake up."

I remember life before I got here. Afghanistan. In my dreams, I remember some journey down an old post road, through heart pine forests where I ventured as a child. Those hanging boughs dead still above me, the first breath of morning somewhere off toward a lake. There the moon waning crescent, tilted empty in its path across the sky, tomorrow coming in measures, a foot, a yard, a mile.

I walk speaking plainly at those night creatures gathering around, the imps and sprites and the stew vermin dug into root clusters, slow lurking cats who move among shadows, dark and haughty in the knowledge that they could take you if they wanted. Down that mossy trail, my imagination expecting the Boo Hag or the ghost hounds of Lisbon to pop out of nowhere, what my uncles threatened of the woods that first expedition, their eyes wide open as they stalked along with their lanterns. That eerie laughter, catching me between the ribs when I am not looking, just the small boy and his terrors their primary source of humor.

"Wake up, we're here."

In the dream, my uncle Mike has a camera. Everything is white. The house, the trees, the sky. Everything except him of course; he is tartan, clean-shaven, and kind. I remember the sound of his laugh and how he carried me through the years, always there or coming.

He's standing on skis and holding the reins to a sled. I remember the smell of wool and rubber Pac boots and something special that I later realize is vodka.

"Wake up, man . . ." Joe says. "We're almost to the border."

There is a trellised arch near the summer garden, rimmed with ice, and a jay out of season, chirping some treble cadence to youth. I remember how that felt. The peace I've sought as long as I can remember. My uncle Mike. He calls me Chrisameechie.

It is just turning dark when we pull into Chaman, a Noorzai smuggling center thirty miles from the fighting. Adobe, dun. There are trucks parked everywhere, an old woman in a wheelbarrow, a man washing his feet from a pail.

"We stay here," Clark says. He pulls off the road, into a dirt lot near a cinder block building that has no windows. There is a gas pump nearby, a single light above it.

"Great." Joe shakes his head. He's used to finer accommodation.

"These man have biriyani," Clark exclaims. Muslims consume nothing between sunrise and sunset during Ramadan, not even water. Not even on long, parchment-dry rides from Quetta to Kandahar. "Kadhi pakora . . . bibita, bibita Haleem. First, we have some tea."

I climb out of the car and survey our surroundings. It is just after 7 P.M., and commerce has slowed to accommodate the only meal since suhur. The air feels brisk against my fevered skin, maybe thirty-five degrees. Joe points to a child walking naked along the road, bleeding from his ears, indifferent to traffic, the cold, men with guns. The night feels desolate; high-desert stars are just visible through the smoke of brickmaker fires drifting across the plain. I notice a small horse pulling a travois loaded with oil cans, a line of lorries Clark claims are full of heroin and RPGs.

"You okay?" Joe asks. He can be thoughtful.

I see border guards nearby and Afghans across the wire. A prickle of

12.7 mm Dushkas, PK chain guns, and AKs in every configuration. Men used to war. The hate feels familiar.

"Yut, I'm good."

The front door to the building is one of those spring-loaded saloon things you see in old Westerns. Creaky hinges, a broken louver. It opens into a single room with four tables to the right, a wide space in the middle, two tables catty-corner to the left. The first thing I notice is a group of men huddled around bowls of soup. Every one of them has a gun. Joe and I are dressed in the traditional shalwar kameez, but I am six-foot-four, ofay, wearing glasses with shiny corners. Joe has the Nikon around his neck and a beard, so he looks a bit more plausible, but his last game of dress-up was wearing a Prada suit with Stella McCartney at Madonna's wedding. It's a tough sell.

The room falls silent. I'm soaked with fever.

Clark ignores the men with guns and leads us to what looks like a dais. He rings a bell for service while Joe and I try not to look American. I feel like we're holding our own until I notice a full-size poster of Clint Eastwood on the wall, the one from *Dirty Harry* with the .44 magnum. The poster alone would have been strange in this part of the world, but right next to Clint is an eight-by-ten glossy of Osama bin Laden with an AK carbine looking like he's ready to go. At first, I think it must be the codeine playing tricks, but then Joe looks at me and shakes his head.

"What's that all about?"

Nobody answers the bell, so we walk off to the corner and sit. Everyone staring. AKs on the tables, AKs in laps, AKs leaning against twitching legs. I'm trying not to look sick, but dysentery has its own agenda. I lean into my palms, the steady drip of fever off the tip of my nose forming dark pools of light in the dust on the table, star-shaped markers of our visit. Joe reminds me that we are not getting on our knees, no matter what. I nod.

Just then, one of the Talib at the other side of the room stands up and grabs his AK and a chair. He walks halfway across the room, sets his chair down in the middle of the open floor, and straddles it. He cocks his head toward us in this bizarre exaggeration of eavesdropping. The whole place silent. Everybody staring. Probably just fucking with us.

Joe mumbles something about the guy looking like Cat Stevens on crack, and I laugh because he's right. And because this whole situation is so ridiculous: the *Dirty Harry* poster, the saloon doors, the fact that we're three days late for a meeting with a warlord named Raziq.

"Right?" Joe says. He's laughing, too, that infectious chug.

"You would know." I nod. When not taking pictures in Afghanistan, Joe owns a prominent casting company in Los Angeles, and though he has no experience in situations like this, he is a keen judge of appearance.

After an awkward moment, Cat Stevens on Crack stands up with the AK in one hand and the chair in the other and walks the rest of the way to our table.

"As-salamu alaykum."

"Wa alaykumu s-salam."

He puts his chair down knee-to-knee with Joe and asks, "Who are you?"

Joe thinks a moment, then points at his camera. "Je suis journaliste."

"French?" the guy asks.

Joe might have said "oui," but I couldn't hear because Cat Stevens on Crack started to parlez-vous français like he'd just flown in from Paris, and all the blood shunted into my nut sack. The only thing French about Joe is occasional dinners at La Tour d'Argent and his Rive Gauche hair. We are screwed.

"I will check the car," Clark says. And leaves.

It is important to note that the first rule of trying not to look like you're part of the intelligence community is never telling obvious lies about not being part of the intelligence community. Especially in a cinder block room full of guys with AK-47s, in a war zone. During Ramadan. Joe has unwittingly violated that rule, so I fall back on my training and start to compose an immediate action plan, what we call a five-paragraph order. In a single fever-honed sequence of assessments, I calculate every contingency from weather to the strength of opposing forces. In this case, it all comes down to numbers. There are twelve of them, two of us. It is a four-hour drive back to the safe house in Quetta. We are one hundred meters from war. I have zero guns.

It gets worse. The only people who know we're here will swear they don't. We have no comms, no credentials, no maps, not even a compass. There is no quick reaction force waiting in the wings, no

Hostage Rescue Team brethren staged to fast-rope in from helicopters, no "blood chits" or satellite phones, no numbers with West Virginia area codes we can call for exfil. No defilade, no smoke to pop. Clark stands up and disappears. We are on our own.

Chrisameechie. It's my uncle Mike. I hear his voice like he's standing beside me.

There are two options: I can wait for these assholes to move and wish I hadn't, or I can seize the initiative with speed, surprise, and violence of action. My only chance is to walk over there and get in the middle of that scrum. If I can snatch one weapon, I will have thirty rounds to spin in circles and mow. Every shot they fire is just as likely to kill their own, and best of all, I happen to know that bullets do not ricochet wildly like you see on TV, they follow the walls, meaning Joe might not die immediately as a result of my havoc. Besides, I have spent nearly ten years of my life practicing close-quarter battle, endless live-fire runs in the kill house, flash-bang grenades and explosive breeches, the mechanism of violence apportioned broadly. I am an expert at open-hand combat, ground game, edged weapons, guillotine chokes, carotid stuns. I have worked the common peroneal nerve with pool cues and Jaeger bottles. I fought Golden Gloves in Washington, D.C., grew up on pink bellies and titty twisters, all the way back to when Bucky Corliss kicked the piss out of me in third grade. I like to fight; I'm good at it.

So, I stand up, squint the fever out of my eyes, and start to walk. Straight at them. Nobody moves. Nobody says a word. The whole room is quiet. The air intimate. Charged.

Twenty feet . . .

My soles squeak across the empty floor, sweat dripping off the tip of my nose.

Fifteen . . .

I feel that close, Norah Jones feeling you get at Phase Line Green, stacked up at the last position of cover and concealment before the breech goes and you enter the room screaming.

Ten . . .

As I pass the door, I glance outside, and in the dim light of the gas pump bulb, I see that the Daewoo is gone. Clark is gone with it. For some reason, I pause to consider the gravity of this disappointment, then take the last step forward. My mind is not working properly because of the fever, but I understand my proximity to the AKs and notice that one of them is lying breech up on the table with the flip lock open, stainless bolt gleaming in a rusted receiver. The owner shifts in his seat and places his hand on the pistol grip. He shakes his head, no, then two men walk past me to guard the door.

So much for speed and surprise.

After an indeterminate period, I walk back to our table, where Joe looks up at me and says, "He's gone, isn't he?" The driver.

"Yut."

Joe shows no fear or anger, he just nods.

Cat Stevens on Crack collects his chair and walks back to his buddies. The waiter appears, then disappears. The room seizes taut, that honest moment when you're in a bar and the big guy shooting tequila won't stop hitting on your wife.

Chrisameechie.

I remember that boy in the snow. My uncle Mike and the sled. There is nothing before that, no imprint of other people nor of myself. I do not care that the recollection is just a photograph in a cardboard box at the other end of the world. In moments when fear reaches in to take me, I go to that picture in search of what I used to be. And though maturity has stained my heart darker, I trust that I can summon the wash of recollection, the cadence of a spry winter jay. I am a child in winter. Nothing else. That is who I believe myself to be.

Joe looks up at me from his chair.

"I gotta tell you, Whit," he says. "This spy shit is getting pretty fucking old."

Earth

Corn tall in rows our
Youth planted East to West
Between granite horizons
This reap cribbed for winter
Where myth precedes us
Nature calling march

We sit there gathered as
New souls born whole into lives
Fully formed not of earth
But its licentions

Here the sheaves stiff in seams
Hopes we shared mornings
When the chance to wander
Glowed apparent

Life now shadows drift
Moments strewn talus and moss
Shadow cairn blazes
These days we stop to remember
That seeds become harvest
In ways we suspect but ignore

I

The Farm

[APRIL 1973]

M y introduction to the intelligence community came midway
through seventh grade. I was standing in a kitchen with three
women and a Great Dane named Siegfried, sorting spoons.

It must have been a Sunday, because Uncle Harold was in town and
the aunts were putting together a big family dinner. Sundays were
often an event at the Farm, with jazz on the stereo, drinks on the veranda, wood fires in the common rooms, depending upon the season.
Today was one of those rare days in the middle, where you could sit
outside and tan, then crawl under blankets for novels, the last of the
snow all corn and sparkle, the spring birds returning.

We were a ski family, and the aunts loved Europe, so they would
build views around worsted fabrics and Campari in decanters, light
conversation about bridge, maybe fashion. It was the last weekend
before the lifts closed at Cannon, and my legs felt strong from exer-
tion, the racing season over but always a race between us, my best
friend Eric, his brother Carl, and Grant McEwen. It was just getting
dark when we arrived, the lamps optimistic in every window, pulling
our skis off the roof rack and arguing about which wax to use, moving
off-piste to the bowl at Tuckerman Ravine. The clop of boots, kids
bragging.

"I'll beat you at pool, too," Eric told me.

"My ass." Just learning to swear.

"Me and Grant against you two," Carl announced. He was the

smartest, fastest, the best at everything. He'd been runner-up for ski-meister that year, ahead of us on his way to Dartmouth.

"Loser," Eric said. He liked keeping the upper hand.

We argued like that, moving in through the garage and up the back staircase to avoid adults, but somebody called out that we needed kindling, a chore that usually fell on me. Then down across the south field to the wood line, away from the light. I never understood why people called it "the Farm." We grew nothing. There was a barn, but it was mostly decoration. There was a long gravel driveway with a gatehouse and men in jackets who always carried guns, a tennis court and a pool. Broad lawns surrounded the place, now piebald with winter rye. A gibbous moon blanched silver in the rusted snow. I walked down to the forest in the loll of breezes, south by southwest, their accents somehow brighter. I could stand outside with my eyes closed and name you the season from the croak of trees. The reverb of woodpeckers, shit-talking crows.

Sometimes I would sneak down there in the middle of the night, find myself a swale where I could spin until I was dizzy, look up and name the stars. I wondered what the first peoples had made of all this, their minds prone to myths and incantations. I thought about the tribes of the great river basins, the Ammonoosuc, Pemigewassett, Androscoggin, their ancestral migrations, bark boat portages down the Saco, west to the Connecticut or farther. The trails I had walked in search of them, my youth spent in mountains.

During mud season, I would stand in the black loam, sunk to my ankles under the weight of adolescence. Awakening. I would lean down to root balls, looking for signs of burrowed things, the bobcats just shadows, the first bears hungry, emerging. I did not fear them, the creatures that lived here, the known and the presumed. I was familiar with their noises, the thump of partridge, coydogs on a kill, moose in rut, even at night, when I would walk out for recreation, those hours alone in the woods. I was never lost because on starless nights I could stop to lean against boulders, run my hands across them until I found their lichen, trust what they told me about relative north.

Sometimes I would not walk at all but just stand there with my arms out to my sides, turn my palms open and try to gather what I could of the world, completely aware that I had been born whole into a life fully formed. That my life would follow adventure, that the adventure would scar me, that I could wait until later to trace those scars like breadcrumbs and find my way home, where I would write it all down.

Even then, I had divided the world into quadrants: earth, fire, water, and air. I would flit among them according to understanding, first using maths, because I loved equations, and then the sciences, because my dreams told me that was the best way to deal with being awake. I collected words as foundation, not just their meanings but their alignment, the sonnets then the prose. I kept new discoveries to myself, but would speak freely when no one was listening, sometimes stumbling into combinations that I considered clever. Trial and error. Simple words like *pace,* odd spellings such as *djinn.* I learned about a tool called etymology and used it to trace all pronunciations back to a place called Babel, where there had been a tower, which apparently fell and spilled out the vocabulary of the world.

When I had collected enough meanings, I turned to books and then to libraries, where I would sit with my back to the playground, honing my senses. I learned to taste reading Twain, Thoreau, and Poe, dousing myself in the slow rivers of the South, sixty-acre ponds, the salty terror of opium-infused tears. I would pour their words into figurative glasses and sip in search of palettes, mine limited to what I knew of New Hampshire, the cress-banked streams.

I learned to feel from two women, Edith Wharton, who had confusing things to say about romance, and that poet Emily Dickinson, whom I never got over. I would imagine her face against a window, staring down at an overgrown garden, hand upon her heart. She called herself fortune's whore, trapped in a slant of light—which I did not understand until I read Hemingway and realized that fear of open places is a common affliction, one I would not suffer. That I would go out into the hard parts of the world and break and most likely heal at the broken places. Then I discovered Conrad, who had been to those places and drawn a map.

I learned about smell reading Plutarch and what he had observed one afternoon in a port called Alexandria, the first place where known things of the world had deliberately been collected. How rigorous minds there would search incoming ships for books and how whole societies of scribes would copy everything down until greed took over, and then the books were just stolen. How Socrates lived there and taught what he had gathered to Plato, and then Plato to Aristotle, then fire had come in the shape of war, and I was back to my quadrants, the knowledge of the earth carried upon water, consumed by fire, eventually becoming air. The smell of that conflagration.

I learned these things in libraries closer than Alexandria: the one at school, the one on Main Street, the one at the Farm. And though I loved books, I sought truth in nature. That time of year, I would walk out into the maple groves where we had already tapped the trees and check that they were running, timing my youth to their invigorating drip. I did not mind the snow falling over the tops of my boots, the cold leaking down between my toes, the wool of my jacket half buttoned, my heart beating joy. I would stop there thinking about the boiled syrup; the snort of horses; how we would sink eggs in colanders and wait for the shells to crack open, the whites turning a special brown, and then nod after they were in us; the quench of melted snow.

Some nights we would go out just to build campfires, then tell stories around them, bugbears in the flames with the night behind us, a curtain we misunderstood. We told stories about Old Nick and his crew, soul snatchers practiced in alchemy and guile. Or we would sit in the hunting cabin, cold creeping up through the floorboards, down from the eaves, thinking about travelers sleeping with the night beasts holding council. That man Three Fingered Willy come in speaking Latin, changing faces at whim, a syllogist explaining species of snake, the husbandry of wolves.

And music. I had one album, which was Led Zeppelin, but there was a player piano in the main house and broad collections of recordings: John Coltrane, mixed with what were supposed to be the extant performances of Jascha Heifetz playing Mahler. The town held concerts Wednesday nights in the summer, on the lawn by the grange. I would lie in those grasses, moving to harmonies I conjured in my mind, the beat all wrong but my own, and because no one had shown me anything finer, I believed them to be brilliant. I was unfamiliar with symphony, but in love with strings. My aunt Sheila had shown me the fundamentals.

"Move your hand up when the music goes higher," she told me, sitting on the couch with her guitar. "If the song goes lower, you move your hand down."

Then the Borealis washing across the sky, rolling like barn swallows but vast, no single hue. I remember the first time I saw them, the

Northern Lights, understanding, even then, what it meant to be human. Those limitations. I would stare up into that distance and shiver, the ethereal wash rising spectral out of the coldest nights. I liked to find a spot free of people, just me and those sprites dancing gavottes, the named constellations most vivid when there was no moon to crowd them. I imagined the souls of minstrels stretched across the heavens; their joy apparent. I imagined what it must be like for them, the sky an inversion. Those timeless rhythms I had read about in volumes, all the impressions of thinkers and feelers and accidental minds.

At some point, the bell rang for dinner, and I remembered that I had walked out for kindling. I felt the air thick and dark around me, realized that I could not always be so distracted, because it was my job to build the fire. Back to the kitchen and those spoons.

"Where's Bullet?" Uncle Harold asked.

He came up behind me, from the front of the house. Though I had not heard him approaching, the entrance did not startle me. Uncle Harold always appeared like that, quiet at first and then the center of attention, an announcement in the form of a question. I was used to it.

"Who?" Aunt June asked.

"Bullet."

I assumed Uncle Harold had been upstairs in his office, where he spent most of his time, sitting behind that big desk with what he thought were secret compartments, pouring over cases of documents and folders, certain things we were not supposed to see. He was wearing a fawn-colored sweater and John Dean glasses with opaque frames. The warm light of the room pooled around him, as did everything else in life, the benign smile a watercolor artist had captured for his portrait on the cover of *Time* magazine.

Uncle Harold spent a good deal of time at the Farm, though he lived other places, coming and going at odd hours, traveling in limousines with a briefcase for luggage and a contingent of lurkers, because people were trying to kill him. His full name was Harold Sydney Geneen, and throughout the 1970s he was the highest-paid executive in the world. In 1971, he made $766,000 base pay as CEO and chairman

of International Telephone and Telegraph, the world's first multinational conglomerate. Minimum wage was eighty cents.

I knew some things about Uncle Harold, but from a distance, the way extended families keep in touch through rumor. I knew that his companies produced everything an average person would need in life: hotel rooms with Sheraton, car rentals from Avis, radios built by Schaub Lorenz. He equipped eighteen-wheelers with shock absorbers by KONI, kept North America connected to Europe with undersea cables. He owned Continental Baking, which made the Wonder Bread for our lunches, the Twinkies we saved for dessert. He had his own private planes, a house next to President Nixon in Key Biscayne, two places on the Cape, a spectacular home in Manhattan. ITT had an entire building on Madison Avenue, offices in San Francisco and Chicago, a European headquarters in Belgium. A fishing camp in Maine.

But it was what I learned later that shocked me. Just prior to Aunt Lillian's spoon-sorting tutorial, I had been crumpling old newspapers to start the cocktail hour fire. We kept a starter box in the garage between some fold-up bikes and an AMC Gremlin in which I learned to drive. Someone had gathered a pile of press clippings and, for whatever reason, discarded the entire collation. I noticed the names first, then the photos. *The New York Times,* page one, above the fold:

C.I.A.-I.T.T. PLANS ON CHILE REPORTED.

Some reporter named Jack Anderson was writing about Uncle Harold in less-than-flattering terms. Anderson called him "blunt" and "ruthless." He quoted a former employee as saying, "I remember one time I got an order from Geneen that said, 'Get rid of two bodies one male and one female. Those were his exact words.'"

The same article revealed that ITT had been investigated by everyone from the Justice Department, to the Securities and Exchange Commission and Federal Trade Commission, to the American Institute of Certified Public Accountants—as if there were such a thing. It said the Senate Judiciary Committee was looking into a contribution Uncle Harold had made to the Republican National Committee to secure an antitrust settlement for a $1.5 billion acquisition of Hartford Fire Insurance Company. It reported that he often traveled with a dozen briefcases, that he sacrificed his personal life for work, which had led to an early divorce before a second marriage to his onetime Bell and Howell secretary, Aunt June.

I knelt there on the hearth, staring at the black-and-white photograph of the man in the kitchen. And I decided it was a good likeness because Uncle Harold seemed monochrome throughout those years, a brilliant and inspiring man born with gifts that did not include warmth. He looked distinguished and knowing in a timeless sort of way, with the kind of face that looks good on coins and stamps. I sometimes thought of him only in profile, the same in any light.

PLOT AGAINST ALLENDE BY I.T.T. AND C.I.A.

The next article alleged that a top official of the CIA had worked with Uncle Harold to prevent the election of Salvador Allende Gossens, a Marxist, as president of Chile. It claimed that ITT had offered $1 million in cash to help the CIA "foment violence that might bring about a military takeover of the country, to use American government agencies to supply anti-Allende propaganda to other Latin American countries, or some combination of these things."

Foment violence. Military takeover. Propaganda. Uncle Harold?

I kept looking over my shoulder, nervous that I had stumbled into family secrets, the way one might discover a diary in a trunk in the attic. It is important to note that in 1973, my parents' house had a television with rabbit ears that received one channel, WCAX in Portland, Maine. *The Caledonian Record* covered high school sports, chimney fires, and obituaries. Now all this stuff about Uncle Harold and the CIA in *The New York Times*. It dripped with intrigue, lured my mind outside the tiny village of Franconia, New Hampshire, to a larger world.

I.T.T. SAID TO SEEK CHILE COUP IN '70.

I read about a cache of secret documents and leaked memoranda from ITT board member John A. McCone, a former director of the CIA. I knew Mr. McCone as a tall, elegant gentleman with an unusually large head. He sometimes came up on weekends. We called him Jack.

C.I.A. AIDE SAYS HE GAVE ANTI-ALLENDE PLAN TO I.T.T.

This article reported that the CIA's director of the Latin American Division of Clandestine Services had worked with Uncle Harold to "plunge the Chilean economy into chaos and thus bring about a military uprising that would keep Allende out of power." It stated, as fact, accusations that ITT and the CIA had jointly staged "a military coup to head off Allende's election."

The White House denied it. The company offered no comment.

I did not know anything about Chile or Salvador Allende, but this explained a lot about Uncle Harold, all those closets full of strange-looking guns and clothes that had never been worn. Hidden compartments in unlikely places; the black case we found behind a closet, full of bugging devices and phone tapping equipment and tiny cameras. Quiet visitors. The times we were sent out to play and the other times we were told to stay inside.

I remember feeling paranoia, kneeling there at the fireplace, and I remember thinking paranoia might not be unreasonable. I was a thirteen-year-old boy growing up in the Cold War, used to duck-and-cover drills during recess and a nuclear fallout shelter beneath the library. I read spy novels, watched James Bond movies, loved a TV show called *The Prisoner,* where a man known as Number Six tried to escape a mysterious coastal village, only to be swallowed by a giant translucent bubble called Rover. Hallucinogenic drugs, identity theft, mind control, dream manipulation. I'd had the Agent Zero spy toys, both the Radio Rifle and the Snap-Shot Cap Gun pistol. At Christmas, I'd asked for decoder rings and Sixfinger, a lifelike prosthesis that shot fragmentation bombs and produced coded versions of SOS. All plastic, but cool.

Suddenly, all the fictions I had imagined became real. I understood, with alarming clarity, that there was a world out there that extended far beyond trees and birds. That the Farm was more than a place to grow up reading books about music and constellations. That I had been born into a life where the line between imaginary and real was less defined than I had thought.

"Work from the outside in," Aunt Lillian coached me. The spoons. "Small to large."

The kitchen at the Farm was a lively space, warm and vigorous, with Benny Goodman just loud enough to move your feet, light turning reflective in the windows. I was standing at the butcher block isle with a pile of sterling flatware, practicing what Lillian had shown me about how wealthy people dine. Lillian, the second of four sisters, wore a gingham apron as she checked the asparagus. The family kept no indoor staff at the Farm, so she saw to meals.

"I wish we could just spring forward," Aunt June announced. She stood at the back window, looking out through the orchard toward the tennis court, which hadn't been swept since Halloween. "This is not our favorite time of year, is it? Can't we move the clocks?"

She had dressed for dinner as she always did, the scent of Youth Dew and Chanel bouclé rich in the air, my favorite concoction. Diamonds here and there, kitten heels. Her skin had the texture of tightly woven silk, and her eyes glowed not from color but with the intellect behind them. She spoke with an accent that I cannot place, even to this day, something more about bearing than location.

"I think we'll try something new this time," June said. She had been wondering aloud among the sisters about a trip to Brussels, where they might stay.

"Ritz Carlton," Uncle Harold told her.

He spoke with no inference or context, as if he were commenting on the weather, the price of hay. He had a round, friendly face and a Bournemouth smile that gathered spittle in the corners when he talked, which was almost all the time.

"We just love the Ritz, don't we?" Lillian said. She spritzed conversations with a steady stream of yeses and nos, depending on the prevailing mood. *We* this, *we* that. She was brilliant at offering no opinion at all, in the most self-assured way. The spinster. "Of course, we do."

Lois, the youngest, wore espadrilles with white culottes and two strands of pearls. She was more beautiful than any of the girls in my seventh-grade class, but taller and older, maybe forty-two. I remember her aura as iridescent, standing there against the sink while her sister tied string around some large cut of beef. Lois had always been the playful one, perfectly put together in childlike ways. Colorful and funny. Duende. Even her son, John Ross, seemed indifferent to her age and relation. He called her Lo when he came up from the Cape in his Alpha Romeo wearing loafers with no socks and salmon-colored chinos.

"Oh, Lo," he would say, "you are such a hoot."

Then Aunt June stepped away from the window to join us. "Hal, why is it always the Ritz? Could we please get this dog out of the kitchen?"

"Because it's the Ritz!" He reached over to the cheese and meat board for a tomato. "Anybody seen Bullet?"

"Hal, please," June scolded. "Who is Bullet?"

"Bullet!" he groused, as if it were apparent. "Jerry!"

"Oh, stop."

"You know that's what the boys call him. I like it. Bullet."

Most of the family referred to Uncle Harold's bodyguard as Jerry, or in salutations as Mr. Sabatino. But thirteen-year-old boys are fond of nicknames, and it didn't take long for us to pick one for the large, quiet stranger who refused to show us his gun. Eric was the first to come up with the honorific, because of the bald head that rose out of the man's shoulders like a copper-jacketed slug, and because "Odd Job" had been taken. "Angelo Sabatino" sounded like some scripted name we'd heard on television; a mobster whom Efrem Zimbalist, Jr., busted Sunday night on *The F.B.I.,* or one of those Sicilians lurking in the shadows around Don Corleone. Eric was good with names.

Bullet seemed an understated yet larger-than-life character to me at that time. I lived two hours from anywhere, in a mountain village of three hundred people, so it was easy to imagine faraway worlds where Jerry Sabatino had been a Mafia hit man, one of those soft-spoken killers Uncle Harold might have met in an alley to offer a bagful of cash to keep us all safe. It was just as easy to later accept all indications that he had come not from the Mafia, but from the CIA.

"Yes, Mr. Geneen," Bullet said. He appeared from around the corner, his specialty.

"Do you know the boys call you Bullet?"

"Yes, sir."

"I like it."

"Yes, Mr. Geneen."

"Would somebody be a dear and fix us a cocktail?" Lois asked. She looked at me and smiled as if I might be the first to agree. I felt her words low in my stomach. She thrilled me.

"Cocktail?" Lillian chirped. Always the fluffer. "We'd love a cocktail, wouldn't we?"

"Kid," Bullet said, cocking his head. He called all of us kid. "Enough with the spoons."

I followed him out of the kitchen, down the hall toward the family room, a long, cheerful space with floor-to-ceiling windows. A massive fieldstone fireplace towered over leather couches at one end, and there were several hundred volumes of fiction and biographies on gloss-white shelves. He took me behind the bar and pointed to the bitters.

"Rob Roy?" I asked.

"Yep."

"Can I see your gun?"

"Hand me the vermouth."

I fumbled around for a bit and then asked, "Are you in the CIA?"

Bullet stopped pouring whiskey. He did not move for a moment, but then tapped some pepper into the mix and poured everything over ice in highball glasses.

"That's what I hear."

"From who?"

"Everyone."

"You mean Eric." There was a jar full of plastic swords for garnish, so I handed him one, and he stabbed a cherry. Those big, hairy fingers. "You've been watching too much television."

The Farm was all about secrets. To visitors, this place was a broad and beautiful estate carved off a Landaff, New Hampshire, hilltop. Aunt June called it the Clear Day Farm because on a clear day you could see forever, just like the song. But to a bunch of kids playing army, the place was a fortress with strategically placed lighting, a shooting range, clear fields of fire.

It would be difficult to overstate the impact of that experience on the remainder of my life. Those claims and revelations. At that age, I teetered somewhere between childhood and not being a child anymore, impressionable, already a romantic. And now, suddenly, my life had turned from skiing to foreign governments, newspaper exposés, houseguests from the CIA.

It felt almost sexual, the intimacy of those discoveries, the smells of Youth Dew and Chanel, Lois in pearls by the sink. I thought about Bullet and his henchmen while rubbing the ink of *The New York Times* between my fingers, conjuring schemes. I could barely stand the excitement rising in ways most boys might associate with the mysteries in a girl's pants or sneaking away for that first cigarette.

I remember tossing those articles into the fireplace and arranging the logs and striking a match. The flames aflicker and then hissing and popping, the bigger logs catching and, before long, nothing to prove that it had ever happened at all. Just smoke up the chimney of a house in New Hampshire. I felt like Plutarch standing witness to the loss of Alexandria.

"Come on, Bullet . . . I won't tell anybody, I promise." Back in the moment, fixing Rob Roys in the bar before dinner. "Tell me about the CIA."

Bullet nodded his head and then shook it, those mansard shoulders moving in concert to that lack of neck. I could see the checked-wood grip of the revolver under his arm, one hand reaching for a glass, the other waving me toward the kitchen, back to those spoons.

Bullet was a professional, but this seemed to rattle him. "Take these out to your aunts," he said.

I did as I was told.

2

Capitol Hill

[FEBRUARY 1986]

I was born on a Thursday in Littleton, New Hampshire, to seventeen-year-old sweethearts, nine months after the junior prom. Many polite conversations would not start with details so personal, but the FBI wanted to know, so I might as well tell you, too. I had been fighting out of Finley's Boxing Gym off Maryland Avenue when the Bureau came calling. To be fair, I had been getting my ass kicked at Finley's Boxing Gym when the FBI came calling, but I was stubborn, and I liked to fight, so every night after work, I would climb into my Jeep and drive Ninth northeast to H, because it was too dangerous to walk.

I'd pull up in front of a body shop called 10th Street Auto Repair and park with my windows rolled down so nobody would break them. Then I'd grab my sparring gear and walk the unlit alley to a beat-up door in back. There was no sign or number, but you could tell you were in the right place by the long, narrow staircase leading up to sounds of men at work. I clearly remember the first time I climbed those stairs, walls papered with fight promotions, the overwhelming smells of Jheri curl, moldy carpet, lacquer solvent from the newly painted cars.

The music was loud and limited to Chuck Brown or Trouble Funk. There was a hand-lettered sign that read, "Through This Door the World Greatest Fighter Will Walk Some Day. Will It Be You?" Right above that, "Watch Your Head."

Mr. Finley and his wife, Mercedes, ran the place. Owned it. He had grown up a sharecropper's son in North Carolina, but even on first impression, he seemed as refined as any congressmen I worked with as a twenty-six-year-old speechwriter on Capitol Hill. He spoke confidently in a low, measured voice that conveyed respect whether you were famous or a felon out on parole. In the years I fought there, we had stabbings, disputes over rankings, gang squabbles, violent girlfriends, robberies, and a gun drawn over delinquent dues, but Mr. Finley handled it all with a mere nod of his head. I never saw any thug stand him down.

Mr. Finley and his wife lived in Prince George's County, but they kept an apartment at the gym, with a kitchen open to the speed bags. He stayed there many nights to read biographies or to cook dinner for guys who would otherwise have gone hungry. There was a television in one corner, and every Thursday, all training would cease so we could watch *The Cosby Show.* No talking allowed. Sugar Ray Leonard started his career there. Maurice Blocker. Olympians and world champions in seven weight classes. Miles Davis showed up to work out when he was in town. Larry Holmes, George Foreman, Ken Norton. Hollywood filmed a CIA thriller at the gym, called *Scorpio,* and *Along Came a Spider,* with Morgan Freeman. But mostly it was kids trying to stay out of jail and punch-drunk nobodies, like me.

"You are welcome to stay," Mr. Finley would tell unruly boxers, pointing to one of his gentleman's rules-of-behavior signs. "Loud and vulgar language must go."

But in the end, gyms are violent places built for violent expression, and despite Mr. Finley's admonishments, the room above 10th Street Auto Repair was an old-school dungeon in one of the city's toughest neighborhoods. At the risk of overstatement, I'll quote a *Washington Post* article that described it well.

"If Beelzebub wanted a coffee break from the nether regions," Thomas Boswell wrote, "he would look perfect leaning against the door to Finley's gym, puffing on a sinner."

I felt like that sinner for a month or two, before one of the trainers finally offered to bring me up in trade for a new pair of focus mitts. His name was Mr. Henry and though he had no teeth, he always wore a tie. He called me a rangy fighter because I was tall and skinny and said I reminded him of Pernell Whitaker, a comparison never otherwise explained. Mr. Henry spent a month working on my jab, walking me in on the full-length mirror and then walking me back out again. Day after day.

"Step into it," he'd bark, gumming the words, spitting on the floor. "Don't be shufflin'."

He taught me to measure distance with my feet, to tuck my chin behind my shoulder, defending against the counter-right. We worked on no other punches, whatsoever, just the jab, with all the other guys wrapping up and watching. Pulling on their gloves.

"Everything off the jab," he'd tell me. "Turn it over, now, turn that bitch over!"

We would get started at about six o'clock, stretching and breaking out the sweat. Then somebody would turn up the music, and Mr. Finley would yell "work," and they'd lean into heavy bags, that rhythmic thump. About an hour later, they'd line up for sparring. Finley's worked round-robin, where everybody would go against each other, the lighter guys showing you speed and the big guys making you handle their weight. I would stand there shadowboxing, watching them watching me. The mirror had a crack where it had been broken during a misunderstanding, but Mr. Finley was a frugal man, so we pretended the crack was a rope line that we would duck under, practicing defense. It distorted the gym around me, like a carnival mirror, all those faces trying to figure out what the hell I was doing so far from where I'd come. I saw them in reflection, chewing their mouthguards, rolling their heads. Everybody wanting to be the guy.

"When's last time you get yo ass beat?" one of them finally asked, about six weeks in.

They called him Big Bob because he was big, and his name might have been "Bob."

"What?"

I'd heard the question, but it stumped me, because I was getting out of the shower when he threw it. The locker room was more like a closet, just big enough for three or four guys at a time. You had to walk through the ring to get to it. There was a door broken off its hinges and a toilet and a little bench where you could drop your towel. The shower was one of those cheap preformed things you can install with glue. It had jury-rigged pipes and no hot water, but there was no air-conditioning, either, so nobody complained.

"You ain't, huh? Ever' swingin' dick in this place fight his way to school, his whole life. Fight his way home, fight his ol' man got there, he had one."

I was going to tell him about Bucky Corliss and how that little prick kicked the crap out of me in third grade, how I took it every day out there under the swing set where Junior Roy had gone over the bars and broken his arm. I thought about how my uncle Mike had come back from the National Guard and taught me a bunch of things he had learned in basic training, about how I called Bucky out and got my ass kicked just the same. Maybe worse. All those kids laughing.

I was going to tell him about the time Ralph Payette kicked me in a fight during recess, broke my hand. Different school, different playground. Fourth grade. How all those new kids laughed even harder because I cried, so I called them jerks and waved my good hand to warn them off, and then I went to the hospital to get a cast, and on the way home I wrote in the journal I kept about the ways it hurt, and I swore, in writing, that I would never cry again. I thought about telling Big Bob how I'd put things square once I got the cast off, because I hated bullies, how I'd fought in basements during high school, bloodied up at bars. That I knew I had no business being there, but that youth had left me with wounds, and those wounds had not healed, and I was willing to take any beating just because. I wanted to tell him about humiliation, but I didn't.

Big Bob said, "We right?" then he waited until I knew that he knew, and he shouldered past me into the shower. Just two naked guys talking.

A couple of weeks later, without warning, Mr. Henry decided it was time for me to try the ring. I waited in the stack until it was my turn, questioning his judgment. Everybody got two rounds sparring, then back to the end of the line, those same guys watching. I worked my way to the front, looking over at Mr. Henry, who had his arms crossed, nodding.

"Work the jab," he told me. "Everything off the jab. Turn that hand over."

I was getting closer and closer, trying to figure out whom I'd go up against. There were five guys waiting, including a middleweight who wore paratrooper boots because he had no other shoes. He lived on a bench near Stanton Park, and Mr. Henry said he was nine and one in professional bouts, but only fighting chumps. Then a lightweight amateur; then Big Bob, who was stepping over the top rope. I rechecked my math and realized I would not face him.

I bit down on the mouthguard to test it, adjusted my headgear, which was brand-new. Rolled my neck. My shoulders. Jumped up and down trying to stay loose. I noticed that nobody else was doing anything at all, just standing there until it was their turn. Used to it.

"Time," Mr. Finley called out. We didn't have a bell.

Big Bob sparred his first round, and then the line moved forward, and the middleweight with the paratrooper boots started to climb in. I breathed a sigh of relief, because Big Bob was eyeing me, sweating profusely. But then Big Bob spat out his mouthpiece, put the open palm of his glove on the top of the middleweight's head, and pushed the man away.

"Uh-uh," he said. Pointed right at me. "I want da white boy."

Then he knocked me clean the fuck out. And my whole life changed forever.

I did not grow up dreaming about the FBI. No one recruited me. I never gave it a thought. In college, I had been an English major who played guitar in a wine bar called Scandies, while studying Shakespeare in London. I had once spent several hours smoking hash out of an orange with guys from my band, Dr. Neptune and the Rare Orchids, trying to figure out the chord changes to some song by Zappa. I wrote poetry in volumes, had hair to my shoulders, once sold my clothes to buy earrings for a girl named Nancy Spellane. I had been detained by police while running naked across the Dartmouth College green. During high school, I drove to Key West, Florida, in a Ford Pinto just to sneak into a titty bar near the house where Hemingway wrote "The Snows of Kilimanjaro."

None of those things would have looked impressive on a law enforcement application, if such a thought had ever crossed my mind, which it hadn't. In fact, I had wanted to work in theater. The concept of proscenium thrilled me, the soft light of naturalism, the allegory inherent in Kabuki masks, the nuanced differences between surrealism and the theater of the absurd. I loved the autonomy of scripted voices in a roomful of viewers who all had opinions but dared not express them. I embraced a life that could exist in the span of two hours with a beginning and an end and predicable interactions that would often prove didactic. That certainty.

I remember the first play I ever attended, standing on the stairs of Dow Academy waiting for the doors to open to *Li'l Abner.* Dow Academy was the primary academic building for Franconia College, a liberal arts experiment where students taught their own classes, walked barefoot in winter, and where a kid who worked for my dad dropped acid and jumped out a window thinking he could fly. I remember the line of kids in front of me, remember waving at one, named Leon Botstein, a tall, skinny local in a corduroy jacket. At twenty-three years of age, Mr. Botstein had just appeared on *The Tonight Show Starring Johnny Carson* as the youngest college president in history. Everyone in town knew him as a brilliant Swiss-born violinist from Harvard, but I was impressed because he was talking to Andy Statman, mandolin player for a local band called Hokey Boker.

"Hey, man, you get up to the mountain today?" he asked me. He skied with my father.

"Yut, wicked icy."

"Tell your old man I said hi."

"Okay."

Then the doors opened, and I found a seat near the middle. The house lights dimmed, the curtains parted, and I realized there were worlds I had not yet imagined. I celebrated every detail, the tap of bare feet on the stage-black floor, characters singing and dancing through the wash of Rosco gels, the corn pone backdrop all earth-tone gouache. I felt invigorated sitting there among smells of patchouli oil, teepee canvas, and reefer, the room filled with long-haired intellectuals from Greenwich Village and Berkeley and other places I had read about but not yet visited. The clogs and bell-bottom jeans and hairy armpits, one carnival of imagination.

There were other productions: high school plays, one-act competitions, Kyd in Gramercy Park. I saw Beatlemania at the Winter Garden, the original cast of *Amadeus* at the Royal National Theater. I watched *Tamburlaine* at the Globe, *As You Like It* in Oxford. I directed a musical at the Berkshire School in Massachusetts, played Puck in *A Midsummer Night's Dream,* threw up onstage during a community troupe performance of A. R. Gurney's *The Dining Room* with Joan Ackerman Blount. I adapted *The Heart Is a Lonely Hunter* for the Carson McCullers Society, covered Athol Fugard as theater critic for *The North Adams Transcript*. I sat next to Paul Newman while Joanne Woodward crushed Amanda Wingfield at the Adams Memorial Theatre.

You get my point. Prior to February 1986, I had not considered life with a badge and a gun. Not before Big Bob knocked me out.

"You ayaite?"

I remember those words floating hollow through my head as I came around. The voice sounded far away, disinterred, like somebody calling down a tunnel or echoes between mountains in the rain. Then I realized it was Othello, the Moor, kneeling beside me, that he had mistaken me for Iago, before the handkerchief, still a general, yet sympathetic. Everything got quiet before rushing back, words changing pitch and volume, blank verse iambs morphing into the Doppler howl of a train. I didn't know where I was, or why. I felt weight in my chest, confusion at the fact that I was lying on the floor, staring at the business end of a broom.

"Git up. These boys need to be sparring."

Which I did. I jumped right up to my feet and then fell right back down. This time I lay there a minute, thinking maybe I'd just rest, staring at that broom. There was a dustpan, too.

A middleweight named Brian sat me against the ropes.

"What did he hit me with?" I asked.

"'Bout everything."

Mr. Henry walked me off to where we watched *Cosby*, sat me down. The fighters went back to work, because getting knocked out in a boxing gym is less exciting than one might think. I sat there unlacing my gloves and taking off my wraps. I unbuckled my headgear and dropped it into a pile between my feet. I thought about taking off my shoes, but I couldn't remember how, so I stared into that jumble, trying to reconstruct the round, every punch leading up to the one that got me. I remembered the impact of his knuckles, bony through sixteen-ounce gloves, my head snapping back, the liver-deep percussion of body shots. How I'd enjoyed it.

"Throw it, throw it out there!" I could hear Mr. Henry prodding one of his other fighters, acting it out in pantomime. "Work that jab. Turn that bitch over!"

I sat in the folding chair with my head down, reconstructing what I could. In my mind's eye, I watched Big Bob circling away from my right, jab, move, jab, move; breathing through his nose, calm as could be. Then he cocked his hips, sat on his heel, sucked a hitch breath, and let it go. White light, a sudden feeling of sadness, then nothing. A dream.

"Bullet tells me you two had a nice talk." It's Uncle Harold's voice. I know it's a dream, even while I'm in it. "Is that right? A nice little chat?"

We are sitting in the dining room, back at the Farm, eating dinner. Uncle Harold is sitting in his regular seat at the head of the table, Lillian at the other end, so she can get back and forth to the kitchen. Jack is there, Jack McCone, former director of the CIA. Bullet staring me down.

John Ross, ever foppish, is complaining about having to wait a day before driving up from the Cape due to the rationing of gas, and Uncle Harold is launching a diatribe about the energy crisis and how ships were anchored off both coasts for no apparent reason. How it was all a scam and that there was plenty of oil to last a thousand years.

I see everything in color, but there's only one color, and I can't tell which. I'm looking down at myself from someplace higher, though I feel Eric beside me, Lois's knee against my thigh. Carl and Grant are across the table with Stephanie. Stephanie, the older sister, is a sweet girl, gifted with eidetic memory for lyrics, which she mimics off-key but with excellent timing. Prone to night terrors and screaming, she rocks in her chair, curling her fingers, some form of dancing. She calls me Love.

"Did we know that Chrissy and Molière were born the same day?" Aunt June asks.

She had said something about its being my birthday, which was in January, so I knew this was different in time and space from previous conversations. I counted the spoons.

"Isn't that right?" She smiled. "We just love Molière, don't we?"

I have no sense of smell in dreams, but I remember how much I loved her perfume.

"What do you know about the CIA?" Uncle Harold asks me.

Suddenly, we're not at the table anymore. We are in the front parlor, where Uncle Harold keeps the framed photos of Haldeman and Ehrlichman, Bebe Rebozo and Richard Nixon, smiling candids from the

White House, his yacht the *Genie IV* anchored off Florida. I see his portrait on the wall, the framed cover of *Time* magazine dated June 18, 1969, the face of coup d'état. I look at my hands, which are still wrapped from the gym, stained black with newsprint. I feel scared.

Then back in the chair at the gym, awake, trying to shake it off. I couldn't have been out for more than a few seconds, but the dream felt longer. And though this whole series of events proved confusing at first, I had been raised on Hamlet, Chekhov, and Cheever, so I understood the transmedial value of mise en abyme, the play within the play. It is also important to explain that I was born a dreamer, not in a Supertramp kind of way, but in terms of subconscious connection to worlds beyond understanding. As far back as seventh grade, I understood dreams to be a gift I could develop into a conscious will of incredible facility. I learned to lie in bed at night using subconscious will to weave the fabric of my life. Things Coleridge introduced to Freud.

"Everybody gets tagged," Mr. Finley told me, coming around. "Part of the game."

"Yessir, I'll see you tomorrow."

I waved and started to leave, down that long flight of stairs, with my bag hanging limp, my free hand riding the wall. About halfway down, I stopped to read the hand-lettered sign: "Through This Door the World Greatest Fighter Will Walk Some Day. Will It Be You?"

Right above that: "Watch Your Head."

It was after nine when I got home. My wife was sitting on the couch, reading Umberto Eco's *The Name of the Rose,* which I found odd, because that was her name, too. Rose. I kept opening and closing my eyes as if that might help. I felt so dizzy.

"How'd it go?" she asked.

I thought about it for a minute, then sat down beside her. My head was throbbing, and I noticed odd smells, weird interactions of shadows and light. My neck was stiff, and my jaw kept popping, but I couldn't tell if it was from Big Bob hitting me or me hitting the floor.

"Okay, whatchu reading?"

She laughed and held up the cover. "Same thing I was reading when you left. You okay, baby? That's a pretty good shiner you got there."

"Yeah, I'm good."

"Hungry?"

"Nah."

"You got some mail," she told me. Then she pulled out an eight-by-ten manila envelope and placed it in my lap. It took my mind a good second or two to process what I was seeing.

"FBI?" I asked her. The envelope had first-class postage; my first name, Jon; and a return address from the Federal Bureau of Investigation, 1900 Half Street, SW, Washington, D.C. 20024.

"What would the FBI want with me?"

Despite some youthful indiscretions, I had tracked a straight and honest life to that point. We lived on Capitol Hill, in a small but respectable English basement behind the Library of Congress, where I had stacks access, my own card. I wrote speeches and handled all communications as press secretary for U.S. representative Silvio O. Conte (R–MA), the ranking member of the House Appropriations Committee. I had been a magazine journalist in California, an English teacher at a boarding school in Massachusetts, a police beat reporter for several papers. I had worked construction, too, tended bar in L.A., and washed dishes at the Dutch Treat restaurant, résumé builders that don't necessarily connote virtue.

"Open it," she said.

I had never been arrested, never gotten detention in seventeen years of formal education.

"Open it!"

I did, slowly, uncertain about what one might discover in an envelope from the FBI. Inside was a form letter verifying that I met basic criteria for employment as a special agent, federal classification 1811, and an application to start the process.

"Special agent?" I asked, somewhat dumbfounded. "Eighteen-eleven?"

The application started out with questions one might expect, like place of birth, Social Security number, mother's maiden name. It was the FBI, so I figured they would want to know where I had gone to college, where I had worked, places I had been. They wanted financial information, memberships in organizations, documentation of successes and failures, a full accounting of scars, marks, and tattoos. They mentioned associations with sovereign powers and the potential to hold top-secret classification, sensitive compartmented information.

"What the hell?"

I thought back on my life, Uncle Harold's secret compartments full of spy paraphernalia, the *New York Times* stories about the CIA, Jerry Sabatino shaking Rob Roys for Lois while refusing to show me his gun. I thought about watching *The Prisoner* on TV, knowing I could evade that bubble called Rover using my skills as a woodsman, about distinguishing myself as an actor, assuming all sorts of disguise. That I had finished high school in three years, delivered my graduation address with aplomb. That I had written well-received speeches about democracy, ridden down Pennsylvania Avenue with Mr. Conte in his GTO convertible for meetings with the Great Communicator, Ronald Reagan. I had eaten jelly beans from the Oval Office bowl.

"Wow," I said, still loopy. "I wonder how they found me."

But of course they had found me. The FBI had probably been tracking me since birth, monitoring my grades and standardized scores. They knew that I had traveled extensively throughout North America and Europe, surfed the K breaks of Baja all the way to Hussong's Cantina. They knew I had skipped Tower Hill history lectures in London to hang out at the Courtauld, later drinking Fuller's over darts at the Drayton Arms. Maybe it would be okay that I had once used CliffsNotes to write a Lit 315 paper and hitched a ride with a guy smoking Maui Multicolor to hear the Allman Brothers at Saratoga. Perhaps the feds had interviewed Elizabeth Taylor or Teddy Kennedy; or Tip O'Neill, whom I had met with Mr. Conte—credible people who would fondly remember our acquaintance.

"This must be how they recruit people," I decided, my vision getting clearer.

"I don't think so, babe." Rosie laughed. "Remember that commercial we saw on TV a while back? I sent in for the application. They're looking for Spanish speakers."

"I don't speak Spanish," I told her.

"Since when has that ever stopped you?"

She had a point.

3

Chiang Mai, Thailand

[THE NINETIES]

She was drinking twelve-year-old Macallan, neat, from a Solo Cup near the pool. She said her name was Jane, that she hated cats and planned to lay over for a couple of days because she had never been to Thailand. She thought it might be nice to check out Wat Phra Singh, do some sightseeing, balance her chi.

I told her my name was Tom, that I would be flying out the next day, that I didn't like cats, either. I had never heard of Wat Phra Singh, so I asked her about family, where she'd gone to school, life's most embarrassing moments, whether she understood cricket. She smiled once or twice, dodging my attempts at humor, but mostly kept shaking her head. I asked her about politics and religion, then turned to porn names and favorite songs that she had danced to on moonlit beaches in Antigua. Nothing.

"Could you help me out a little bit," I asked her after a while. "I'm dying over here."

"All right." She nodded. "Two Truths and a Lie."

"What?"

"Two Truths and a Lie. The game."

"Never heard of it."

"Jesus, where did you come from?"

She reached under the table and pulled out a couple of those little bottles you get on planes or from the minibar. One was Dewars, and I think the other was Old Grand Dad. I hadn't seen a purse, but she had a fanny pack on the floor. I could hear the zipper.

"Want one?" She poured them into her cup. "I've got plenty."

"No, I'm good." I liked beer, so I waved to the short guy in the flowered shirt.

"You tell me two truths and one lie; I try to figure out which is which. Then vice versa."

"Okay, you go first."

She thought about it while I looked around. It was a brand-name hotel, nothing special. String lights, early evening, luk thung. There were a couple of newlyweds getting handsy near a candle in the corner, the usual cast of business travelers: two nonassociated white males, a Chinese guy reading *The Economist,* three Africans in suits. The Africans were speaking Esperanto and were most likely on some kind of fact-finding junket from the United Nations. I assigned them all identities, judged that none of them was close enough to listen in.

"Let's see," she said. "I know all the words to 'Sara Smile' in Farsi, I keep a vial of anthrax in my desk, and I have a steel plate in my head."

"Wait, Hall and Oates? You don't mess around."

"Your turn."

"All right." Game on. "I have a master's degree in physics; I played college hockey, Division One; and Prince Charles almost ran me over playing polo at Windsor."

"That's two lies and a truth."

"Huh?"

"You don't have a master's in physics, and you might have played hockey, but not D-One."

She was right; I had it backward.

"You're trying too hard," she told me. "Go again."

I looked at her for a long minute, attempting to size her up. The basics were obvious because these gigs always went pretty much the same way. You show up in a civilian car at some FBO, in this case a municipal airport near Manassas, Virginia. I had an old brown Dodge Power Wagon with bench seats and a bumper sticker that read, "Fight Crime: Shoot Back." It had a diamond plate toolbox bolted to the bed with a mount-out bag containing C-4 slap charges, a chopped-down M14, a plate carrier with six magazines, night vision goggles, and a bag full of grenades. My job in those days was to be good at hiding in plain sight, and our compound at Quantico was secure, so I felt the factory lock would be sufficient. Oh, I forgot: I also had duct tape and jumper cables, because you never know.

In those days, nobody had G-550s or the Global Express, so our ride would typically be a Lear or maybe a Falcon with generic paint and a tail number that came back as corporate lease. Heading east, we would stop for gas in Gander, Newfoundland, and then Shannon, and then any number of places depending on the mission.

Packing was easy, because you would show up wearing plain clothes that specifically did not include Royal Robbins cargo pants, Oakley sunglasses, or any kind of vest. I had grown my hair out, and I had a respectable goatee, think Lemmy Kilmister meets Van Dyke.

In my experience, there would usually be seven or eight people on the plane: two air force sergeants; an arrogant, out-of-shape State Department liaison; an arrogant out-of-shape assistant U.S. attorney; a linguist; and two or three shooters, one of them, of course, being me. Oftentimes, I would nod to the other passengers while navigating the cluttered aisle, trying to find a seat that reclined or an open couch, almost always upholstered in leather. We had Walkman devices back then, with plug-in headphones and extra batteries. I carried paperback novels because they fit in my ruck, and I could burn them when I was done, to avoid leaving prints. The only question I ever asked was whether we'd be flying for more than eight hours or less, so I would know whether to drop a whole Ambien or a half.

"Okay," I told her. "Let me think."

"Don't think. It will throw off your timing."

Jane was not out of shape, but not athletic, either. She was left-handed trying to use her right. I guessed her to be forty-three years of age, mostly Slavic, though blond. She had no accent, no unusual mannerisms, and had chosen a truth involving Hall and Oates, so midwestern, a breakaway Catholic. She was neither as arrogant nor as punctilious as most CIA officers, and she had not once mentioned going to Harvard.

"All right . . . I once changed the clutch of my Harley in a parking lot outside Sioux Falls, hiked the Appalachian Trail, and Prince Charles almost ran over me playing polo at Windsor."

She shook her head.

"Still trying too hard?"

"Maybe parts of the trail, not the whole thing."

"Give me one last try," I said.

"You're very competitive."

"I got in a fight at the Louvre, was in a high school band with Stuart Hamm, and all that stuff about Prince Charles at Windsor."

"You clearly want me to ask about Prince Charles."

"Should I try to figure out your lie?" I countered. "Let me take a shot at this."

"Good luck."

"Sing the first line. 'Sara Smile.'"

She did, in a confident voice, loudly enough that the African guys from the United Nations turned around. One of them gave her a thumbs-up, so I guessed she wasn't faking translation.

"Who is Stuart Hamm?" she asked.

"Best bass player in the world."

"What did he hit you with?"

"Who?"

"The guard. The guard at the Louvre."

"How did you know it was a guard?"

"I didn't, but that's three truths. You're not too good with games, huh?"

"Shit. Okay, my turn. How did you get a plate in your head?"

"Skydiving. High-speed failure to open. It's titanium, not steel. I should be specific."

"So, anthrax? What the hell? Why would you have anthrax in your desk?"

She shrugged, took a healthy whack at the Solo Cup.

"You think about it for a sec." She nodded. "I gotta take a leak." She reached down for her fanny pack, then stood up looking a bit wobbly.

"You all right?"

"It's the titanium," she said. "Sometimes it acts weird in the heat. And you know what, you seem like a decent guy for FBI, so I'm going to let you in on a little secret. My real name isn't Jane; it's Constance. You can call me Abby."

She walked away.

. . .

Okay. So, the pool, the minibar bottles, and the three Angolans might or might not have been in Thailand, and if so, not necessarily in Chiang Mai. I could call it an undisclosed location, but that would be both snide and pointless. The conversation is real, and after a lifetime touring the notional world of shelled operations, I honestly believe it all looks the same. A mountain is a mountain, a beach a beach, a passport entry something I have to stare at for a while trying to remember classification. I have had similar conversations over naqe'e al zabib in Yemen, camel milk in Somalia, rat wine in Hanoi, absinthe in Tbilisi.

What mattered most to me during those years was that I stay peripheral to all of it. I wanted to remember no trip by location, no association by name. I did not want to comment on my day to hotel clerks, enter polite conversation in elevators, explain my destinations to taxi drivers, or engage tourists with directions or recommendations or any opinions at all. There were no par avion posts home, no Moleskine introspections I would someday read to my kids, no photographs or vocal recordings.

I did not want to go sightseeing because I did not want to look over my shoulder strolling scrub routes along cobblestone alleys or rely on napkins in defense against hard surfaces where I might leave something to prove I had ever been there, no sidebars with pretty strangers asking directions, no sightseeing introductions on tour buses full of people pointing lenses. No off-campus massages or free drinks in expat bars watching MotoGP or any substance whatsoever that could be served in a hookah. I avoided everything that might spike "inconclusive" on a lifestyle polygraph some random afternoon in Virginia. It was easier staying anonymous.

Imagine a thirty-year road trip where everyone you meet asks the same obvious questions and you always have to take a minute thinking about the answers.

What's your name? Where you from? What do you do for a living?

At first, it's kind of entertaining, because you have a legal alias and a wallet full of pictures of somebody else's kids, a Blockbuster video card, maybe proof of insurance. But then you wake up one morning and you're so jet-lagged you say fuck it and, just for entertainment, you tell the barista your name is "Serge." You lie around your room until the bar opens, then you find a seat in the middle, you order some non-American cocktail involving Pimm's or grappa and fake an accent strangers might find interesting though not distracting. You see how many drinks you can swallow before noticing changes in your own behavior, staring at the guy in the backbar mirror, trying not to bullshit yourself.

When I started, I told people I was from Stringtown, Oklahoma, because I had been there a time or two and I felt confident no one else had. I made up blue-collar occupations because most people want something simple, something they can relate to. I would say I shoed horses, because I loved some years I pretended to be a cowboy, but then one day in Macau, I got sick of being the low man on the totem pole, so I promoted myself to team roping champion of a four-state area. I told them I was a header, that I preferred King ropes, and Ford over Chevy, that I rode saddles made by Reid Flatten in Livingston, Montana. For a while I said I was a bullfighting coach from Laredo, then a fluffer at bar mitzvahs, for quite some time a door gunner on the Space Shuttle. I entertained no one but myself, because most everyone answered with "Oh that's interesting. I sell flooring for Monsanto."

At first, the alias is a plaything, something you might have to stand behind at customs, but disposable in a bar. Sometimes I would wake up on a two-day layover, go down to the concierge, and say I was looking for tickets to the opera. That my name was "Alpaca" or "Monday" and that I was staying in 603, which I was not; that's the area code for New Hampshire. They would nod officiously because they didn't care if my name was "Monday"; they were just lining up tickets. But the days roll into years, and somewhere along the way you forget what you tell people, because you have become anonymous, not just to them but to yourself.

There was a time in my life when I enjoyed the game, those early adventures before there were Krispy Kreme donut shops in the Istanbul airport, no Gap in Nairobi, no heated saltwater infinity pools whatsoever in Mozambique. The counterterrorism community was small and anachronistically secret in those days. And it was a young trade, built on innovative tactics, including close-quarter battle, or CQB, which we ran interchangeably at the only four kill houses in the United States: Delta's complex at Fort Bragg, the SEAL Team Six beach site at Little Creek, the CIA's facility in Williamsburg, ours at Quantico.

We traveled three hundred days a year, practicing surreption during missions and in training. We stayed to ourselves, running jungle hits in Puerto Rico, dive trips to the Caribbean, tea in Gaza, infiltration scenarios in Germany, goat hunts in Argentina. I swam the Dead Sea, traversed mountain ranges, floated the Med, lived spartan with interesting groups from the Šar Mountains to Jordan. I held passports in blue and red but did not need a black one, because we were seldom official, and my skill set required conversations with exactly no one.

Countersurveillance was simple then, something you could figure out reading John le Carré novels. Everything came down to cash and a plausible story that had been backstopped by a roomful of clerks on the fifth floor of headquarters. But that was before intelligence agencies started running metadata-mining algorithms on signals intercepts, sifting imagery captures from satellites in space, processing DNA onsite in minutes, recording sound in the most ingenious ways. Even sitting by a pool with Abby would be difficult now because newlyweds like to post selfies on Twitter, threatening photobomb exposure that can get you killed.

Lots of things were different in the nineties. Thanks to an 1878 statute called the Posse Comitatus, military units were prevented from deploying to law enforcement operations, so HRT stayed busy at the fringes of what has been publicly disclosed. Terrorism was considered a criminal enterprise prior to September 11, the domain of Justice, and extraordinary rendition was a relatively new concept, waterboarding a poorly understood tactic, black sites mere speculation.

Even now, few people know that the U.S. government's first extraterritorial snatch was not the work of Seal Team Six or Delta, but a joint FBI-CIA operation in 1987 called Goldenrod. The Reagan administration used two secretive laws to go after a terrorist named Fawaz Younis, who had been hiding in Lebanon: the Comprehensive Crime Control Act of 1984 and the Omnibus Diplomatic Security and Antiterrorism Act of 1986. In action that Kathryn Bigelow would admire, a couple of hot feds in bikinis lured the murderous hijacker onto a yacht off the coast of Cypress. Hostage Rescue Team swimmers Drägered up, stole him over the horizon to an aircraft carrier, and flew him back to the United States in what at the time was the longest military flight in history.

After that, things kinda took off. The Bush administration eventually declared "war on terror," built a bunch of cages in Guantánamo, and hired two psychopathic assholes to enhance interrogation of just about anybody caught wearing a beard. A few names have been advertised—Ramzi Yousef, Mir Aimal Kansi, and Abu Anas al-Libi—but during the 1990s, renditions had become so common that we flippantly called them "grabs."

The basics have never changed. Some guys get brought back for prosecution, some are taken to off-grid spots for palavers, some stay right where you find them because things do not always go according to plan. As a contemporary CIA counterpart Bob Baer once said in a public forum, "If you want a serious interrogation, you send a prisoner to Jordan. If you want them to be tortured, you send them to Syria. If you want someone to disappear, never to see them again, you send them to Egypt."

I'll rely on his words, here. No agency is going to ding me for mentioning details that have already appeared in the public domain. Rules about spilling secrets in books.

At any rate, I was thinking about none of this while Abby went to the bathroom. I was trying to focus on which of her truths was a lie; trying not dwell on the complications of flying in private as one person, out commercial as another. The differences between those lives. I was trying to focus on what would be my truths, here, and during my layover in San Francisco on the way home. What I'd buy for cover gifts to get the family to forgive my absence. What adventure I'd create to tell my kids.

I looked over at the Africans and those sweethearts huddled around the candle, and I thought about Rosie opening the front door at the sound of my truck coming up the driveway. Mick and Jake running toward me with their arms wide open, yelling, "Dad's home!"

How I'd hug them all and hand the boys Giants hats, and we'd go out on the lawn after dinner to toss around a ball.

"Dad's home!" they'd holler. "Dad's home!"

I'd smile, pretending I was there.

"So? What do you think?" she said when she got back.

"About what?"

"Two truths and a lie. Anthrax, steel plate, or Hall and Oates?"

I had not noticed before, but she was wearing baggy shorts with a drawstring bow in front and cheap shower sandals from the hotel store. She was used to traveling light, skilled at fitting in. Could have been a tourist from anywhere, a substitute teacher.

"Well, those Angolans over there seemed to understand your Shangri-La karaoke, and most folks don't care about the difference between titanium and steel, so there's that."

She took a sip. "So, you're going with the anthrax?" she asked, then sat down.

"Easy now," I told her. "The jury's still out."

"Classic FBI." She nodded. "Always linear. Adductive, inductive, deductive, everything an investigation. What are you, a lawyer or an accountant? You're so obvious."

"Oh, and you're not?" I laughed. Waved for another beer. "You guys always think you're so clever, that nobody knows who you are. All that sneak-and-peek shit leaving chalk marks on poles, lurking around cocktail parties at the embassy every Wednesday night, playing Spot the Molester. Some poor bastard with a gambling problem."

It was the first time she laughed out loud.

"Spot the Molester?"

"Come on," I said. "You think we don't have the same schools? Every FBI agent gets rated on ability to recruit snitches, just like you do. Assets, agents, confidential informants, whatever you call them, it's all the same thing. That's our stock-in-trade. Blackmail. Vulnerability. Human compromise."

"Jesus."

"You don't think we hang around peep shows trying to find losers who would do anything to keep their wives from finding out they're addicted to porn?"

"What's yours?" she asked. "What's your vulnerability?"

"Velcro. I love that sound, sticking shit all over me and tearing it off."

More laughter, another beer, another reach into the fanny pack for a nip.

"Want to hear a funny story?" I asked her.

"I guess?"

"First time I ever went to Jerusalem. Some gig with Shin Bet."

"Never heard of them."

"Like maybe ten of us. I can't remember what we were there for, but it was some secret squirrel thing, so the station sends one of you guys over to read us in. An older guy. He tells us that our rooms are wired full audio and video, that we would be followed everywhere we went, and that we should not assume we were any better-looking just because we were in a foreign country. You know Shin Bet."

"No idea what you're talking about."

"So, this guy on the team, we called him Scarhead, says, 'I'll show those assholes.' He goes straight back up to his room, drops his pants, rubs one out to show them who was boss."

"Rubbed one out?"

"He could do it on command. Said, 'That'll teach 'em.'"

"I don't get it. What does this have to do with anything?"

"Nothing. I just thought it was a funny story."

"Are you sure you don't want one of these?" She pulled out a couple more bottles, and I poured one into my beer.

"I'll bet I've spent more time at the Farm than you have," I told her. "Harvey Point. Red Stone. Stations all over the world. One of the first times I went to Camp Peary, we were doing live-fire car hits out on the racetrack. We were staying out in the Quonset huts; I think it was Pine Cabin. Anyway, we were practicing mobile assaults, and we had this new thing where we were running flexilinear axle wraps that would blow the wheel assemblies clean off and set the car down at a specific spot so we could stage an ambush. Very effective but messy, so we were covered in shit, spall, and brake dust and flash-bang powder and everything. And it was hot, so we were sweating our asses off. Soaking wet."

"Is there a point, here?"

"You got something better to do?"

"Pine Cabin. Continue."

"So, at lunch, everybody drives over to the chow hall, right? Probably six or eight blacked-out Suburbans, everybody hungry. And all you geeks walking around in your khakis, studying neurolinguistic programming or how to write cables or some shit like that, and we show up wearing Nomex flight suits tied around our waists, smelling like MOUT. Fifty meat eaters standing in line for a cheeseburger, and all the CTs drinking Kool-Aid out of that machine over by where you drop off the trays. Everybody trying not to stare."

I finished my beer-whiskey combo and waved for another. I was still jet-lagged and starting to feel pretty loose.

"One of the guys on my team, named . . . who cares . . . he's a good-looking guy, so we're just shuffling along, talking whatever, and these two women in front of us keep checking him out. Whispering, checking him out, whispering. Finally, one of them turns to us and says, 'Who are you guys, anyway?' And we didn't know what to say because, you know, we were told never to talk to anybody about anything down there. But these two chicks just crossed their arms, waiting, so finally Raz says, 'We're with the Justice Department.'"

I paused for dramatic effect.

"And?"

"And one of them smiles, winks at us, and says, 'Good cover.'"

We both laughed. Out loud.

"Right? I mean who the hell ever knows who anybody is anyway?"

"What does that have to do with me?" she asked.

"I'll tell you what it has to do with you, Abby . . . It means you know there's a Pine Cabin at the Farm, and that it's a Quonset hut in the woods. That you remember being a CT wearing khakis, drinking Kool-Aid from that machine where you dropped your tray. More important, it means you know what Nomex is and that you have no questions whatsoever about MOUT or staging live-fire ambushes on the racetrack at Camp Peary. So, I'm guessing you went DO somewhere along the way, that you might have augered in on a jump or two and added a titanium plate to your brain housing group. Which means there's no way you took a desk job at HQ riding dirty on a bottle of anthrax. Two truths and a lie. I win."

"Wow," she said. Sat back in her chair. "Not bad."

"We're not all adductive and linear."

"How did you get into this?" she asked. "Recruited out of high school?"

I laughed. During all my years in that world, I never met a single person who had been recruited. Not that way. Recruitment is one of those myths popularized in movies and books by people who want to believe that they are so special that a highly classified working group has been developed just to find them. In my experience, most people just apply.

"My wife saw a commercial on TV. I had a concussion, so she filled out the application for me. What about you?"

"Don't know what you're talking about. I'm a colonel in the army."

"You guys never lighten up, do you?"

"Iowa State. ROTC."

"Bullshit. I'm guessing you were captain of the field hockey team, National Honor Society, decent SATs, and a hard worker, but your parents couldn't afford full Ivy, so maybe Virginia or UVM. You read a few books, took the Foreign Service exam, got approached by a teaching assistant at the Kennedy School midway through your master's at Georgetown."

"I was ROTC. I'm a colonel in the army."

"Gimme another one of those bottles."

"Back to the game." She nodded. "Did you really almost get run over by Prince Charles playing polo at Windsor Castle?"

"Sure did. Playing some guys from Brazil. Couldn't have been more than a dozen of us on the entire field. He had just started dating Diana. Things were different in the eighties."

"Is your name really Tom?"

"No. It's David. Want to know what he said?"

"Who?"

I looked around and noticed that everybody else had gone to bed. It was getting late.

"Prince Charles. He said, 'One must keep his eye on the ball, mustn't he.' And then loped off. Nice guy."

She thought about that for a minute. We were both kinda hammered.

"Look, I'm sorry," she told me, finally. "But you know how it is. My name isn't Constance or Abby. Or Jane. It's Sue."

"Final answer?" I asked. "That's your I'm-a-professional-but-we're-all-in-this-together-and-I-been-drinking-a-six-pack-an-hour-so-I'm-gonna-let-my-guard-down truth?"

"Six-pack name." She reached out her hand. "Pinkie swear."

I wanted to tell her mine, some honest representation of who I was at that place and time. Not the stranger in my wallet or the asshole ordering opera tickets calling himself Monday, or some bar mitzvah fluffer pretending to be a team rope header. I wanted to admit we were both patriots, hanging all the way out there for a country that had no idea, trying to do a difficult job in a hard world that, despite all the training, still gets lonely and confusing and cold.

It didn't matter that sometimes vulnerability peeks through when you're sitting around pools, drinking whiskey from Solo Cups, and waiting on planes. No matter how hard you are, deep down, where it matters, a time bomb waits, ticking, and that tick sounds like a heart. We hate to admit it, but we know our lives will not be defined by wins but by losses, because mistakes make us human.

"Pinkie swear," I told her. "My name isn't David, either. It's Mark."

4

Quantico, Virginia

[MARCH 1991]

Hostage Rescue Team selection. Day four. Black Thursday.
The most important moments in a life fully formed do not always line up in chronological order. Sometimes they lie dormant for years, hidden in prayers and addictions, waiting for the proper perspective to set them free. But then someone pulls a trigger, and a specific experience pops up out of nowhere to become our center, the point in our lives when everything else is relegated to before or after. A middle, a fulcrum. Our deepest identity. The geometric mean.

Mine is a steel chair on a carpeted floor in a windowless room. There is an incandescent bulb dangling above my head. The room is silent except for subdued breathing, the sound of water dripping, an occasional cough. I reek of dog shit, pluff mud, and untended groin. My feet are bleeding, and I understand that I am shaking, that my body hurts deep down in unfamiliar ways. I think about the first time I walked into a prison, the sally port door creeping closed behind me, walled off from friends and family; the warmth of my former life cruelly refused.

"What's your name?"

I know they're out there, but I can't see their faces. They call themselves operators, maybe forty or fifty of them, and they never go away—lurking, watching, trying to figure me out.

"What is your name?"

Sometimes they wear white shirts with logos and cargo pants bulging at the pockets with three-by-five cards on which they record my failures. Never an expression, no cheers or condemnations. Sometimes they wear black, gather us together in smaller units, note attrition, and then mix us into unpredictable associations. We wear pinafores colored red, blue, or green and shorts or pants depending on the terrain. Armbands denoting rank. There are no watches or jewelry of any kind, not even your wedding ring.

"This is an individual event of indeterminate duration," One of Them will read aloud from written instructions. Always male, always a face we have not yet seen. "Your objective is to follow the man in the yellow shirt. Are there any questions, go."

They refer to our suffering as evolutions. We call them events, but it doesn't matter what you call things, because every day is a competition, and they score us in ways that seem difficult to figure out. Sometimes we race dashes around a corner; other times, we shoot targets for score or build GP Medium tents to sleep in, then grab a four-foot length of rebar to carry above our heads as we run in circles for hours trying to get back to a moldy cot for slumbers. But there are no slumbers. No food. Comfort is a ruse.

"Chris, what is your name?"

Sometimes we do nothing but fly around in helicopters or climb tall ladders, jump off platforms into water, blindfolded. One time they put me in a cramped black hole wearing scuba gear, where I sat patiently until I realized it was a puzzle and that I could sit there forever, but the whole point was to escape. The hiss of my regulator, the sense that One of Them was there in that hole with me. Always under observation.

"This is an individual event of indeterminate duration."

"What is your name?"

But now they have placed me dead center in a circle of light, which reminds me of a stage production I directed after college, *Doctor Faustus,* by Marlowe, the final soliloquy. I had blocked the scene using gaffers tape and an old carbon arc spot loaded with a popular gel called Bastard Amber, which seems appropriate here, a protagonist contemplating act five in hell.

This is an interrogation, and I am aware that it is an interrogation, but I have forgotten what interrogation means. There is a clock on the wall, though I can't make sense of time. It reads 03:22:52, those blink-ing red digits counting cadence to the pounding in my head. It re-minds me of Amsterdam, my mother's birthday.

"What is your name?"

A long silence. "Chris, what is your name?"

And I would agree that the mean is not a place but a number. Then I would counter with the premise that in looking back on our lives, we might count the days and the experiences as integers that add up to a small but nonzero set of revelations. A Reuleaux triangle of ifs. Proof that life itself might be seen as a line graph built with addends, fractions, and constants, bound to equivalence using any number of functions.

"What is your name?"

"Is this a dream?" I ask One of Them. The clock ticking. "Am I in a dream?"

"What is your name?"

This guy keeps asking me the same question over and over, but my mind is so tweaked, I can't decide whether to shit or steal third base. Delirium is a subjective condition, difficult to describe. I had experi-enced it twice, the first time, working construction one summer dur-ing college, building a tramway at Cannon Mountain for a company called Pizzagalli. We had been working twenty-eight hours straight when, sometime after midnight, the stars circled that moonless sky, sat down in rows as Leonard Bernstein waved the Boston Symphony Or-chestra through Tchaikovsky's Symphony No 5. I was cold and tired beyond reason when the music came over me, standing that summit, the music swelling in my head.

The second time was at a D.C. hospital called Providence, near Catholic University. Rosie was passing in and out of consciousness, thirty-two hours into labor with Jake. Induced. No epidural. I'll never forget the way she would pass out between contractions and then wake up exhausted, stare into my face, lost to reason and herself in a wilderness of pain. Things women know.

"What is your name?"

One of Them wants me to tell him who I am, not the face I showed up with, but the identity hiding behind it. He wants sordid confes-sions, revelations not yet unveiled, even to me. He wants the middle truth, and I am willing to help him, but all this running around in circles with no food or sleep has done a number on my head. I am out of my fucking mind.

I look down and notice that I am wearing camouflage pants bloused into dark leather boots. I have a gold terry cloth band on one wrist, a T-shirt covered in mud. My skin is striped from abrasion, macerated where wet, cracked where it has dried. I remember being stripped naked, some days ago, standing in front of a man with a clipboard who noted evidence of an appendectomy, prominent clavicles, no other scars, marks, or tattoos. I don't know why.

"What is your name?"

My pinny is blue, like my shirt, though thinner. I can read C-10 printed in silkscreened letters, and I think that might be significant.

"Chris, what is your name?"

The voice is male, deep, monotonously benign. It sounds recorded, like it is coming out of some cheap speaker, and I realize it must be the assistant principal of Littleton High School calling me to the office. His name is Mr. Smith, and I met him just once, shortly after a fight. It was not a fight so much as a dispute during gym class with an older kid named Asshole, who did not appreciate me cutting in line at the water fountain. I remember that we had words, then that we tussled a bit, and then the sound of shattered glass as we spilled across the hall into a classroom door.

"Boys will be boys," Mr. Smith had said, the disciplinarian. "But somebody has to pay."

"What is your name?"

I fidget in my seat, clench my hands into fists, because that's what I do. My mind wanders down a different hallway, peak foliage, right after my ski team physical, when the guidance counselor, Mr. Daley, motioned me aside. He was angry because he had seen the results of our eighth-grade IQ tests, probably the Stanford-Binet. He waved a piece of paper in front of my face, and though I could not read the score, he called me lazy and scared. Scared of endeavor, he told me, scared of taking a chance at what I might accomplish if I tried.

"What is your name?"

I remember other times people have circled around me: baptisms, courtrooms, fighting in the mud. I remember my first public performance as a musician, an open mic in a rathskeller beneath the Franconia Inn. I was playing "Helpless," by Crosby, Stills, Nash, and Young because it was the only three chords I knew. I wanted to play Hendrix, but all I had was an acoustic guitar and a Maybelle Carter book of fingerpicking techniques my dad found at a campground. All those people looking on. Painfully shy in a small town where the biggest celebrity was Eddie Splude, who ran the town dump.

I remember glasses of wine, the encouragement of a pretty woman in a peasant shirt who smelled of popinac and thyme. Trying to line up my fingers with the strings, the thump in my heart, the way I couldn't move my tongue. I hear a voice far away in my head, somebody saying my name, people clapping. *Chrisameechie.* Then my first amplified notes and thinking about how I wished I was in the woods hiking or dryland training in the fall, when the ground was hard but not yet covered with snow.

"Chris, what is your name?"

My real first name is Jon, like my dad, who turned eighteen the day after I was born. He was a bright student, a member of the student council, vice president of his class. I have a photograph of him in 1950s attire, hours before my conception. The photo appeared in *The Little-ton Courier,* with a story about the prom, which described him as follows: "Height, 5 ft. 10 in.; color eyes, brown; color hair, brown; real sharp dresser. Likes to ski, play basketball and baseball, school and girls. Crazy about hotrods and fried clams."

The *Courier* noted my dad's favorite song: "My Special Angel." That he had a '36 Ford.

"Favorite saying simply, 'Baby U Doesn't Like to Dance?'"

My mother enjoyed poems, and when I was young, she liked to sing me an old fortune-teller song so I would understand the effable aspects of destiny. "Wednesday's child is full of woe." She would nod, then point her finger accusingly. "But Thursday's child has far to go."

I remember her singing as my father picked us up after work in the Valiant, driving her to Leavitt's restaurant, where she turned double shifts as a server. Jon T. mowed ski slopes, off-season, swinging a scythe eight hours a day. At night, he would lead rescue operations in the Presidential Range, high-angle accidents on the Cannon cliffs, where tourists were most susceptible to weather. He was a powerful, charismatic man who wore Peter Limmer boots with rawhide laces. His scent, the musk of labor. He had fallen in a field when he was nine years old and gone partially blind to a goldenrod stem. He had a wall-eye that was not corrected by glasses.

"Friday's child is loving and giving," my mother would tell me. "Saturday's child works hard for a living. Your mother was born at midnight, between them."

"Your mother," she called herself. Third-person omniscient. Enough said.

My parents could have chosen a different life, but they dropped out of school and went to work showing courage, selfless dedication, and restraint, foundations they hoped I would build on. Which I did, because I was born into a perfect youth, a ward of the earth. Mountains and trees. Long slopes, my skis gaining speed.

"What is your name?"

I want to give One of Them an answer, divulge secrets about the child alone in winter with Uncle Mike and a sled. But to give them a name, I must search farther. I must decide if there is anything earlier than the black-and-white photo I keep in a cardboard box at the other side of the world. My answer must be truth, and truth evades me.

"This is a outa-state check, sir," she told me. "Do you'ns got any ID?"

The first time I introduced myself as a special agent with the Federal Bureau of Investigation was in the number three checkout line at a Kmart in Springfield, Missouri. Rosie and I had arrived a couple of days earlier from New Agent Training with our whole life crammed into the back of a shiny CJ-7. That life included two suitcases, Jake in a car seat, and several sleeves of Saltine crackers for Rose, who was sick with a bun in the oven, our second child, Mick.

"You'ns?" I asked.

"Yes, sir, this is a outa-state check. It ain't no good without no ID."

I started to reach for my driver's license before realizing it was from the District of Columbia, same as the check.

"ID? It's two bags of Huggies, some Similac, and a Mr. Coffee," I told her. "What's that, twenty-seven eighty-nine? You won't take a check for twenty-seven eighty-nine?"

"We got rules."

Rosie kinda sighed. It was a Saturday morning, and there was a line of people stacking up behind us. Hot outside. Jake was getting impatient. Everybody staring.

"Look, we just moved here," I told her. "I haven't had time to get a local license."

"Sir, I done tolt you, Kmart ain't gonna take no check without no ID."

We had a brand-new USAA credit card with a one-thousand-dollar limit, but it was already tapped out from the move, and if there were any ATMs in those days, I had not seen one.

"Can you call your manager or something?" I asked. "This is ridiculous."

"Hey, buddy, what's the problem?"

"Relax, man."

I was getting annoyed when Rose tapped me on the arm and pointed to my back pocket.

"Oh, wait a minute," I told the cashier. Then I reached for my shiny new wallet, the one with the gold-embossed insert sporting a blue seal and my official likeness, clean-shaven, wearing a tie.

"What's this?" The woman shrugged. "I don't get it."

She was about forty years old and looked like most people I had met in the Ozarks: white, rodeo buckle, average in Midwest ways. She held my spanking-new credentials between her fingers, turned the leather case over a couple of times, trying to figure out what I had tendered.

"I'm an FBI agent," I told her. "We just moved here from Washington, D.C."

"Sir, I can't . . ."

"That's my name right there, my picture, see where it says 'FBI'?"

"FBI?"

"See, right there? Federal Bureau of Investigation. That's why we're buying all this stuff," I told her. "We've just rented a house, and the movers don't get here until Wednesday."

She stood at the register dumbfounded, complete overload. And I thought about explaining how the FBI transfers personnel based on the needs of the Bureau, that there's a day during the tenth week of New Agent Training when all the first office orders are sealed in envelopes and stacked in alphabetical order behind a lectern. How when the class counselor reads your name, you walk up front, state where you want to go, where you think you're going to go, and finally where the Bu says you're going to go. I wanted Dallas, thought it would be Chicago, got KC.

I wanted to tell this woman how, immediately after graduation, I picked up my Bureau-issued Smith and Wesson Model 10 revolver chambered to .357 magnum and headed west. How we had driven 1,117 miles in a Jeep with a lift kit and mud tires but no air-conditioning in the middle of July. How Rose was five months pregnant, and Jake was eight months old, neither complaining.

"Ma'am?" I asked her. "Ma'am."

Then she snapped out of it, called for a manager to checkout number three, and I explained the whole thing all over again.

"FBI?" the manager asked. "You don't look like no FBI."

"What's that mean?"

"You're wearing cargo shorts and a Yankees hat."

"It's Saturday, ma'am. We're buying diapers."

"I don't know, sir. This is weird."

"Look, we've been staying at the Silver Saddle motel for a week," I told her. "It's so goddamned hot, the air-conditioning won't keep up, so we've got to walk around the mall trying to stay sane. Give me your phone; I'll call someone to sort this out. We've got things to do."

"Silver Saddle? On Glenstone? Why in the world would you stay . . ."

"And you know what? On top of all that, I got in an armed altercation in Kansas City last week, my first day on the job. The baby's getting impatient; my wife is pregnant, as you can see. We need these diapers. If we're going to have a problem, you need to tell me right now."

"I never met no FBI agent before," the manager said. "How do I know if this is real?"

"Because that's my photo and that's where it says 'Department of Justice' and 'By Order of the Attorney General of the United States.' Who would make this up? It would be a felony."

"Felony?" she said, all woodsy. "I heard that!" Then she handed back my creds and nodded to the cashier. "Take the check. We ain't need no trouble."

· · ·

"Do you solemnly swear that the testimony you will give this subcommittee will be the truth, the whole truth, and nothing but the truth, so help you God?"

"I do."

The sign on the door reads "Room 215 Hart Senate Office Building." I'm standing behind a long wooden table with one hand in the air, looking at a wall of variegated marble. There is a large seal in the middle that reads "United States Senate," seven men beside me; five stage left, two on my right. The lighting is Bastard Amber. A roomful of groundlings.

"Please be seated."

I recognize Senator Dianne Feinstein from television, Senator Fred Thompson from the movies, and Democrat Patrick Leahy because my sister lives in Vermont. I have never seen Senator Kohl or Abraham, and the legendary Strom Thurmond, though advertised, has not made an appearance. I know all about Chuck Grassley, the senior senator from Iowa, because he has made a career of disparaging the Bureau, but his chair remains empty.

"This committee will now proceed."

The man doing all the talking is named Arlen Specter. He's chairman of the Senate Terrorism, Technology, and Government Information Subcommittee, a Republican from Pennsylvania. He has just announced plans to run for president, and this certainly has all the gravity one might expect of events leading up to an election. Cameras, mics, stern-looking faces.

Everyone is here, all the networks, CNN, *The Washington Post, The New York Times.* I count three feed cameras, two marked "C-SPAN," which is broadcasting the whole thing live. The chyron reads "Ruby Ridge Incident, September 14, 1995."

"We will have two panels today," Senator Specter announces, looking around the room. "The eight sniper observers from the Federal Bureau of Investigation, and then the pilot of the helicopter together with the deputy U.S. marshal who was in the helicopter."

The FBI snipers are Hostage Rescue Team operators from the blue and gold sections, five former marines, one navy Underwater Demolition Team explosives expert, a defensive tackle from Annapolis, and me. I am the only one at the table who has no military service, but I have written speeches for politicians, directed theater, and covered

both as a print reporter. I understand this kind of stagecraft, the plot-
ting of narrative truth. I have been here before.

"The eight sniper observers are present today at the request of the
subcommittee," Mr. Specter reads for the record. "It's my understanding that there are the seven with counsel provided by the Department
of Justice, and one of the sniper observers here is without counsel." He
looks us up and down. "And which individual is that?"

I raise my hand.

"And Mr. Whitcomb, why have you elected to appear without
counsel, if I may ask?"

Every other shooter at the table has one or more attorneys. They
are lined shoulder to shoulder behind us, dutifully focused not just on
these proceedings but on three years of criminal investigations, media
scrutiny, administrative inquiries, civil cases, and a U.S. attorney who
has convened a federal grand jury, trying to put us in jail for murder.

"Yeah, it just didn't seem necessary to me."

C-SPAN cuts to my face. I'm wearing a suit from the Springfield
days, white shirt, a club tie striped blue and red. Capitol Police made
me leave my gun at the magnetometer, so I'm sitting slightly askew.
I've groomed down to a regulation mustache, businesslike hair.

"Didn't seem necessary?" the senator asks, incredulous.

And I appreciate his concern. But I am a special agent of the Federal
Bureau of Investigation, sworn to protect the United States from all
enemies foreign and domestic. I swore an oath to the Constitution. I
believe in this stuff.

"You just want to put that on the record," Senator Specter says,
quite respectfully.

I use that pause to look around the room, at the cameras and the
lawyers and the staffers and politicians and the exhibits they have
brought to show, including a topographical model of Naples, Idaho,
posterboard graphs on easels, and a wood door with a window and a
curtain and a .308-caliber hole through a single pane of glass.

FBI agents report investigations on what are called FD-302s, and I
have a stack of these forms in front of me, four different statements
documenting two rifle shots on a mountain in Idaho, the deaths of a
federal agent, an unarmed mother, and a fourteen-year-old boy. The
first FD-302 is my own, six sentences in two paragraphs, dated August 22, 1992. The second is six pages, my sworn statement to a shoot-

ing review board, conducted nine days later, while I was sitting in the woods on a log. The third document is dated September 23, 1992, and was written by an agent I do not know, clarification of previous claims. The fourth is stamped December 7, 1993, my ten-page statement to an assistant inspector-in-place named Powers. It states, "In the course of this inquiry, certain information may come to our attention indicating that a violation of criminal law has been committed. Information may also come to our attention that violation of administrative rules or procedures has taken place."

I look down at the fourth report in the pile, a paragraph where I say, "I have been advised of my rights and responsibilities in connection with this inquiry, as set forth on a Warning and Assurance Form (FD-645), which I have read, I understand, and I signed."

"I know you've been informed that you can have counsel if you want counsel," Senator Specter tells me.

"Yes." I nod. Yes, I know.

And we're going to pause this whole thing right here because a couple of things need explaining. First, as I have said, the most important moments in a life fully formed do not always line up in chronological order. Sometimes they lie dormant for years, hidden in prayers and addictions, waiting for the proper perspective to set them free. But then someone pulls a trigger, and a specific experience pops up out of nowhere to become our center, the point in our lives when everything else is relegated to before or after. Our deepest identity, the geometric mean.

In my case, the trigger involved the death of a woman on a mountain in Idaho, not the shot itself, but its reverberations through society, through what I had been taught about justice, through what I believed about myself. I felt that trigger in Arlen Specter's words, standing between walls of cameras and lawyers, testifying before the U.S. Senate, Room 215 in the Hart Senate Office Building, the Ruby Ridge Incident. I felt that trigger, both literally and figuratively, as the truth behind my identity, what HRT wanted me to reveal, Black Thursday, during selection.

"What's your name?"

About halfway through the hearings, we took a break, and I had no lawyer to consult, so I walked outside for a breath of air. I looked around that lovely autumn day and realized I was standing three blocks away from my old desk in Mr. Conte's office, where I had crafted speeches for political gain. Mr. Finley's boxing gym was a brief walk east, our old apartment even closer. I could see the Folger Shakespeare Library, just up the street, an early inspiration. And in that moment, I found my way back to a steel chair on a carpeted floor in a windowless room.

"What's your name?"

I remember the moment my role in life changed, stepping up onto a stage as a kid from New Hampshire, being handed an FBI badge and a gun. It was a proscenium stage in an auditorium with velvet curtains and lots of doors. I was wearing a suit, white shirt, a club tie striped blue and red. There were hundreds of people in the audience, a long table covered in packets all neatly arranged. My parents were there, my sister, my wife and son. My shoes hurt. My head was clear.

A tall, elegant man with close-cut hair and good posture moved toward me; his name was Assistant Director Glover. I reached out to shake his hand, smiled toward a camera. Then he presented me with one of those small packets from the table. It was about the size of a wallet, leather embossed at the edges with cheap gold filigree, folded in the middle. It had "FBI" printed in bold letters on one side. There was a blue seal, a photograph, and my name.

"Special Agent Christopher Whitcomb," AD Glover announced.

I thought back on growing up a good kid, independent and kind. That the only crime I had ever committed before joining the FBI was stealing a piece of candy, a root beer barrel from Aldrich's Market, when I was six. I ate that piece of candy, and I enjoyed it, but when the guilt came for me, I took the empty wrapper and left it in the fresh produce section, hoping someone would find it and guess that it had fallen out of the box. I watched until it got stuck on an old lady's shoe, and I followed it with my eyes as she walked away. I wanted to believe that it wasn't my fault, to make up a story about how things happen in the world, things that are wrong but possible to explain. That good humans fail, though not forever. That we are learners.

"What is your name?"

I thought about a friend once telling me that the first step toward sanity is acceptance of a higher power, that it could be anything: a doorknob, a pierced ear, Saskatchewan. Mine is that mongrel little prick Bucky Corliss kicking the shit out of me every day at recess. I hated him, the humiliation, the disdain. So, one day, I picked myself up and made a conscious vow that I wasn't going to be that guy getting his ass kicked on the playground anymore. I realized that the higher power in everyone's life is not always good. That it might take a monster to fight monsters. That I would be one.

"What is your name?"

Delusion passes. I realize that this is Black Thursday, day four of a two-week selection for the FBI's Hostage Rescue Team. I am sitting in a steel chair on a carpeted floor in a windowless room. There is a lightbulb hanging above my head. I am no longer shaking.

"What is your name?"

At that point in time and space, I could have told them what they wanted to know. I could have stated my given names, the one I was born with, the ones I had acted in stage plays and childhood games. I could have listed nicknames, epithets hurled in fights, intimate whispers, beautiful things like "Daddy" and "son." I could have pretended I no longer knew who I was prior to Black Thursday, pretended I didn't know who I would be from that day forward. But I did not, because I was born whole into a life fully formed, which is a role, not a limitation. I am an actor unbound by proscenium, wearing a mask of ego, speaking lines of id.

I am Thursday's child, and I'm just getting started.

Fire

In the evening when life
Gathers across miles
The spark of recollection
A flit among darkening coals
Snow melting mansard eaves
This fieldstone chimney a
Séance of truthful past
A steamy hiss
Shine trapped in panes

You think you remember
The yellows and reds
Now blue
Just light until you listen

It's not what we see that burns
Not flames nor heat
Not fear nor regret
It's what we stare too long into
Believing God just Nature
The hopeful tithe of moments
There before us pyres we built
Then stoked to conflagration
Watching Heaven burn to
Cold, cold night

5

McLean, Virginia

[OCTOBER 2001]

There are two ways into the George Bush Center for Intelligence at the Route 123 entrance. The left lane is badge access for CIA employees, contractors, and cleared associates. The other lane breaks right to a small parking area behind the guardhouse. Visitors are directed in clearly worded signs to check in and get a day pass before proceeding up the long drive to sprawling lots designated North, South, West A, West 1, 2, and 3. There's a parking deck, too, but I never got to use it.

. . . Too many rookies, not enough pros . . .

It was a beautiful day, my first time back at Langley after the September 11 attacks. The leaves were turning, my Giants were 3–1, Rosie and the kids were busy decorating for Halloween. I had the Targa roof off my car and the wind in my hair, the cassette player boisterous through upgraded speakers.

I had just bought the fancy new Nokia 8310 with the pictographs and monochrome screen, and I was talking to my old HRT sniper partner about a tee time Saturday morning. The speedometer climbing past 103, weaving through traffic. Persol glasses, tinted green.

"What's that you're listening to, Whit?" he asked.

. . . Ashes to ashes smoke or get smoked,
We come by the masses, you come and get choked . . .

"Ludacris, brother." The wind a roar. "Game Got Switched."

"Sweet." That kinda mood.

"Stand by," I told him. "I gotta shift."

And shifting was the issue at hand, because I was driving north on I-495 in a Porsche 911, running way too hot for the 193 exit. I had the Nokia in my left ear and one of those cool Motorola car phone handsets in the other, with Art Cooper, editor in chief of GQ magazine, yelling at me for unrelated reasons. I couldn't hear for shit, but the big center gauge on a 911 is a tachometer, so I was trying to downshift by the numbers, steering with my knee.

"What is that noise?" Art demanded, a fan of Sinatra. "Is that rap?"

"I have a meeting, Art. I gotta go."

"The hell you do!"

It was almost noon, and Art sounded like he'd had too much coffee or not enough Stoli. I guessed he was on his way to Four Seasons for lunch, maybe Gore Vidal dishing on the Clintons; Henry Kissinger and David Granger gossiping over silver plates of fish; Gloria von Fürstenberg hopping tables with a flute of champagne. Things he'd shown me.

"Who are you talking to?" my partner asked, a calm voice in the Nokia.

"Doesn't matter."

"What?" Art rasped, the chain-smoker. "Turn it down!"

To be clear, racing toward CIA headquarters in a Porsche 911 with an HRT sniper in one ear and the editor in chief of GQ magazine in the other did not make much sense to me, either. But I'll mention that whole life-fully-formed thing, again, and ask for a little slack. This stuff is hard to explain even when you're in it.

"I'll call you back!"

"Don't you hang up!"

First things first. We're going to call my old HRT partner Pi because he might read this someday and it will make him laugh. Second, Pi was not just a world-class shooter; he was my brother. He finished my sentences, had the keys to my house. We competed at crossword puzzles, hated cleaning guns, and kept adjacent lockers at the Fredericksburg Country Club, where we often played golf. Mick and Jake told everybody their "Uncle Pi" had been bitten by a shark because of a gnarly surgical scar he'd gathered after rupturing his spleen.

Second, I have rubbed up against every kind of killer, from Marvin Hagler and Joe Bonamassa to a serial murderer named Oscar Ray

Bolin, who drowns his victims with a hose. Art Cooper had that same distance in his eyes, things he knew about the world but kept secret from others. He was bright and urbane, calculating, oddly humorous, mildly derisive. He knew every swinging dick worth knowing and feared not one of them. I loved his seething curiosity, the great whiskey bar in his office, that literary mind.

Woofers thumping, the whine of tuned exhaust, life racing through me.

"How 'bout you turn it down just a little?" Pi suggested, calm in every situation.

"Hang on, brother. I'm just pulling into Langley."

"Langley?"

"Long story."

"Ten-four."

I had a lot on my mind that first time back. Three weeks earlier, I had been supervisory special agent in charge of a little-known intelligence cell within the FBI's Critical Incident Response Group, which housed HRT, negotiators, and the National Center for the Analysis of Violent Crime.

Under the auspices of Presidential Decision Directive 39, we had operational jurisdiction over all acts of terror, and I mean everything. But now I was flying back and forth to New York a couple of times a week to do book signings and appear on television, mostly NBC. For reasons that now seem difficult to swallow, I had resigned from the FBI, handed in my badge and gun.

Life was changing in shudders. I had a plan.

"Where are you?" Art asked. He was used to being in charge, though not in charge of me.

"Doesn't matter."

"Who are you talking to?"

"Don't worry about it!"

I could see the main gate coming up fast, so I downshifted with my elbow, popped the cassette, and checked my tie in the mirror, all one flail of arms.

"We go off at nine," Pi told me. "You gonna make it?"

"I'll meet you at the range."

Then up the left lane like always, until I remembered I no longer had a pass. Art was still yelling, so I didn't realize my mistake until well

past the turn, and because the brake and clutch pedals are so close together on a 911, I missed the downshift, locked up the tires. That
squeal.

"Shit."

"What's going on?" Art asked. "Are we on for Tuesday or not?"

"Yes, we're on!" I told him. That was the whole point of this trip.
"I'll call you back."

"When?"

"I don't know, a couple hours. I'll call you back."

I shifted into reverse and chirped the tires, again.

"What a pain in the ass," he growled.

"I'll call you back!"

I clicked off the phone, checked my watch, then pulled into one of
the diagonal parking spots behind the guardhouse. I was just about to
open the door when I saw a guy come up behind me in the rearview
mirror. Then another, then a couple off to the side. They were wearing black Nomex flight suits and body armor, MP5 sub guns aimed
pretty much right at my head.

"Hands where I can see them," one of the guys told me. All business.

There were six of them circling around. I had seen the same ma-
neuver a million times, taught it, done it for real. We called it a felony
car stop, and these fellas looked proficient.

"It's all good," I called out. "I went down the wrong lane."

"Put your hands up!"

I did.

"Don't move!"

I did not.

One of the men to my right poked his muzzle through the open
roof, scanned the passenger seat for threats. The two in the back moved
to five and seven, clearing the space behind me. One reached to open
my door, which made me happy, because HRT just breaks out the
windows.

"Guys, look, I'm sorry . . ." I started to say, embarrassed. Every government installation in the country was on high alert, and the CIA
might have been near the top.

"Step out of the car!"

I focused on compliance, trying to transition from the arrogance of my former life to the hubris of this one, but it was hard, because they had Aimpoints leveled right between my eyes.

"Let me see some ID."

I reached for my FBI credentials, as I had on countless occasions, proof that everything would be just fine. But I no longer had FBI credentials, because I had tendered my resignation just days before al Qaeda killed 2,977 innocent human beings and started what would become the longest war in U.S. history. All I had was a driver's license, same as anybody else.

"Slowly," he cautioned.

Then one of the guys on the other side of the car stepped to where he could see me.

"Jesus Christ, Whitcomb," he said. That look of recognition. He dropped the muzzle of his MP5. "You should know better than that. You trying to get yourself killed?"

September 11, 2001, is one of those seminal moments in American history: Everyone can tell you exactly where they were and what they were doing when it happened. In my case, it was a windowless room on the second floor of a nondescript building near I-95 in Stafford, Virginia. I was sitting on the edge of my desk talking about terrorism with FBI agents in charge of preventing it.

"This is ridiculous," I griped.

I had flown in from London the previous night, front row in the upper deck of a 747, watching first-class passengers argue over who was going to sit in the jump seat for landing.

"I had a wood-handled steak knife in my hand, looking at the back of the pilot's head," I told the guys. "Somebody has to figure this out."

Then one of them pointed to a TV on my credenza and said what you and the rest of America was saying at the exact same time.

"Wow . . . did you see that?"

I turned to my left as CNN broadcast the horror of American Airlines Flight 11 crashing into the North Tower of the World Trade Center. Then Flight 175 a hundred yards away. My phone erupted with reports of an explosion at the Pentagon. Then the towers fell one after the other while I was getting briefed on events unfolding over a field in Pennsylvania. Everybody was running in and out of my office, because we oversaw terror, and I oversaw intel, but mostly because I also had Fox and MSNBC.

"I need answers," my boss told me. "I need them now."

So, I made calls to sources, typed cables to counterparts, phoned my buddy Terry Quinn, a New York City firefighter standing at Ground Zero who told me the whole decade was on fire, you could smell it in your clothes.

"Al Qaeda," I assured my boss. We all knew that, of course. "It's bin Laden."

Yes, I can remember precisely where I was and what I was doing on September 11, 2001, but odd as it sounds, my salient memory of those tragic events did not occur until one day later, when I found myself standing in a different office in a different city, another windowless room. I was waiting to appear on *Larry King Live* with Tom Clancy sitting on a yellow midcentury sofa with a well-dressed Asian woman on the floor between his legs. She was massaging his feet.

My last day in the FBI.

"Can I get you anything?" another woman asked. She was wearing a headset with one of those little jaw mics, some kind of producer. "Water, tea?"

I turned around to answer, but she stepped past me like I wasn't even there.

"Oooh yes . . ." he was mumbling. Tom Clancy. "Mmmm, right there."

That's what I think he was saying, because he was leaning back with his eyes closed, mumbling baby talk, and the woman on the floor was speaking baby talk, too. They seemed to understand each other in some private language that included purrs and coos and stuff that made me wish I had a camera or wasn't there at all.

"That's it . . ." he said, and some other things I couldn't quite make out.

It didn't seem inappropriately sensual or erotic; it was just weird. An Asian-style foot massage in a greenroom, the day after September 11, waiting to appear on *Larry King Live,* with Tom Clancy mumbling baby talk on an Ikea version of a very stylish couch. I shit you not.

I stood there in the doorway, trying to figure out how one might proceed in a situation like that. I'd met plenty of celebrities: A-list actors, models, athletes, a Medal of Honor recipient, a teacher of the year. At the risk of name-dropping, I'll come right out and admit that I had once thrilled at meeting Bruce Springsteen in a corridor beneath the Brooklyn Academy of Music, waiting with Sheryl Crow for her performance on MTV. Shook his hand. Nice little chat.

"Mr. Clancy?" the woman asked. She had a clipboard. "Can I get you anything?"

I should not have thought about interrupting a man during a foot rub, but this was the greenroom for a call-in talk show, and I had just published my first book. Tom Clancy was the bestselling author of a generation, the novelist who summoned HRT to save Jack Ryan in *Patriot Games*. I had met Fred Thompson while testifying about Ruby Ridge to the U.S. Senate. My mother was a Clancy. We had so much to discuss.

"Yes," the producer spoke into her headset. Then: "Yes, Mr. Whitcomb is here."

He ignored her. She ignored me. The Asian lady ignored everything except Mr. Clancy's feet. Then the producer shook her head and disappeared into what looked like a janitor's closet.

"Oh, yes, that's it . . ." Mr. Clancy said in baby talk. I just stood there, staring.

"Sir?" someone else asked. I heard a door open. "I'm ready for you."

I turned to my left and saw a very attractive woman motioning with her hand.

"Let's get you done."

So, I walked over to where someone had installed a linoleum countertop with a blow-dryer, a suit coat steamer, and some tools I recognized from my theater days as makeup brushes.

"Right here?" I asked, pointing to a tall, white vinyl chair.

She nodded and said her name was Andrea and asked if she could take my coat.

"Nah, that's all right."

I sat down, and she tucked tissue paper into the collar of my shirt. The wall behind her was a brightly lit mirror with those big bulbs you see backstage at gentlemen's clubs. It smelled like Pond's Cold Cream and Coco Mademoiselle, which was all the rage.

"Are you here to talk about the attacks?"

"Kinda. I wrote a book. This is part of the press tour. My name is Chris."

"Nice to meet you, Chris. An author, huh?"

"I am now."

"I always wanted to write a book. You probably hear that a lot. What's it about?"

"I'm in the FBI," I told her. "I used to be a sniper on this counter-terrorism unit called the Hostage Rescue Team. The book is about my experiences."

"Oh, wow. Is that why you didn't want to give me your jacket?"

"What do you mean?"

"Your gun. I don't mind, I see 'em all the time. Which show are you doing?"

"*Larry King Live.* I thought it would be bigger."

"No, he's in L.A. We do feeds, here, all kinds of shows. Is this your first time on TV?"

"Pretty much."

I closed my eyes while Andrea worked on my face. Such a strange sensation.

"How long have you been in the FBI?"

"Almost sixteen years. But this is my last day."

"What? After all this? You're leaving?"

"You can't write books about the FBI and stay in the FBI," I told her.

"Oh, I guess that makes sense. Is it hard? Leaving?"

"Hard? Everybody I know is working 'round the clock trying to save the world from Osama bin Laden, and I'm sitting in a makeup room getting mascara. No offense, but it sucks."

"None taken."

I sat there with my eyes closed, trying to make sense of things.

"My first book signing was supposed to be tomorrow afternoon at the World Trade Center," I told her. "There's a Borders in the mall there. Well . . . there was."

"No way."

"Can't make it up."

We didn't say anything for a while. Then the producer called out that I was up in three, so Andrea pulled the tissue paper out of my collar, and I stood to leave.

"It was nice meeting you," she said, dabbing my nose with powder. "Break a leg."

I took one last look at the guy in the mirror, turned around, and followed the lady with the headset past Tom Clancy and toward Larry King in the janitor's closet at the other end of the suite.

CIA headquarters is every bit the stark campus of cubes you have seen in movies. That huge seal in the chessboard floor, stars on the wall, those tall, boxed pillars. You know what I'm talking about, the grand foyer with the high ceiling and the drop-bar turnstiles, all those anonymous faces marching eyes front, heavy with secrets, wrought by angst.

"Good morning," I said to the front desk receptionist. "What a pretty day."

I strolled in like I owned the place, because it's just another office building if you belong there and because Langley always struck me as a clubhouse through which a special crowd passed, a good place to run into friends you'd met near pools in places like Chiang Mai.

"Good morning."

What they do not tell you in movies is that you don't get a decoder ring or a secret handshake to move from one air-gapped space to the next. Every embassy, field office, station, offsite and underground installation has a gatekeeper. Even FBI HQ required me to sign in and wear a clip-on visitor badge because a gun and credentials were somehow insufficient.

"I'll need to see your ID."

Something about Langley always struck me as brighter and less confusing than the J. Edgar Hoover Building. Maybe it's the broad forest stretching to the Potomac or the lighter cut of stone. Maybe it's the *Kryptos* sculpture, which has inspired decades of spirited thought because what you don't know is more interesting than what you do. Maybe I enjoyed Langley because of its original art or the inscription that reads "And ye shall know the truth, and the truth shall make you free." I mean, what could be more optimistic than that?

By contrast, FBI headquarters is a dark labyrinth of cluttered halls, steel doors with keypad locks leading to other doors that are also locked, then into vaults full of people skulking around as if they're in on something special, which they probably are not, because clearances are clearances, and I have held them all.

"Do you know the way?" she asked me, once I had signed in. The lady up front.

"Yes, thank you. Have a nice day."

Maybe I found the CIA brighter because I never officially worked there. Government buildings come across as a bit more pleasant when nobody thinks they can boss you around. Regardless, the time has come for me to let you in on our first little secret. That army colonel drinking minibar whiskey out of a Solo Cup actually *was* an army colonel. She did attend ROTC, though not at Iowa State. Her name was none of the three she offered during our game of two truths and a lie, but we'll still call her Sue. It's easier.

"Seriously, Whitcomb?" she asked when I arrived at her office. She had a cluttered desk in a suite focused on weapons of mass destruction. "SWAT team? You know better than that."

CIA headquarters is a maze of secrets until you fuck up. Blame is loud and instantaneous.

"I forgot!" I told her. "Quit dicking around. We're late."

I took a minute to say hi to everyone, then she waved me toward the door, and we started the walk from her bunker to the executive dining rooms. This was the meeting I had mentioned to Art without saying the word *CIA* or explaining surreption in any meaningful way. I swear.

"What the hell are you doing?" I asked her, about halfway to lunch.

"Don't worry about it. I get a little vertigo."

It turns out Sue did have a plate in her head. It was also true that she got the plate during a parachute jump, a high-speed failure to open. It affected her balance, not just in Chiang Mai.

"You're such a pain in the ass."

The trip from Sue's office required passage down a very unusual hallway that I have seen only at the CIA. And because I have not found these hallways mentioned in the public domain, I will not describe them further. I will only say that Sue could not move well through certain geometries, so she had to walk sideways with her eyes closed and her hands against the wall.

"I'm blaming this on you," I told her, checking my watch. "Being late."

"Wait till you get a plate in your head. See how much you like it."

And then, finally, to a nicely decorated dining room behind a door marked "ADR-2." We sat near a window looking out over brilliant foliage, at a linen-clothed table with patterned china and properly arranged spoons. Wicker-back chairs. I thought about Aunt Lillian and ordered steak.

"Nice to meet you," I said to the two people who joined us. Mid-forties, both male.

And then a bunch of small talk about sports and people we might know in our parallel worlds. It was all quite informal and polite. Just lunch.

"I saw you on *Larry King* a few weeks back," One of Them said as we were finishing our salads. "The *Today* show. *Imus in the Morning.* Your spread in *GQ.* I just got your book."

The other male nodded. "You're all over the place, huh? What's it like on TV?"

"I'm not sure what I expected, but the learning curve has been steep."

"Well . . . see one, do one, teach one, right?"

I nodded, then I explained what I could of my ill-timed transition from fifteen years in clandestine service to life as a talking head. Uncle Harold, my interest in maths. Big Bob.

"What did the FBI think about it?" One of Them asked. "The book."

"They were supportive." I shrugged. "I think they thought it might help with recruiting."

"How'd you get it published?"

"I sold it in a poker game with Brad Pitt," I said. "*GQ* excerpted it and put me on the masthead. The editor's name is Art Cooper, and he wants to fly me to Afghanistan to find bin Laden, write an article about the shadow war. So, here I am."

"Sure, you did." One of Them laughed. Then the other. "Brad Pitt."

Their toplofty response reminded me of those two women needling Raz near the Kool-Aid machine at the Farm. How he'd told them we were in the Justice Department, and they'd nodded, assuming everything in the world was good cover. Two Truths and a Lie. This snide game.

"So . . . I've got something to run by you," I told them. "Speaking of *GQ.*"

Then a server brought the entrées, and we turned to the matter at hand, my pitch. It started off simply enough with me saying I still stood for the national anthem watching NASCAR races, even when there was no one else around. I mentioned the phrase "special access program" and certain classifications I'd held. I listed denied areas I might have visited, identities I may have used; team roping, no mention of bar mitzvahs. I summarized my weapons expertise, explosives training, work in Elizabethan theater, arcane and specialized skills. And eventually I told them what I thought I could accomplish moving through the tribal areas of Pakistan with a press credential as discussed over maps with Art Cooper at 4 Times Square in Manhattan. I mentioned single malt whiskey, how Condé Nast was more than willing to front business–class tickets and reasonable expenses. I needed targets and objectives.

"That's quite interesting," One of Them said when I had finished. "But I see a couple potential barriers to success. The first, of course, being the issue of tasking."

"Tasking?"

"Tasking."

He was kind enough to thank me for my visit, but explained that the U.S. government already had a Joint Special Operations Command, B–52 bombers, and sixteen intelligence agencies who felt quite confident they could handle things without me. He took a minute to discuss the differences between Title 50 authority and Title 18 jurisdictions, how the CIA gathered foreign intelligence for clients like the White House while FBI agents like me chased thieves. He spoke with that polite condescension you'll find at all three–letter agencies.

"Gotcha." I nodded.

But then I reminded him that perhaps he had missed a couple of things while he was chewing broccoli, specifically the windfall potential of my plan, which I ran through all over again. And when I was done, the other guy said, "You know what? This might dovetail nicely."

He reached into his pocket for a business card and, on the back, jotted down a room number at the Pentagon. A name.

"This is the person you need to speak with," he told me. "You should go there, now. I'll call and tell him you're coming."

After lunch, Sue and I walked back to her office, slowly down that odd-shaped corridor, her hands on the wall. When we got to her desk, she said, "Want to see something cool?" She reached into her top drawer and pulled out a small glass vial full of what looked like about three grams of blow.

"Hall and Oates." She smiled. "My lie. I figured no way the HRT guy knows Farsi."

"What?" I shook my head. "You have frigging anthrax in your desk?"

"It's inert, but it has all the basic properties." She rolled the vial between her fingers, and though a powder, it seemed to flow like homogenized milk. "Cool, right?"

"Piece of work," I told her. "I'd put you in my next novel, but who would believe it?"

"Two truths and a lie, babe," she said. "Gotta keep 'em guessing."

I looked around at what could be any place of business, piles of folders and coffee cups and family candids on desks in three-by-five frames. Computer screens with privacy filters and ergonomic chairs. The walls were dotted with inspirational prints, chrome-framed golf courses sparkling with dew, sunsets at sea. There was a fighter jet going vertical with the caption "Integrity," some others about teamwork and pride. I saw a .50-caliber bullet casing holding a Bic pen, the spent launch tube for an M72 rocket. She had a bobble-head Jesus, various WMD graphics like you'd see on a Slayer album or fallout shelters when I was a kid.

"It's called *Black*," I told her. "The novel. I'll make you the hot karaoke singer from Iowa State. Anthrax assassin from CIA. What do you think?"

"Who cares?" She shrugged. "Just don't call me Sue."

When we got to the janitor's closet, the producer handed me one of those clear plastic earpieces HRT used on protection details. She clipped a small microphone to my tie and ran the cord down the back of my jacket to a battery pack clipped to my belt.

"This is your book, right?" she asked. Had it in her hand. "I'll put it on the shelf behind you, so it shows up in frame. L.A. will also have it in graphic, so you'll get plenty of coverage."

"Okay, thanks."

Then she pointed to a cheap fold-up chair. "You're hot. L.A. will cue you in."

It was a tiny room with library wallpaper and bright lights and a small camera like you used to have for home videos. Someone had taped an eight-by-ten piece of paper right beside the lens. They had drawn an arrow with a Magic Marker and two words: "LOOK HERE."

I sat in the chair as the producer pulled the door closed behind her. I heard background noise in my earpiece, a commercial for L'Oréal, then some music and Larry King's voice introducing his next guest, a special agent with the FBI named Christopher Whitcomb.

"Mr. Whitcomb," I heard him say. Larry King. And then he asked a bunch of questions, about al Qaeda, bin Laden, the World Trade Center, what had just happened to innocence.

I sat there for a long beat, trying to decide what to make of all this. For some reason my mind conjured flames: campfires in Franconia; Thermite pyres in Kosovo; the ember-charred remains of children at Waco; smoke rising off the USS *Cole* in Yemen; muzzle flash at Ruby Ridge. I thought about L.A. burning in the Rodney King riots; the small, red glow of a cigarette in the mouth of a bad man I had quartered in a jungle near El Yunque. Door breaches, grenades. I remembered my uncle Mike, always there or coming, a wife raising four kids without me. I thought about my friend John O'Neill, who had spent his career fighting al Qaeda and died at the twin towers, Terry Quinn and the guys from Ladder 22 combing rubble for survivors. My brother and my father grieving the loss of heroes because they were firefighters, too. Bodies falling. Americans grieving. Everyone connected.

I thought about leaving a job that had been the cornerstone of my identity since I was twenty-seven years old. The shock, the rage, the resolve. Black Thursday, that horrible Tuesday.

"Hello, Larry," I answered.

They say it all passes in a flash, that last moment, right before your eyes. And it did, my life in the FBI. But that's the thing about being born whole into a life fully formed, there are no do-overs. You take the good with the bad.

"Feebie, huh?"

The man at the Pentagon was wearing a knit tie and khakis, his shirtsleeves rolled up to reveal three separate watches. Sue had told me he was a warrant officer with a military occupation specialty that had no nine-character code. The name on the card from lunch was "Fred," but he did not introduce himself, and I did not ask.

"I used to be."

We shook hands, and I looked for a place to sit, but all he had was a freestanding blackboard and a couch covered in boxes. He had a window that looked out onto other windows. There were no family photographs, nothing on the walls.

"Well, you come recommended," he told me. "I won't hold it against you."

The blackboard was a jumble of words and smudges where he had been mapping his thoughts. There were three columns, more or less, which started on the left with the heading "Mission Program Plan" and bullet points such as "democracy," "economy," "justice." The middle column listed B platforms with the names "Minot" and "Al Udeid," distances in kilometers, specific types of munitions. The column on the right had a bunch of refrigerator poetry combos, things like "Objective Gecko," "Vector Strawberry," "Hammer Down." I'm kidding, of course, but not really.

"I hear ya have a proposal," the man told me. Fred. Heavy Boston accent.

"You from Boston?"

"No."

We talked for more than an hour about tasking and essential elements of information with specific reference to the concepts of client, narrative, and agency. We had a frank discussion about outdated inferences I might have carried with me from the FBI, the scope and intent of the Constitution, matters of surreption, the authority of George W. Bush. He used a bewildering series of acronyms to describe subsets of affiliations that would specifically not be financed by, nor in any way tied to, the CIA. He mentioned blood chits, a phone number in West Virginia.

At one point he said, "Yut, that Rumsfeld is a real pissah."

Then he read me into Pakistan, the differences between lines on a map and ancient alliances involving the Pashtun, Tajik, the Nuristani. He detailed the reach of Musharraf and his Inter-Services Intelligence, the ISI, known strategies of America's initial deployment. We discussed our own individual interactions with terror, relevant notes on culture, climate, and clothing.

Finally, we went over logistics involved in any trip to Afghanistan, including cash, shot cards, waterborne illnesses, visas, and fixers. When I thought we were done, I thanked him for his time and asked him if there was anything I had missed. I wanted to know if he had any advice, something that might help me fully accomplish my now better-delineated goals.

"I have one suggestion," he said.

I found him to be a thoughtful man, though brusque; keenly insightful. He reminded me of the Wizard of Oz, a small and ordinary man hiding behind the booming voice of the DOD, a patriot doing his best at wheels and levers.

"What is it?" I asked.

He turned to his blackboard and resumed his scribbles. The warrant officer with no MOS, the spook with three watches.

"Never trust a man who squats to piss."

6

Islamabad, Pakistan

[NOVEMBER 2001]

G etting to the war was no picnic. Conventional wisdom held that one could fly to Uzbekistan and travel south in trace of soldiers, or to Islamabad and then north through the Khyber Pass. The problem with Tashkent was Pentagon flack Torie Clarke, who was putting journalists into Humvees with seventeen-year-old M60 gunners from Detroit because war is easier to pitch from the inside out. The embed route worked well if your name was Geraldo Rivera, but mine was not.

The problem with the Khyber Pass was that it was full of bad guys who did not discriminate between cameras and guns. They were killing everybody. Some print media types were flying into Tajikistan and weaving their way west along the tortuous route from Dushanbe, but that was a perilous fourteen-hour grind under the best of circumstances. Ramadan in a time of jihad was not the best of circumstances.

"You're the FBI guy with all the connections," Art Cooper had told me, our last meeting in his office. "Do you think Alan Richman bitches about booking his own flights?"

I had never heard of Alan Richman.

"There's a lot of moving pieces, Art. We are invading a country."

"Call Travel, for Chrissake. Sign for some cash. Just figure it out!"

Figure it out? I had flown private for the past ten years, Falcons and C-17s full of pipe hitters with beards and tattoos who would not have been caught dead stooping to logistics. Fred and I had not even discussed travel, because nobody books their own flights in spy movies, and compared to finding his office at the Pentagon, a trip to Kabul should have been child's play.

Uncle Pi was no help, either.

"*GQ*?" he'd laughed out loud during our Saturday round of golf. "You want to mount out to Trashcanistan with a bunch of pouters wearing calfskin loafers?"

"It's complicated," I told him, halfway down the third fairway.

"Oh, yeah. I'll bet. You and Markie Mark roping into Tora Bora wearing camouflage tighty-whities. Calvin Klein goes to war; the guys in the back room are gonna love this."

He lined up on his ball and started that weird cocked-head waggle. "I hear Ashleigh Banfield is still over there," he said. "Promise you'll steal me a pair of her panties, and I'll call my buddy at the embassy. Now watch this shot."

My last option was burgers and beer in New York City, a Chelsea bar called the Half King. "That's a tough one," Sebastian told me. "I'd probably fly into Lahore, work north through the Swat Valley."

I'd first met Sebastian Junger leaning against a Leopard 1A5 tank in the Italian sector near Dakovica during the war in Kosovo. He was a household name at that point, due to his wildly successful book, *The Perfect Storm.* He owned one of the coolest watering holes in the city, had a tough-guy shadow, literary chums. He was on the masthead at *Vanity Fair,* provided the jacket blurb for my first book.

"Want another beer?"

"Sure," I said. "I gotta tell you, man, you and I have done some crazy shit over the years, but I always had backstops and weapons. This solo stuff is a whole new adventure."

Sebastian was not much of a talker, but he had a timeless stare, a present laugh. I considered him the best war writer since Herodotus, which is saying a lot, because you know I love Hemingway.

"How's the book doing?" he asked.

"Fine. Baldacci is taking me out on his tour. Great guy. You know him?"

"Nah. We gotta get you scheduled, here, for a reading."

"Cool."

I did not go to Sebastian Junger seeking help with sales or promotions. I wanted advice on how to walk alone. He had a rare understanding of hollows, the dark defilade where a writer might look for truth, in bomb craters, hearts and minds. I reminded him of a town in Kosovo called Peć, where an old man had stopped us on a bridge. The man was crying, and we couldn't understand, so he pulled down his pants to show us that somebody had cut off his dick. That raw, weeping stub. I had asked Sebastian about it over a cup of tea, and he'd said something like violence is done by man, not to him. Violence is man. There will always be war.

"I plan to cross near Chitral," I told him. "There's a mullah named Sufi Muhammad."

"You'll figure it out," he told me. "Please pass the ketchup."

I was still trying to figure it out when I met Joe at Heathrow. He was standing at the bottom of a long escalator outside the British Airways lounge, with a phone to his ear, the first guy I ever knew who had an American Express Black Card. That meant he also had a twenty-four-hour concierge who sounded earnestly chipper about helping Sheryl Crow's former boyfriend find vegetarian restaurants in Herat.

"Get me a beer," Joe said, pointing with his thumb. "I gotta get these bets in."

I was still trying to figure it out when we arrived at the Islamabad Marriott twelve hours later. Every journalist in Central Asia had posted up there, looking for an angle on the story. The parking lot was crowded with Prados, windows cracked so the drivers could smoke; Hilux pickups full of plainclothes guards with fake Ray-Bans and prominently featured guns.

Inside, the lobby was bristling with people on sat phones and walkie-talkies, everybody yelling with an urgency that corresponded to nationality and the prominence of affiliations. The loudest offenders, of course, were American: network producers, specifically ABC. Then came cable news, a crew from CNN and everyone associated with Ashleigh Banfield, who had arrived as MSNBC's blonde du jour but was now a prime-time sensation. She had that Catherine Deneuve vibe, big glasses, and a way with words. She used phrases like "quite conversely" and "no less rattling" to describe ugly things, the blunt filth of invasion. She had dyed her hair brown and wore a scarf to look less glamorous, but this was not a glamorous place to begin with, so she was easy to spot. Which was good, because I had promised Pi I'd steal her drawers.

"Four hundred a night?" Joe said, louder than anybody else in the lobby. "In this shithole? You gotta be kidding me."

"Yes, sir. Please, sir." The clerk nodded. "I am sorry, sir, there is a war."

I had slept poorly on the flight from Dulles and even less coming in, which meant I was out of sorts. Joe lived in L.A. but had been staying with his most recent love interest, near Marylebone, in the West End, so his head was only five time zones east of GMT. Joe called himself a citizen of the world, was a pro traveler if I'd ever met one. He was good with logistics.

"War?" he growled at the kid behind the counter. "I don't see any goddamned war."

"Yes, sir. Please, sir . . ."

Joe waved his hand around the lobby as if to prove his point. "All I see is a bunch of tourists in safari vests. Holy shit, is that John Burns?" Then he just walked away.

"We'll take it," I told the clerk.

I had been to these parties a million times, of course, on both sides of the rope. Crisis response is remarkably similar whether you're the FBI or *Der Spiegel*. Everybody flies in with a bunch of padded cases, experts in their field, heartfelt resolve. It does not matter whether you represent Justice or the fourth estate, both sides wield imperative. Invariably, it becomes a pissing match between the people who hold the perimeter and those trying to wriggle through.

Regardless, I finally checked in, got Joe away from John Burns, and made it to the room.

"Fucksakes, Whit, that's a lot of cash."

I had pulled ten thousand dollars out of my pack and tossed it onto the bed. Two bricks of fifties.

"They don't take Black Cards where we're going," I told him.

"We should split it up."

"Yut. Here, put this in your sock."

Joe and I worked well together, and simply. I had met him during happy hour at a Best Western near Davis-Monthan Air Force Base in Tucson, Arizona, my first year on HRT. He had been trying to break into Hollywood writing scripts, and I had a novel, so a mutual friend made the connection. That mutual friend was a Charlie team assaulter named Magnum who could jump flat-footed to the top of any bar wearing cowboy boots and a Browning Hi-Power. He was winning bets with business travelers when Joe arrived. We'd been thick ever since.

"What's next?" he asked me.

"The embassy."

"All right. Let me hit the head."

Joe traveled light and always looked the same. He wore James Perse T-shirts, Blundstone boots, and one of two Prada jackets, depending on the weather. Average height and build, a hockey player from Minnesota who passed the bar but never practiced law. He read Bukowski; collected penguins; lived east of Lincoln, in a midcentury bungalow on a double lot in Venice, California. At that time, he owned a casting company specializing in real people. He'd found the world's most interesting man for Dos Equis, a Latin-looking fellow named Goldsmith.

We showed up at the embassy about thirty minutes later, in the Pakistani version of a rape van, the only ride left to hire. Pakistan presents British, so the driver was on the right, Joe in the middle. A soldier walked up to my window because I had waved, the stranger coming in.

"Yessah," the guard said. Heavy local accent. He had a red beret and a bolt-action rifle.

"I'm here to see a guy."

"Which guy."

"A guy."

"You here for conference?"

"No."

"Why are you here?"

"I need to see a guy."

"Please step out of the car."

And here is where we can agree that I am a complete frigging moron. If I had ever previously visited the U.S. embassy in Islamabad— and I am not saying I had—it did not have an outer perimeter staffed by Pakistani soldiers with bolt-action rifles. I had not considered such a thing because traveling on the down-low with X-ray snipers meant you just pull in with your blacked-out Suburban and follow some guy in cargo pants to your meeting.

Things had changed.

"Seriously, Whit?" Joe groused. "A guy? You want to see a guy? What the fuck."

I didn't know what to tell the guard: He was Pakistani; his uniform didn't even fit. There was no way I was going to give him the names of my contacts, not in front of the rape van driver, not even in front of Joe. And what the hell was going on, anyway? FBI agents on foreign soil do not explain themselves to locals. I was used to VIP status, a backstage pass to the world.

"Wait here," I told Joe. "I'll be back in twenty minutes."

Which proved to be optimistic, because it took all of that just to get past the marines to an office with a big desk, some chairs, and two men I had never met. Overseas FBI offices are called legal attachés, or Legats. This was a small one.

"How do you know Pi?" I asked the big man after pleasantries. He was an FBI agent named Charles, wearing one of those gold rings everybody buys for their twenty-year medallion.

"We worked white collar together in San Diego," Charles told me. "Bank fraud."

The office looked like anywhere: plaques, framed memorabilia, GSA furniture. But two things alarmed me. The first was a copy of my book, *Cold Zero,* on the corner of his desk. The second was the September issue of *GQ* magazine, open to a full-page spread of me sporting camo pants and too much product in my hair.

The caption read, "Trained to kill with a license to do so."

Neither man said a word, but the message was clear. They'd highlighted it in yellow.

"Great guy," Charles said. "We played on a bar league softball team called My Dick Is So Hard I Don't Have Enough Skin Left to Close My Eyes. He is the only agent I ever met who rolled up from the Academy sporting an eighteen-karat Rolex Presidential."

"That's Pi." I laughed. "He still wears it everywhere, even CQB, breaching doors."

"Terrible golf swing. How can I help you?"

From there we sat down and had a frank conversation about where I planned to go and the basics of what I hoped to accomplish. Because that's how things worked in those days: You'd knock rings, tell a few jokes, and then, if everything went well, turn tidy and get down to business.

"First things first," the other guy told me, the short guy who did not offer a name. "The tribal areas lie outside our sphere of influence. The war goes back and forth across the border up there, and the ISI is fully engaged, so don't think they won't know who you are."

"All right."

"We can't keep you from going, but if anything happens, you're on your own, and you need to know that. Second, this is one of the most corrupt countries on earth, and if you want to get anything done, you're going to need to grease a few palms. Stay here. I'll be right back."

While he was gone, Charles read me in on important aspects of America's new global war on terror. He talked about the true nature of Musharraf's cooperation, the influence of mullahs. He told me the Taliban had fallen at Mazar-e-Sharif, Taloqan, Bamiyan, that the Northern Alliance had seized Kabul. He said three Germans had been killed waving press passes in Khyber, that I was a fool if I thought anyone gave a shit about me holding a camera.

"Who's the short guy?" I asked, but Charles ignored me. Then the short guy came back holding two bottles of Johnny Walker Black.

"Pakistan is a dry country," he said. "This stuff is liquid gold."

"Thanks." I nodded.

"Thank the CIA. I stole it from the bar."

When we were done, I stood up to leave, and we all shook hands.

"Before you go," Charles said, "I gotta ask, how the hell did you get a book about HRT past prepublication review? Seriously, how did you sell a goddamned memoir?"

So, I told him.

"Hey, Chooch, pass me a beer," Joe said.

"Hand me one while you're at it," I chimed.

"Fuck yourself, Whit," Chooch told me. "Let me see that pistol."

I have always loved New York. I remember the first time I saw it from the Cross Bronx Expressway during Mayor Beame's era, an entire borough of rubble. In college, I visited the Met and attended dinner parties on the Upper East Side. During my years teaching English at the Berkshire School, Rosie and I would drive in from Western Massachusetts to watch plays, rummage for books at the Strand. We stayed with friends at the Hotel des Artistes; strolled the park down to Random House, where Cormac McCarthy sold his books—I remember looking up, imagining editors behind those mirror-black windows— then over Forty-eighth Street to the Scribner Building, where Maxwell Perkins had squired Fitzgerald and Thomas Wolfe. I loved the rumble of trains, graffiti-tagged walls, dirty water dogs, picklebacks at three in the morning, after Elaine's had closed. I loved the art, the music, the words carved into buildings, the utter sex of it all.

"What's the game?"

"In-between," Chooch decided. "Mixed with a little Red Dog, ten-dollar ante."

In the late nineties, my home and professional lives were centered in Virginia, but social interactions had moved to SoHo, a stark-white lobby in André Balazs's new spot, the Mercer Hotel. It was a Friday in November 1999. I had taken the train up to New York because some buddies were in town. I had just flown home from Macedonia, and it wasn't yet Christmas, so I had the weekend to blow off a little steam. Most of my friends lived in Tribeca but ate at Raoul's, where you could still buy an eight ball of crack and go sporting for hookers. There was a great bar called Fanelli, where we'd sit afternoons drinking Brooklyn Lager while listening to Bob the bartender talk about fighting Larry Holmes at Madison Square Garden.

The lobby of the Mercer Hotel was the hottest seat in town in those days, and to be fair, the only reason I ever got through the front door was a buddy we will henceforth refer to as L. Bellagio. I had met him six or seven years earlier, in a sandwich place off Abbot Kinney, in Venice, California. He was best buddies with Joe, who was unemployed at the time. L. Bellagio was unemployed, too, but he was an actor and had just auditioned for a TV show called *Chicago Hope*. I recognized him from movies like *Shocker* and from my favorite ski flick, *Aspen Extreme*.

"What was it like to do full-frontal nudity?" I asked, referring to that memorable scene where he runs naked down a road in the snow. "Like swimming in cold water? Because, damn."

"You know, Whit," he'd sniffed. "If it weren't for your job, I wouldn't even talk to you."

We had fallen into an alpha male pose-off because he was a face; I carried a gun. But now we were buddies posted up on couches at the Mercer with the rest of the crew filtering in.

"So, what are we doing later?" I asked. L. Bellagio usually called the shots.

"Playing cards."

"Yeah, right. Where we going?"

"We're playing cards."

I had driven up thinking we'd go out for a big dinner, like we usually did, ten or twelve fascinating people at Rao's or some new restaurant where nobody else could get a table. My life was truly out there in the nineties, bouncing between T-ball games, black ops in Third World shitholes, and a novelty seat among a whole bunch of household names.

"What's the buy-in?" I asked him.

"Don't worry about it. I got you covered."

We started around nine. The Mercer staff had decked out one of the bigger rooms with a table, several buckets of Corona, and a whole bunch of Patrón. It was Joe and me and L. Bellagio and some new guys I had not met. One of them was named Steve Scher, whom I will introduce by saying he is dead as of this writing, and his name is tattooed on my arm. There was a disarmingly articulate guy from Harvard, two tagalong yucksters and their buddy, Chooch, whom I did not know well enough for nicknames, so I called him Brad or Mr. Pitt.

I had ended up at the head of the table, Joe, Scher, and Harvard on my right, Brad Pitt to my left, then his buddies. We played around the table for a couple of hours, breaking out the cigars and the taunts and the goofy things guys do in a card game. I told Brad Pitt I had a T-shirt from Kickapoo High School because Springfield, Missouri, was my first office; he'd grown up there.

"Oh, yeah?" he said. "Go, Chiefs."

The room was raucous, full of smoke and money, men drinking irresponsibly.

"Come on, Whit, show him your gun," Joe told me at one point.

I had a big Les Baer .45, so I pulled it out, dropped the mag, and ejected a round into Brad Pitt's lap. Harvard picked up the pistol and aimed it at the ceiling, Joe announced side bets on speed-loading. I would swear Jennifer Aniston and Courtney Cox stopped by, but I

have been told I'm wrong. Yes, I am aware that this was appalling behavior, but I'll make sense of it later.

"What's the game?"

"I just told you," Chooch said. "In-between with a little Red Dog,
too."

"What do you mean a little Red Dog, too?"

"Scher, quit dicking around. You in or out?"

"Blow me."

This was before Texas hold 'em, so games could get exotic. In this
case, the deal went clockwise, each player getting two cards face up
and betting on the third in between. If you got a two and a three, you
would pass, because there was no way to win. If you got a two and an
ace, you'd bet the pot, because aces were high. The problem was that
if you matched either of the two original cards, you would have to
double the pot, which had already happened several times. The game
just kept going until someone took it all, so, by the time it came back
to me on the fourth or fifth cycle, there was a pile of cash on the table.
It was a big pile, several thousand dollars.

"You lucky bastard," I heard Brad Pitt say. I had drawn a two and a
king.

"Pot," Scher decided, as if it were obvious. He was a bet-the-pot
guy.

"Pot," the entourage agreed, everybody nodding.

"Of course he's going pot," Brad Pitt decided on my behalf. That
pikey look.

The problem, as I saw it, came down to maths. This was a new
deck, which still had three kings and three twos. Quick calculation put
my odds of stepping in shit at 6 in 48, or about 13 percent. I also understood that 52 factorial placed risk somewhere around 1.2 to the
power of 60, which is a very big number. Even drunk, I knew it would
be a nice win, but way too much to lose.

"How much is in there?" I asked, pointing.

Brad Pitt looked at me, then looked around the room. Think *Joe
Black* meets *Twelve Monkeys,* that man-child confusion. Tongue between his teeth, like he's about to whistle.

"How much?" he said. "Who cares how much?"

"Pot," Scher decided again. Puffing on a Cohiba.

L. Bellagio nodding. "Go pot."

"Son. Of. A. Bitch," Chooch taunted. "You don't have the balls, do you?"

It wasn't a question of balls. I was a government employee with a mortgage, four kids, a 401(k), a social worker wife. I did not have eight thousand dollars in my pocket, which is pretty much what a bad card would cost me. I still owed a hundred dollars for the buy-in.

Joe started laughing, that infectious chug of his. Harvard called me Limp Dick. Then it went around the table like contagion, epithets and taunts, stuff no one's supposed to say.

"You don't, huh, Whit?" Chooch said. He stood up and pointed his finger, the pretty boy from *Thelma and Louise* calling me out. "Mr. Tough Guy FBI sniper doesn't have the stones!" Then he reached into his pocket and yanked a bankroll of hondos. "I'll bet two grand Mr. HRT doesn't have what it takes."

Furious side bets ensued, everyone high-fiving and laughing and casting aspersions. Guys doing shots, all the server girls laughing, too, like they were in on some kind of hotel lore.

"Pot!" I announced. "Pot! Fuck you guys!"

The room went dead silent as Chooch picked up the deck and made stage drama out of the flop. When I opened my eyes and saw that it was a ten, I jumped to my feet with both middle fingers in the air, and pandemonium ensued. It was epic. Everybody yelling and jumping around and paying those side bets, cash a cloud in Mercer air. I scooped up every bill on the table and then held out my palm to Brad Pitt, who owed me for side bets also.

"Who's got the stones now, Mr. Fight Club?" I asked him. We'd all seen the trailer.

"Lucky prick." He's such a great guy.

When the frenzy had subsided, I broke the cardinal rule of card games involving famous actors and serious gamblers. I took the money and ran. It was still early enough to go see Bob the bartender at Fanelli for a beer and a couple of stories about how he'd robbed a bank. I grabbed my .45 out of L. Bellagio's lap, loaded it up, and left the guys to their cigars.

"Fuck you, Whit!" is the last thing I remember. Sticks and stones.

I took the elevator down to the stark-white lobby, out through those tall leather curtains onto Prince. The night felt new and vibrant. I could not wait to call Rosie and tell her the story.

"But how did you sell the book?" Charles asked when I had fin-ished. "I don't get it."

I told him how, the next morning, L. Bellagio called me down to breakfast with two brothers named Stone, who found me an agent at William Morris, who sold the book to Little, Brown. That *GQ* bought excerpts, took me to lunch at Four Seasons, put me on the masthead. How everything was great until asshole bin Laden blew up the towers the day before my first signing and I couldn't go back to the fight, so I had to think up new ways to contribute.

"So, here I am."

"Hmmm." Charles nodded.

I picked up my two bottles of Johnny Walker Black, and we all shook again, but then the short guy put his hand on my shoulder and said, "They probably told you some crap about blood chits and phone numbers in West Virginia, but don't believe 'em. If anything happens, you're on your own. Nobody is coming to get you. It's important you know that going in."

"Thanks, man." I nodded. Then I walked away.

It was dark by the time Joe and I got back to the hotel.

"Can you believe this shit?" he groused. "This country has nuclear weapons, and you can't buy a beer?"

A very polite concierge had just informed us that Pakistan prohibits alcohol consumption for all Muslims, making it a felony for 97 percent of Islamabad to hit the bars, even after thirty hours of flying and a long visit at the station. There were only two places in town where one might find a cocktail, the concierge told us. One of them was the Serena Hotel, which was too far to walk, and because this was the first day of Ramadan, all drivers were home enjoying Ishtar with family.

"That sounds like a hundred-dollar problem," Joe said. He reached into his boot.

"Please, sir, no, sir." The concierge raised his palm in protest, all very professional.

"More?"

"No, sir, please, sir."

"How much?"

I tried to diffuse the situation by comparing things to Lent, but that was pointless, because Joe knew all about Ishtar and didn't care about Lent; he was an atheist.

"I just spent two hours sniffing curry-flavored ass," he told me. "Because you had to go see 'a guy,' and now you've got two bottles of hooch we can't drink because ten grand isn't enough cash to work things out. Spare me."

As luck would have it, the Marriott catered to the international traveler, so the other bar in town was right beneath our feet. We took the elevator to the basement, followed signs to a door at the end of a hallway. The place was empty except for a bartender who refused to serve us until we'd registered in a government ledger. All patrons were required to list full name, passport number, and a signature attesting belief in any god except the prophet.

"Is he watching?" Joe asked, meaning the bartender.

"Nope."

"Good. Fuck these guys."

He signed in as "L. Bellagio," and I signed in as "Team Rope Header." Back to the bar.

"Good evening, gents. How may I help you?" The bartender was professionally trained and well put together, maybe twenty-seven.

"What is Murree?" I asked.

"It is whatever you'd like, sir. We have beer, whiskey, vodka, sherry."

"All Murree?"

"Yessir. We are a Muslim country: Alcohol is not allowed."

"Wait a minute," Joe said. "You only have two bars in the whole country, but you make your own booze? How's that work?"

He reached into his camera bag and pulled out one of the Johnny Walker bottles, and I shook my head, because I knew where this was going. I had seen it before.

"What about women?" he asked, looking around. "Are they illegal, too?"

"Joe."

"I mean it is Friday night, and we're in town for only a couple days."

"Come on, man. I'm tired."

And we must pause here for a moment, because there is no way to continue without a little backstory. Everyone who knows me will state unequivocally that I know nothing about women, except that they all love Joe. I'm talking about famous women, infamous women, notorious women, unknown women, rich, poor, young, old, married, and single. Joe found love in dive bars, on three-hundred-foot yachts, along bike paths. And yes, there were women in the hotel, but they were all busy filing stories or setting up feeds on the roof for morning shows in New York. He needed options.

"Relax, Whit," he said as we drank. "Let me work."

I could walk you through the whole process of bartering CIA liquor for women of negotiable morality during Ramadan, but that would be misprision. It would also be pointless, because just about the time the bartender hung up the phone and told Joe he had girls on the way, a haggard-looking man in street clothes walked in and tapped me on the shoulder.

"Mr. Jon Christopher?" he inquired.

I just looked at him.

He handed me a folded piece of paper. "Please you to meet friend mine here."

I took the note, saw that it listed a time and an address.

"What's that?" Joe asked.

"I don't know," I told him. "But finish your beer. There's no time for hookers."

Turns out the address was only four blocks away, the corner of two oddly quiet streets. We got there just before 11:30, but everything was closed, so we stood quietly waiting until a four-door sedan pulled up and the man in the passenger seat told us to get in. We did.

And I will digress, again, to say that I know you have watched this scene play out in bad movies a hundred times. It is full-blown cliché. Granted. But I will also point out that we still have many pages to go, and if you don't believe me, here, there's no sense hanging around for the crazy shit that lies ahead. Trust me, I know what you're thinking, but I have all the receipts.

"I got no service, zero bars," Joe said after about forty minutes of driving. He had our only phone. "Just so you know."

Which made sense, because cell reception was spotty even in the city, and the city was now barely a glow behind us. The sky was cloudy and cold, and it was well after midnight when we turned off the road to what the sign said was a polo club, now deserted. I could see nothing but headlights until we parked near a modest single-story building. Shrubs. There was light in a window, three SUVs in the lot.

"Just you," the man in the passenger seat stated once we got out of the car. He pointed to a table on a veranda where Joe was supposed to wait, then led me inside to what could have been a community center in Tulsa. I counted four men wearing black cable-knit sweaters, sidearms holstered, two long guns, various styles of hat.

"Nice to meet you," a man said, the one wearing a topi. Rural clothing, rubber shoes. "As-salamu alaykum."

"Wa alaykumu s-salam."

We shook hands, and he motioned for me to join him at a table, just the two of us.

"I have never met anyone named Team Rope Header," he said. I looked down at the table where he had a photocopy of my passport. "Is that a common name in Northern Virginia?"

"How can I help you?" I asked.

"How can you help me?" He spoke in a firm voice but was cordial. I felt discovered though not betrayed. "I'm not sure why I'm here."

"I am not, either," he told me. "But I can guess."

Then we had a polite conversation that was rather one-sided, because I did not say a single word. I could see Joe through the window, and they had brought him tea as well, so I listened while our host explained that Pakistan was a new country in an old part of the world. That Musharraf was a general who had seized power based on intelligence from clever sources in withdrawn places. That we were surrounded by enemies; my confidence might be misguided.

"Tell me," he said after a while, making a circle with his finger. "Do you like this place?"

"You mean the polo club? Sure, I'll bet it's nice during the day."

"Not during the day. Do you like it now, alone in the middle of the night, chatting with armed men who are fully aware that you mock Islam by attesting faith as Team Rope Header."

What was I going to say?

"You are a visitor, here," he warned. Then he read me into a country briefing of his own, and when he was finished, he said, "Please enjoy your stay in Pakistan writing articles for your fashion magazine. GQ magazine. I trust you will remember us well."

Joe and I did not talk at all on the way back to town, lights on the horizon growing brighter as we rode across fields, then through the streets of Islamabad, to the hotel. My mind was an unsettled murk of sleep deprivation, Murree beer souring in my gut and a slight vibration I sometimes get when I'm cold.

"Good morning, sirs," the man at the door greeted us. An empty lobby. Two A.M.

Then up to bed. I took the cash out of my sock, laid it on the nightstand. Johnny Walker on the dresser. Joe killed the lights, and I lay there a long time staring at the ceiling. The only thing I could think of was that we had been in-country one day at the start of a longer journey. That I'd seen it all, but maybe not this. That the ISI was everywhere.

They wanted me to know.

7

North-West Frontier Province

[NOVEMBER 2001]

The road to Chitral passes through Thana, capital of Malakand District, which might have been Nebraska for all I knew, because the entire region was a cloud of smoke. There was no GPS or Google Earth in those days, and though I can now tell you every detail from terrain to demography, all I knew at the time was that we were headed north through what were called the tribal areas, beyond the reach of chaperones. I didn't even have a map.

"How much farther?" Joe asked.

Our driver's name was Jan Alam. He spoke English, eschewed Western music, and looked remarkably like Robert De Niro, which resonated with Joe, of course, because Joe's business was casting. As you might imagine, Jan Alam knew where to take us and what to do once we got there. He spoke only in answer to our questions, kept a machine gun under his seat, and came well recommended.

"We are close, Mr. Joe. Maybe one hour, no more."

"Step on it. This smoke is killing me."

Smoke was an issue because Malakand is a poor agricultural region of loamy soil and jagged mountains that I could describe further, but there's no point, because you've seen rocks and fields. Sugarcane was the primary crop, and for some reason, the locals had decided to burn everything for two hundred miles, choking us on acrid gray road all the way back from Peshawar.

"What's the name of this place?" Joe asked me at one point. He was bored because he had last been in London with his girlfriend, and there was nothing to photograph except me.

"Doesn't matter. We're looking for a guy, not a location."

"Great. Another guy."

In November 2001, Sufi Muhammad bin Alhazrat had risen to the top of several lists for one specific reason; he was leading thousands of Pakistani militants out of the tribal areas to help the Taliban kill Americans near Kabul. On paper, Sufi Muhammad was founder and First Emir of a group called Tehreek-e-Nafaz-e-Shariat-e-Mohammadi. My initial briefing stated that he had been born in Maidan, Lower Dir District; had received his education at Panjpir, Swabi; that he was sixty-eight years old. I knew that his sect of Islam was Sunni Salafi, that he controlled young men's minds from Abbottabad to Kashmir, that he had issued fatwas shortly after 9/11.

The good news was that he would be easy to spot because he wore a bright orange beard, a head wrap, and "birth control glasses." The bad news was that he lived in a denied area that frowned on people who looked like me. Whatever illusions I'd had regarding the global war on terror suddenly escaped me; a press pass from *GQ* magazine seemed like silly cover.

"Thana," Jan Alam told us once we had pulled into town. "You are here."

The first thing I noticed was a roundabout with a large statue of a large man on a rearing horse, waving a very large sword. Then I noticed a surprising number of Punjab Police, who stood out quite prominently with their khaki trousers and epaulets on charcoal-colored shirts. I had been warned that this bucolic farming community was known for an iron fist of corruption, what the locals called Thana culture. One of my sources had compared it to driving through Mississippi in the 1960s with Massachusetts plates. Other than that, it looked pleasant enough, with the sun setting over mountains, and the streets closing for the big meal of the day.

"And you wonder why I don't eat meat," Joe said.

He nodded toward one of the last open markets, a butcher shop next to a place that sold motorcycle parts and small engine repair.

There was a dead goat hanging upside down from a hook over a pool of used motor oil. It had been skinned and was missing a shoulder, but it still had its head. The carcass looked shiny in the long, yellow light, and a man with a knife stared as we drove by, carving some neighbor a stringy fillet. I noticed dead birds dangling unplucked by their feet and a bar ditch full of trash, entrails, and what must have been sewage based on the smell.

Then we turned right onto an unmarked street and up a winding dirt road to the top of a small mountain where Jan Alam parked in a cobblestone lot.

"Your professor," he told us, then climbed out to retrieve our rucks.

"Not bad," Joe decided, looking around. The view sprawled majestic.

"Let me do the talking."

At that point, a man walked up wearing white from head to toe, including his eyebrows and long, bushy beard. He welcomed me with a hug and called me Mr. Christopher and then hugged Joe, who he referred to as "my friend." He was probably sixty years old, was heavy-set, erudite. He had a warm, honest smile but was missing two incisors and had a real problem with his gums.

"As-salamu alaykum," he said.

"Wa alaykumu s-salam."

Then: "Welcome to my home," walking us around the garden.

The professor lived high on a ridge overlooking the Swat River Valley in a lovely old house that was masonry construction, painted white on a landscaped excavation. The house showed a large portico in front, louvered windows with stained glass transoms in hardwood frames. There was a broadly curved staircase leading from the lawn to the veranda, where his staff had arranged six chairs in the open air, beneath a forty-watt bulb.

"This is not an Afghan issue," he told us, once we had sat. "It is not a Pakistani issue. It is a Pashtun issue."

He had invited three other people to dinner, including his brother Bashir and two murky men who had not come to share Ishtar. I see no point in naming them.

"Millions of Pashtuns live along both sides of the border," the professor said. "They feel more allegiance to their tribe than to any government. We have only been an independent country since 1947. Our people go back to the beginning of time."

"What about the Taliban?" I asked. "Are they part of the tribe?"

"*Talib* means 'student,'" the professor explained. He held a PhD in economics but lectured history at a local college. He seemed quite comfortable delivering his lessons as Joe recorded. "A Talib is a student of Islam, but from the very lowest classes of society. They have no money for schools, so the only education they receive is in mosques, the madrassas. All they know are what mullahs tell them, which makes them vulnerable to fundamentalism, even extremism. Revolutions begin in the classroom."

"Tell me about Pir Sayed Ahmad Gailani," I said as our conversation careened among politics and war and religion, sometimes all one thing.

"He leads the National Islamic Front of Afghanistan. He wants to be prime minister of the new government. He has no chance."

"That is what he told me." I nodded. "I met with him before coming here. He said he offers peace, but the American government wants men with guns, which is strange, because he seems to have lots of men with guns. He had nothing good to say about the Northern Alliance."

Gailani lived behind twelve-foot-high walls on a dead-end street in a closed cantonment. He had a large security detail, including a sandbagged sentry post with a belt-fed RPD. He kept all his windows closed behind dark, heavy curtains with music blaring against SIGINT intrusion. His guards met us at an offsite, searched us, and only then drove us to the meeting. When I asked the well-known politician about seeming paranoid, he told me Afghanistan is a violent place and that it is not paranoia if people are trying to kill you.

"Everyone has guns." The professor shrugged. "What Gailani does not have is an army."

"He said Washington has no interest in peace, so he went to Rome for an audience with the king, seeking reunification. I didn't know Afghanistan had a king."

"Zahir Shah lives in exile. He is an old man, a sentiment." The professor thought for a moment. "Be careful who you ask about Sayed Ahmad Gailani, Mr. Christopher. Everyone knows he works for the ISI, therefore the CIA. He had a Peugeot dealership in Kabul."

"But he fought with bin Laden against the Russians, right?"

No response.

"He told me a friend of his had been blindfolded in Kandahar and taken to a cave several hours away. A doctor. He said bin Laden was sick but not dying, that he was in mountains but didn't know where."

"This man has been hiding since 1979. The Soviets did not find him; neither will you."

Then a servant brought glasses of water, two big trays of figs and cheeses and fresh local fruits. There was meat, also, but all I could think about was that goat.

"Why does the Taliban protect bin Laden?"

"To understand this, you have to understand Pashtuns," the professor explained. "We have a custom that when you invite a guest into your home, he becomes your responsibility, in all ways. You must feed him, clothe him, offer him a bed. It is a great honor for us to have guests, and we will protect them with our lives, if necessary. I think it would be easier to give up a brother than a guest. We say Pashtunwali."

"You are our guest," Bashir pointed out. "Osama bin Laden is a guest of our cousins in the Taliban. The decision is made at the beginning; things sometimes change before the end."

The servant followed up with tea, which we drank steaming, encircling parlor tables pushed together. The skies dazzled with the moon ascending, such a lovely evening.

"When bin Laden came to Afghanistan, he was nobody," the professor explained. "Just another Arab. But then he brought in money and made a name for himself fighting the Soviets. When Sudan pushed him out later, he needed a place to go, and the men he had fought with took him in as a guest. His mujahideen had become Taliban, focused on sharia law, a caliphate. Your president Clinton could have intervened; he did not."

"So, you're saying they had to protect him? The Taliban."

"Yes, of course, as I said. The Taliban are Pashtuns. They will not give up their guest. They cannot. It would be against everything we stand for."

"You say 'we.' You mean Pakistani Pashtuns?" I asked. "Will you protect bin Laden if he flees across the border once the Americans close in?"

They all thought quietly for a minute. Tora Bora was less than sixty miles away.

"The Taliban are all Pashtuns, but not all Pashtuns are Taliban," Bashir decided. He seemed to be growing ill at ease, wary of me and my questions. I noticed him deferring to head movements from those two men I have not named. Furtive looks, loaded gestures.

"There is support for Taliban here, but I don't think so for bin Laden."

The two quiet men sat there watching me, watching Joe, watching us watching them.

"What about Sufi Muhammad?" I asked. "He is not hiding. He is leading men across the border to fight. Pakistani jihad?"

"War is sport for these men," Bashir responded. "They like to fight."

"With what?" I asked. "All I have seen is farmers."

They all laughed.

"Everyone has weapons." The professor shrugged. He motioned to a servant and mumbled something in Pashto. "People who have nothing to eat will have a rifle."

The men talked among themselves as the servant went into the house. Joe got up to change the tape in his recorder, and then the servant came back with a Red Army–issued Kalashnikov. He handed it to the professor, who removed the magazine, cycled a round out of the chamber, and set the gun on the table in front of me. It was all very casual, a familiar routine.

"How much?" I asked. "How much for one rifle?"

"For you?" Bashir interjected. "Two thousand five hundred rupees, forty U.S. dollars."

"With the bayonet?" I asked.

"Yes, of course, you have the bayonet, as you see it there. I will give you three magazines, ninety regular bullets." He thought this was a negotiation, that I wanted to buy it. "Maybe less for people who live here, of course, more for invaders. You are in the middle."

"He means foreigners," the professor corrected his brother. "Not invaders."

Everybody nodded. Very matter-of-fact.

"Thank you," I told them. "What about other things: explosives, belt-fed RPGs?"

"Yes, of course, there is everything." It seemed obvious. "Some things cost more, some less. The British left bureaucracy, but the Soviets left weapons."

"I'm told Sufi Muhammad has thousands of soldiers. Where does he find them? How does he get them across the border?"

"Look out there." Bashir pointed. It was dark, but the harvest moon had opened the mountain horizon to easy speculation. "There are checkpoints, but only for foreigners like you."

Then one of the quiet men spoke. "Why Sufi Muhammad? Why you want to know?"

"He is difficult to understand for Americans who think of Pakistan as an ally," I said.

"We are your ally. Do not mistake our customs just because they confuse you."

"I'm not confused. I just want to be accurate," I argued. "What I tell people matters."

"Osama bin Laden is not Pakistani," Bashir jumped in. "He is not Afghan. He is not Pashtun. He is an Arab offered refuge because of his help against the Soviets. He helped your government, too. I have seen photographs of him with Americans, smiling. That is accurate."

I did not respond. Our tea had cooled.

"Excellent," the professor decided, as if wrapping up his lecture and sending everyone off to homework. "It's late. You must be tired from your travels. I will show you to your room."

"I want to meet these people," I told him. "I need to go to Chitral. It's important."

They looked at each other and spoke Pashto. Their conversation seemed contentious.

"You are my guests," the professor said, finally. "If you want to follow Sufi Muhammad across the border all the way to Kunduz, I will take you. We leave in the morning."

The first person who ever called me nuts was a psychiatrist from Johns Hopkins University, the lead clinician on a panel of five mental health professionals. It was my third year on HRT, maybe six months after Waco. I was sitting in the back row of classroom 214, a tiered lecture hall on the second floor of the FBI Academy building in Quantico, Virginia. The entire team of forty-seven shooters had been assembled in white polo shirts and well-polished boots. I was clean-shaven, had just cut my hair. The front office told us not to show up wearing guns, so I kept mine hidden.

"Confidentiality is important," the doctor said. His team had finished its fitness-for-duty assessment as directed by FBIHQ. "I feel it important to tell you all what I will report."

He was a willow of a man, with a pedantic voice, just taller than the lectern where he stood reading from prepared notes. His panel of shrinks stood off to the side with their hands clasped in front of them. There were three men, two women. All of them wore glasses; one had a beard.

The clock on the wall read 16:05. A Tuesday. You could hear a pin drop.

"You seem to have a significant issue with anger," he told us, because psychiatrists never use the word *nuts*. "I believe this anger is deep-seated and pervasive, the result of broad causality involving constant and sustained violence in training, appalling loss of life during successive deployments, and a wolf pack culture that discourages any display of emotional vulnerability, which you seem to misconstrue as weakness. Your anger has become rage."

He looked up from his notes as if assessing our reaction. Nobody said a word, but I stared back, seething. I could feel my heart beating with hatred for him and his crew. I hated the people who had sent him. I hated people in general. I kinda hated myself.

"I think this rage is culturally entrenched, self-similar, and very dangerous," he continued. "I believe this rage . . ."

"Rage?" one of the guys in the back row started yelling. "Rage?! You want rage? I'll show you rage!"

It seemed there was a difference of opinion between the docs and the operators. At that point, two things happened almost simultaneously: The doctor of psychiatry and his entire panel shit themselves on the way out the door, and my buddies fell into a bit of an intramural row.

The good news in all this was that my first *DSM*-III diagnosis of mental illness was delivered professionally in front of my closest friends, my peers and colleagues, people I most admired. The bad news is that the doctor was right.

It starts with night sweats—at least, it did with me. I would wake up at three in the morning levitating somewhere between a wet bed and the cold, hard floor, which I would hit in the Weaver stance, known at work as "ready gun." If you're lucky enough to have someone in bed with you, they wake up, too. Scared. Then they try to coax you off the ledge, because the kids are asleep down the hall, and it can get loud sometimes, if you're yelling; and they're young, so they don't understand what's wrong with Daddy. Then you come around a little bit, shake your head, apologize to no one in particular. You rinse off your face in the sink and climb back into those soaking-wet sheets, staring at the ceiling fan until it's time to go to work. Which is tough, because work is the only place you feel better, even though work is the problem to begin with.

There was no such thing as post-traumatic stress disorder in the nineties. Everybody had a crazy uncle Frank who had come back from Vietnam a little tweaked. Nobody cared, because he'd take you to the strip clubs on the back of his Harley in a leather vest covered with patches that read "Kill 'Em All, Let God Sort 'Em Out." It was kinda cool.

If CTE had been discovered, I had not heard mention. Depression wasn't a thing, because Boomers never got enough hugs growing up to begin with, so we handled mood swings with our fists at recess, in bars on weekends when we got older. Resilience had not been invented. Employment assistance programs were called Get Your Shit Together or You're Fired. Prozac was an option, but not really, because men who got stressed went bowling; women bought shoes. Cops beat their wives, but nobody cared, because wives had side squeezes and martinis.

The only real problem with mental illness, as I saw it, came down to secrecy. Every FBI agent holds top-secret/sensitive compartmented information, or TS/SCI. But due to the nature of our work, most HRT operators also read into augmented "permissions," for special-access programs, research projects, and even individual operations. I held a Q clearance, for example, which is now discussed in the public domain, but it was a felony to mention when I got it. There's one called COSMIC, which I never had; ATAMOL, which is similar to Q; and YANKEE WHITE, which is specific to dealing with the U.S. president.

Before you think this all sounds fun, understand that every classification comes with more ways to accidentally step on your own dick. There is the whole issue of lifestyle polygraphs, word traps where you can say things but not in certain configurations. Different agencies have different rules and often do not play nicely with others, which leads to jokes and miscalculations. When I pulled Q, for example, I had to sit through a black-and-white video from the 1950s that did not instill confidence in the intelligence agency that showed it. Black-and-white, I swear.

Plus, it's easy to make mistakes, because sometimes it just seems silly. Fast-roping was classified when I joined HRT, for example, certain types of bullets. You could get fired for mentioning technologies that your eighth-grader now keeps in the back of her closet. And then some guy shows up from DARPA with the prototype for a sonic cannon. It's cool if you're popping watermelons with high-powered speakers, but a pain in the ass if you're in a bar trying to talk about it with your partner while spies listen in. Then there's the chopper-mounted rifle platform that stabilizes shots using inertia to create artificial mass. Briefcase nukes, black staging areas in Cypress, sources and methods. It goes on and on.

Which brings us back to dreams, which I mentioned earlier because I once considered them helpful, and I need to make clarifications. When I was a kid, I had a recurring nightmare where a wolf would sneak into the house, put me in a sack, and steal me away while my mother was weeding carrots. It was terrifying, so I'd scream as hard as I could, but nothing would come out. Then, one day, I realized I could steer my dreams by calmly saying, "Mom, the wolf has me in a bag." She beat up the wolf, Bucky Corliss left me alone, the nightmare went away.

But then came the migraines. I remember sleeping on the seat of my Power Wagon because I'd get tunnel vision, making it impossible to drive. It would usually hit right after training, which made sense among guys who shot 250,000 rounds a year, entering every room with a flash-bang on the overpressure of C-4 charges that hit you like a fullback coming through the dive hole. We sparred daily at strikes, kicks, and ground game; jumped out of helicopters into the ocean at twenty feet and twenty knots. A steady diet of impact, one bell ring after another.

Which is a problem, of course, because all this stuff is hard on the brain, and the brain is critically important when it comes to secrets. Nobody knew how to react when guys like me started doing odd shit in public, because hostage rescue is a nuts-and-bolts game with nuts-

and-bolts solutions. If you get shot or break your leg, you just go to the team surgeon and get a bunch of Tylenol, but if you start wearing a hoodie in August or scaring new agent trainees in the lunch line, they bring in a psychiatric SWAT team from Johns Hopkins and take away your clearances, because you might be unstable. Can't hold Q if you're unstable.

So, I hid it. Or tried. In lieu of bitching, I figured out that the best feeling in the world was knowing I was going to die but surviving. Which was easy at first, because hostage rescue revolves around the surgical application of violence, presenting daily opportunities for excitement. CQB is live fire, for example, a game of inches where you get used to the feeling of bullets brushing against your cheek. But maybe you want to get a little closer, let those hollow points scratch your itch. So, you lean in.

I was on the climbing team, so I started a game called Toes Over, where I would get as high as I could and walk out to the edge, balancing death on the heels of my boots, hands out to my sides, teetering in the strongest wind I could find—cliffs, buildings, towers. And we lived in helicopters, of course, which we would fly in steep orbits with our feet in space, nothing but gravity for tether. Centrifugal force pins your ass to the deck, but I love physics, so I would push my head forward in the steepest banks, that thwomp of rotors providing comfort as I leaned forward until I became weightless, tiny fractions of formulas away from being spat out into the blue morning sky, one miscalculation from going home in a box.

But in the end, death is like any other addiction: The more you do, the more you need. And the more you need, the harder it is to find. So, sometime around 1994, I decided to give up on trying to steer dreams, to embrace more fully a life of hazard. I let Rosie deal with the kids while I turned off the lights completely, got used to lying in the dark, staring at the fan.

I awoke in Thana feeling a bit unsteady. Part of it was fitful sleep on a webbed cot in an unheated room. Part of it was the bright sun tapping at the window to remind me there would be nothing to eat or drink until dinner. Part of it was knowing we were heading north almost to

the Himalayas in search of zealot mullahs foisting jihad among madrassas full of teenagers who had rifles but no news of the world, only the
Koran.

"You good?" Joe asked, once he knew I was awake. "Made a lot of
noise last night."

"Jet lag."

"Copy."

Maybe it was because my plan had made better sense in the comfort
of a Porsche 911, all swole with Ludacris, racing up to lunch at the
CIA. Or perhaps that I would have felt safer with a red passport in my
pocket instead of U.S. dollars in my boot. There was a certain sobriety
in knowing that a press pass from GQ magazine would provide no
more protection than a forty-dollar AK-47 with a bayonet and three
magazines. Whatever the professor and his crew had been told or paid
by my handlers, they were smart men, and my true agenda was lost on
no one. Joe and I stood out like diamonds in that skun goat's ass.

"Time to get going."

"Ready when you are, pal."

I got up to wash, but there was no running water, so I stepped behind a curtain. There was a tiled hole in the floor with worn prints
where other visitors had placed their feet. I saw a plastic bucket full of
water that had iced over, a ladle hanging from a nail to wash your
hands.

Joe was up by the time I emerged. He was loading his camera,
dressed and ready to go.

"That's nice," he said, pointing to the sewer drain, which was an
open gutter in the concrete floor, everything flowing outdoors through
the wall.

"I'm going to have a look around," I told him.

"What time are we leaving?"

"I'll find out."

"My friend!" I heard someone say, shortly after I walked outside.
The professor was standing on a bare patch of earth on a hill behind
the house. I walked up there noticing things I had not seen the night
before: foliage in the trees, landscape pots, husks of dormant bougain-
villea.

"How was your rest?" he asked. A gracious host.

"Fine, thank you. What's that you've got there?"

He had a small transistor radio in his hand, with a bent coat hanger for an antenna.

"The BBC." He smiled. "*Breakfast with Frost.*"

"I thought so," I told him. "Believe it or not, I was a guest on that show once, myself."

"Yes, I know." He nodded. "I remember your discussions."

"Why are you up here?" I asked.

"This is the only place I have reception. George Bush thinks Osama bin Laden is running an evil empire from a cave in Tora Bora. I am a fortunate, well-educated man in a city of one hundred thousand people, and this is my only connection to the world. You should write about that."

We stood looking out over mountains. Joe had emerged with his camera and was walking around the garden, doing his thing.

"Sufi Muhammad was arrested last night at Landi Kotal, coming back across the border," the professor told me. "He left Khyber two weeks ago with thirteen hundred men, but he came back with thirty-seven. People are very upset. I think it is not a good idea to visit Dir."

"How do you know that? About him being arrested?"

He ignored me. "Perhaps we spend the day here. There are people you can meet."

"No. I want to meet the families of the men who died," I told him. "I want to see the madrassas, talk to the mullahs. I need to document their perspectives."

"It is very dangerous there. I think you misunderstand."

"No. I understand, completely," I told him. "That's why we're here."

He thought a moment like any professor of history might. Then he turned off his radio. "As you wish," he said. "We are ready. Please meet me at the car."

It was a five-hour drive from Thana to Chitral, and we got two flat tires in the first thirty miles. Joe and I sat in the back of the professor's sedan while Bashir and his two quiet friends kept pace behind us. The road was mostly paved but rough in places, an old route through verdant fields dotted with mud huts that had high boxed windows but no glass against weather, not even shutters. The view of mountains struck me as spectacular, almost artificially stunning in some places as we drove long stretches through unpopulated valleys where men would appear out of nowhere and stand near the road for no discernible reason. White rivers, popcorn clouds, wing-bound birds of prey. I loved it.

The tribal regions looked feudal, medieval, and though I had questions about traveling back in time, we talked very little until the professor pointed his driver to a two-track road leading off to the right. He leaned back over the seat and told us there was something we needed to see. The two-track got smaller and smaller, passing through swales until it came to a stop near a steep, grassy embankment leading into foothills. Bashir pulled in behind us, and we all got out to stretch our legs. We were in the middle of nowhere, but it was sunny and getting warmer.

"What is this?" I asked.

"Pomegranates," Bashir told me. "*Anaar.* Here where they grow."

He walked around to the back of his car, opened the trunk, and retrieved three AK-47s like the one he had shown us the night before. He handed one to each of his quiet friends and motioned with his hand. No guns for me or Joe.

"Please, this way."

Bashir walked point, and we started out into the shadowed forest with the two quiet guys behind us. Joe and I walked shoulder to shoulder in the middle; the professor stayed in the car.

"Pomegranates?" Joe said after a few minutes.

Then higher, farther away from the lot, five minutes, ten minutes, maybe a mile through a sprawling grove of trees that could have been an apple orchard in Vermont. Eventually, Bashir stepped out into a broad gravel pit with a steep bank like where we used to go shooting when I was a kid. There were three more men waiting for us when we got there. They had guns, too.

"As-salamu alaykum."

"Wa alaykumu s-salam."

Joe told me we were not getting on our knees, because it felt a whole lot like that might be an issue, and I would have agreed, except the life-fully-formed thing had brought me here before. I felt perfectly at ease, though I need to explain.

Hostage rescue requires constant practice for few actual missions. To stay sharp, HRT occasionally accepts other assignments, including what, during my era, were prominent criminal interactions: drug raids, fugitive hunts, armed standoffs at Ruby Ridge and Waco. We did other things, too, renditions and overseas deployments, quiet gigs in Africa, doper hits in Central America, high-value-target assessments throughout Asia. In 1994, we even took up babysitting.

I remember that Gold Section snipers had just finished shooting movers on the rifle deck when word came down from HQ that the New York Field Office had a source they called Tom Clark, and that Mr. Clark needed protection. It turns out that Tom Clark was a former Special Forces colonel in the Egyptian Army named Emad Salem, among other aliases. He worked undercover as a Joint Terrorism Task Force confidant of "the Blind Sheik," Omar Abdel-Rahman, following the 1993 World Trade Center Bombing. He worked Ramzi Yousef and a whole other cast of shitbirds, too.

The first problem with Tom Clark/Emad Salem was that U.S. Attorney Mary Jo White and the Southern District of New York wanted to keep him alive for trial; al Qaeda wanted him dead. The second problem was that he was a six-foot-two, 275-pound national judo champion with a violent, mercurial temper. He had become very unhappy with HRT because we would not let him leave our safe house for recreation. One morning, after almost shooting him dead in an elevator during a fight, we decided to take him out in the woods for a little walk.

"This is far enough," I remember him saying. A firm voice. "You do it here."

We had driven Salem out a long dirt road, stopped near a similar orchard. We had placed one guy on point, two covering the rear. We all had guns, except him.

"I go no farther," he told us, about ten minutes in. "Kill me here. I walk no more."

That's how they do things in Egypt. If you piss somebody off trying judo moves in an elevator, they walk you out to an orchard and shoot you in the head. And I was thinking about that when Bashir led us out of the trees and into that gravel pit, how things can look one way and be something else altogether.

"Mr. Christopher, you want to buy our weapons. You should try them first," Bashir said.

Then we all gathered in a circle. He introduced us to his friends, one of whom handed me his carbine with a red wood foregrip and a folding stock. I held it in my hands as I had held countless others on countless occasions, but then I looked at Joe for guidance, because we had reached the point in every tour where the comedian guide asks if anyone is from New Jersey.

"Thank you," I said—then the obvious dilemma: Do you continue pretending to be a GQ writer who has never fired a gun, or do you trust that they knew your name before you arrived and expect you to be a highly trained marksman? That dilemma.

"Please," I said. "This is your home; these are your weapons. You go first."

It didn't help that Joe and I had traded our Western clothing for shalwar kameez and pakols, which we'd purchased at a bazaar near the hotel, and that it was cold as hell, so I'd kept my North Face fleece and Joe his Prada. Everything about us presented contradiction.

"As you wish." The man nodded.

Then he flipped the bolt brake and rolled a mag of 7.62-by-59 mm rounds full-automatic into a patch of dirt. I ran a mag, Joe ran a mag, Bashir ran a mag, then the others. After a while, we all laughed and hugged it out and hiked back out to the cars. A nice morning at the range.

"How did you find the shooting?" the professor asked. "You see? Everyone can fight. Even the farmers."

"Didn't look like farmers to me," Joe told him, the casting director. We headed north.

Nobody said anything all the way to Dir. Eventually, traffic grew heavier, and those lovely fast-running streams turned to side streets lined with open-front buildings full of plastic pails, brightly colored fabric, Nestlé water bottles, and fresh, exotic produce we were not allowed to eat. Joe's spirits seemed to have been buoyed, because now he had plenty of places to point his camera, and I was glad to make our first stop on a much longer drive.

"We are here to see a mullah named Sharif," the professor told us once we had arrived. "He is Sufi Muhammad's hand in this region. A very powerful man. You must be careful."

The driver pulled into the local equivalent of a strip mall, basically a bunch of square, brush-painted caves. There were bearded men everywhere, dressed in Cantabrian brown, full of agitation. It looked pretty much the same as Thana, another day in a world I knew nothing about.

"Stay in the car." The professor got out and walked to a concrete dock where a man sat next to another man who had a live monkey on a chain. They nodded to each other and then walked away, into shadows.

"You American!" someone yelled in decent English. "Why you come here?"

And I realized that, in the moments since the professor left us, we had been found.

"Bin Laden is a hero to all Muslims," the man called out. "America hates Islam!"

I'd love to draw you descriptions of how things looked or what I felt, but it all happened so quickly, I didn't have time to think. What had been an open lot swelled shut around us almost immediately, maybe sixty or seventy men yelling Pashto, a flash mob of disbelief. Confusion, rabid ire.

"Use the recorder," I told Joe, but he was already there. We needed faces, and it seemed to make sense that we'd have a better chance outside the car, so I pushed open my door and jumped into a sea of dirty-brown shalwar, zealots twisting up with rage.

"You make bin Laden!" someone yelled. "Americans make bin Laden to fight Islam!"

Then an old man, a very old man, stepped forward, close enough to poke his gnarled finger into my sternum and hurl accusations, which I understood without understanding a word. He had rotten remnants of teeth that had grown together in a face of rice paper skin, and his breath made me turn my head. He had a ratty beard and rheumy eyes, and I was six foot four, 225 pounds to his ancient frailty, but he came at me hard, ready to go. Joe was standing on the seat with his elbows on the top of the car, indifferent to anything except getting his shots. Younger men were elbowing toward us, the way your buddies appear out of nowhere when you're in a bar and it's about to go off. And then somebody's tooth pops out, and the bartender reaches for his Louisville slugger—and within an eighth of a second, the first punch at the far side of the room turns into a rugby scrum at the door. Sometimes the war on terror is just a misunderstanding.

"This is not good for us here," the professor said, somehow back at the car.

Bashir and the two quiet guys behind us were honking their horn like it was time to exit, and I was thinking I wished our guns weren't in the trunk. I can see that monkey on the chain losing his shit, then Mullah Sharif there on the concrete step, elevated above the cloud of parking lot filth and dun kameez, staring down with no expression whatsoever. Yes, a monkey, two ugly Americans, and a riot—this shadow war playing out a thousand miles from nowhere.

"Fuck this, man," I told Joe. He was still standing on the seat with his elbows on the roof, indifferent to the mob. I noticed that he was recording the whole thing but had the Nikon, too, and that 50 mm lens gathering faces because he loved getting close. "Let's go!"

Then, just as quickly, we were bouncing out of the cratered lot, racing north toward larger peril, Joe shooting through the back window as the younger men chased after us, up the road, waving opprobrium, chucking stones. Bashir and the others close behind, just another day.

"This is not a safe place for you," the professor said, choosing Churchill-like understatement. "These people have lost brothers. They are angry."

Then back to silence for another hour, until we came to a truck blocking the road with two men waving for us to stop. One of the men had a uniform and a badge I had not previously seen. They looked bored, and we would not have stopped, except we were in line behind a bus moving slowly, and one of them caught me trying to hide my face.

"ISI, maybe Special Branch," the professor said. He seemed genuinely concerned. "Stay in the car, no matter what they tell you. I do not know why these men are here."

They waved us to the side of the road, which wasn't much of a road to begin with.

"Where are you going?" the man in plainclothes asked once we had stopped. He was looking through the car, like cops do, searching for probable cause to go deeper. Then he looked at me.

"Chitral," I told him. "We are journalists."

"It is not safe from this point forward."

"No shit," Joe said.

"Many bodies come back from Afghanistan. It is dangerous for Americans."

"They are with me," the professor told him. I still don't know why that mattered.

The man looked around for a moment, then said, "Sign here."

Joe and I signed his book using real names, because it would be the only proof of our crossing. Then the professor pointed for the driver to continue, and we headed farther away from the world. After about a mile, once the road had faded back to the stark beauty of the tribal regions, Joe pointed his Nikon out the window, and I looked over to see what had caught his eye.

It was a man in his thirties with his pants down at the side of the road. He was squatting to piss.

8

Guantánamo Bay

[APRIL 2003]

"Behind this concertina wire sit six hundred fifty Taliban and al Qaeda members brought to Guantánamo Bay by U.S. officials who believe information gathered here could prevent future terrorist attacks."

It was still early in the war when I spoke those words, but late at night. I was standing at the edge of an ocean inlet with the stadium lights of America's most notorious prison as a backdrop. I was sunburned, sweating profusely, wearing a ribbed-white Guayabera shirt I had bought at El Norte Mall in San Juan, Puerto Rico. There was a camera crew in front of me, an army major off to the side, and two well-armed guards sporting M4s, body armor, and woodland utility cover. The words were my own, though fully scripted, the set piece in a larger story.

"Let's try that again, man," my producer said. "Maybe put your hands on your hips. You're looking kinda tense."

You could hear screaming from prisoners in chain-link cages, so he held up his hand until things quieted down. Then he pointed to the sound man, who gave him a thumbs-up. "Chris Whitcomb, Camp Delta, night shot two, take three," he said. "And . . . roll video."

Oddly enough, my first trip to Gitmo was not the result of some black ops rendition in Sanaa gathering EEI during interrogation of a high-value target. I did have to sign an "area clearance" before getting on the plane, but I arrived using my full Christian name. I flew in via

Roosevelt Roads, on a military hop from Norfolk, Virginia, wearing civilian clothes with no suppressed weapons, no odd-color passport, no air force sergeants from the NSA to scramble comms. Sue, Fred, and Art Cooper all knew I was there, but none of them offered to help, because I had an award-winning producer from CNBC named Jeff Pohlman to keep everything in line. I did have to take care of my own hair and makeup, and laptops were prohibited, so I had to write my stories on a legal pad. But everything else was great. Gitmo had a McDonald's, beautiful weather, and plenty of appalling visuals to help us frame our shots.

"Relax, big man," Joe coached. He was there, too, just because. "You got this; pretend we're talking in a bar."

Anyone who has been to Guantánamo Bay knows it's nothing like talking in a bar. In fact, it's not like anywhere at all. I have interviewed offenders in broadly diverse lockups, from Missouri's Polk County jail to the kennels of Timor-Leste, and I gotta say, Gitmo sucks. Language was the first speed bump, because only the guards spoke English, and they were strictly off-limits to journos. The guys in orange jumpsuits spoke Dari or Pashto, maybe some Arabic, but they mostly just hurled invective, which was not a language but easy to interpret.

The man in charge of Camp Delta, Maj. General Geoffrey D. Miller, spoke bullet point jargon but gave us access to a small subset of prisoners in a facility called Camp Four. That seemed encouraging until I realized the prisoners in Camp Four hailed from twenty-seven different countries, including Chad, Sudan, and the Maldives, where they speak Dhivehi, which is a whole other can of worms.

I should not complain, because getting to Gitmo at all in April 2003 was impossible unless you were an E-3 reservist, because the army, of course, needed guards. It was easy if you had cargo pants and a six-pack name, because the Bush administration was way into interrogation. And getting to Gitmo was no problem at all if your name was Hadji, you had a beard, and you'd gotten caught holding an RPG outside Herat, because Donald Rumsfeld was all too happy to put a bag over your head, strap you to the floor of a C-17, waive visa requirements entirely.

Invitations were hard to come by if you worked for the Red Cross, the ACLU, or the Geneva Convention, because those organizations were banned. Congress was not interested in looking unpatriotic on fact-finding junkets; NATO reps were busy attending pressers at the Hague. UN interests were treated with respect commensurate with freedom fries. As one might imagine, requests from TV news organizations were laughed at, then filed in the trash.

The good news for me was that my buddy Jeff Pohlman was the world's greatest cable news producer, and of course that whole life-fully-formed thing. I mean, how else do you explain the fact that I ended up being the first broadcast correspondent in Joint Task Force Guantánamo Bay, after being the first writer chasing Sufi Muhammad spawn up the Swat River en route to Taliban interactions in Spin Bolduc with a warlord named Raziq? With a forty-dollar AK-47, a photographer named Joe, and ten thousand dollars in my boot. For *GQ* magazine.

There's no other way to explain the fact that within days of my break-in-service from the FBI and my fateful appearance on *Larry King Live,* plenty of news programs were trying to book me for war stories about al Qaeda. Howard Stern called early, then *Imus in the Morning, Meet the Press, The Daily Show* with Jon Stewart. The list went on and on: BBC, NPR, Bill Maher, the *CBS Evening News, Coast to Coast AM with Art Bell.* I once saw myself, forty feet tall, on a huge TV screen in Times Square; another time, eating wings at a Hooters on Kauai. It was surreal.

The only way I can make sense of my life in the two years after September 11 is that America needed someone to explain terror, and I was available. Maybe it helped that I brought FBI credibility or that I appealed to bookers as a voice of calm in a world of chatter. It did not hurt my popularity when some homicidal scumbag started mailing anthrax to Tom Brokaw, and I had a friend named Sue at the CIA who kept a vial in her desk. It didn't hurt that I had spent two years teaching interrogation at the FBI National Academy, or that my first book was about fighting terrorists around the world with the Hostage Rescue Team. And then, as luck would have it, I met Elena Nachmanoff, the legendary senior vice president of talent development for NBC. She and I sat down to talk just days before the D.C. sniper started around-the-clock news coverage, all over again. Turns out the networks were in hot competition for talking heads.

And so, as improbable as it might sound, within a year after leaving the FBI, I was offered a job co-hosting a nightly news show called

CheckPoint CNBC, with Martha McCallum. Calling myself co-host might seem a bit presumptuous, considering Martha's now remarkable success at Fox, but that's the way it was pitched to me at the time. Thirty Rock was already paying me to appear seven days a week across their platforms, everything from *Today* to *Hardball with Chris Matthews* on MSNBC. They treated me like a king: put me up for six months straight at the Essex House, on Central Park South; gave me car service, a nightly bottle of wine, and a nice basket of fruit, because that's the way they treat you at NBC.

"Fair, firm, and impartial," a man in camo said.

But then, of course, CNBC sent me to Cuba.

"Fair, firm, and impartial."

The first thing I noticed at Guantánamo Bay was a whole lot of Pashtuns and a complete lack of Pashtunwali. Gitmo looked like a giant dog pen wrapped in that green stuff you see around tennis courts. The walls were twelve feet tall and topped with razor wire; there was a big sign that said, "Honor Bound to Defend Freedom." Even on the army's sterilized tour you could smell human excrement, which detainees tossed freely, and therefore the smell of bleach. Joe kept pointing to black-and-white placards warning against photography, shaking his head. Some things stood out: the iguanas and banana rats, huge frigging rats; concrete floors at the old Camp X-Ray, all broken and stained; a plywood guard tower with a big American flag.

There were three prominent colors at Joint Task Force Guantanamo Bay: BDU camo, bad guy orange, and head-to-toe white for a select group of enemy combatants who had bought into what Camp Delta called the Road to the Haj. Our Pentagon minders explained that all detainees were given the opportunity to earn their way to Camp Four by "cooperating with investigators to provide information that enhanced the national security of the Homeland." There were posters everywhere, which we were allowed to read but not allowed to film.

"The Road Home Is Paved with Truth, Brother," some posters proclaimed. Big posters with compelling images, like what I might have had above my bed in junior high. Imagine Frampton on *Frampton Comes Alive,* but with a beard. "The Road to Haj Depends on Cooperation."

Our CNBC tour of the world's most notorious prison had been

completely staged, of course, all interactions plotted. The flack in charge of our visit was a stern, humorless man named Maj. John Smith, and though I had never met him during my time at the Fourth Psychological Operations Group, I recognized his behaviors. He walked us through pristine blocks of extruded steel cells, every one of them a model unit of religious tolerance that included a shiny new Koran, a bar of soap, and an arrow pointing prayer mats toward Mecca. We were shown Camp Delta's air-conditioned medical facilities but not the prisoners being fed with tubes during hunger strikes, nor the survivors of self-induced hangings. We were reminded of things we already knew: that these terrorists were the "worst of the worst," so dangerous they had been flown from Kandahar with bags over their heads to keep them from chewing through the plane's hydraulic lines. As if that were even possible.

We were walked through the outdoor spaces to a row of single-wide trailers where the doors had been left open so we could glimpse friendly conversations between white people in polo shirts chatting with nonwhite people who did not have polo shirts. Major Smith explained that many of the detainees had arrived wounded or ill with diseases ranging from tuberculosis to schizophrenia and abscessed teeth, that they were all bathed, deloused, shaved head to toe, and then treated by doctors. Head to toe? I was wondering what infraction some poor private first class would commit to get the job of manscaping scrotums, but then someone said, "Fair, firm, and impartial," and I snapped to.

"Fair, firm, and impartial." I nodded out of habit.

I caught a glimpse of the ocean between cracks in the green tennis court screen, and I thought back to that episode of *The Prisoner* where Number Six was stuck in a coastal village with a giant bubble called Rover trying to swallow him whole. Then, just as quickly, something else caught my eye: a face I knew from someplace real. A woman wearing no jewelry.

This happens sometimes when you're on the job, a moment when you're walking down the street with your family and you recognize a face but can't immediately decide if they are a friend you met at a barbecue or some felon you put in jail. This particular woman saw me at the exact same moment I saw her, carrying a legal pad of her own while walking with several soldiers. We knew each other from the

Academy, my two years teaching interrogation in the Communications Unit. We had both been special agents, but now she was trying to coax confessions from terrorists, and I was walking around in a Guayabera shirt with a camera crew from CNBC. We traded that look of recognition, the choked-down smiles, the infinite distance between where I had started and what I had turned out to be.

"Fair, firm, and impartial," one of her colleagues said, nodding.

I just kept walking.

"I love Coltrane," Inge said with a sigh.

Joe and I had just finished dinner in a Santa Monica restaurant, two weeks after escaping our Chaman altercation with Cat Stevens on Crack and his bearded friends. All those AK-47s.

"This is Bird."

"What?"

"Charlie Parker," I told her. "I love Coltrane, too, but this isn't him. It's Charlie Parker playing 'Yardbird Suite' with Miles Davis; Dodo Marmarosa on piano."

"Are you sure?"

"Am I sure? You want to know who's playing bass?"

"Let it go, Inge," Joe said. "Whit knows his music. Don't get him started."

"Wait, wait, wait . . ." the woman sitting beside me interrupted. "What about the guy with the orange beard? Sufi something. And what the hell are 'birth control glasses'?"

"You can't get laid when you're wearing them," Joe explained.

"Did you find him?" a third woman asked. "The Sufi terror guy. And I don't get it. What about the Clint Eastwood poster and you getting hallucinations in a safe house, all those Taliban dudes staring at you with bowls of soup and guns. Where did Cat Stevens on Crack go?"

"This is so confusing," Inge and a third woman said almost simultaneously. "Is Kashmir near Afghanistan? And what is ISI, anyway? Special Branch of what?"

Then one of the women punched me in the arm and said, "Whit, you suck at telling stories. Cut to the chase. How'd y'all get out of there alive?"

"Good luck with that, Big Man," Joe said. He waved to the waiter for another round of drinks, stood up, and walked away.

Okay. Maybe I am getting a little ahead of myself, here. Let me back up.

Remember how I said Joe loves women and women love Joe, and the part about him being a casting director in L.A.? Well, it turns out that Joe knows a lot of supermodels and famous actresses, and as luck would have it, models and actresses love going out to nice dinners at exclusive restaurants with guys who have full-page spreads in *GQ* and who just got back from the war in Afghanistan.

It is also true that getting invited out to dinner with supermodels and famous actresses is a whole lot like getting a TS/SCI clearance with Q permission. Both forms of access require adherence to strict protocols, including surreption, compartmentation, sangfroid, and specific brands of sunglasses. It's kinda like one big club, the Q and the celebrity hang. They go well together. Both are invitation-only, and the dues are steep, though not limited to money. Some places take reservations only under the name "L. Bellagio"; others, "Team Rope Header." Both lifestyles involve private jets, a fascination with guns, and that fantastic feeling that comes with knowing there is nowhere you can't go, because there is such a thing as an All-Access Pass to the World, and you've got one in your wallet.

"Whit!" Inge was saying. "What the hell? Finish the story!"

And I was just about to when Joe marched back to the table. He looked pissed.

"You all right?" I asked.

"Some pretty-boy asshole won't let me out back to see What's Her Name."

"Back where? Why not?"

"Says it's a private party. What the hell? I built this place. There's no 'private.'"

Sorry. I forgot to block the scene.

Every club has a clubhouse, and in 2001, we had several. The West Coast office was a bisque-colored building along a creepy section of Olympic Boulevard in Santa Monica, where one might go to get their car reupholstered, maybe a knife fight and a taco. It was a rough part of town in those days, mostly taquerias, and pit bulls scratching for bets behind razor wire lots.

As luck would have it, a very successful TV producer named Tony Yerkovich had gutted a dive bar near Sixteenth Street and filled it with mahogany, leather, fine linen, and the best pot roast in L.A. Joe had chosen the Buffalo Club for several reasons, one being its unlisted phone number and lack of signage, meaning normal human beings had no way to find the door. The other was outstanding quinoa, because you might recall that Joe is vegetarian.

It did not hurt that Tony Yerkovich knew absolutely everyone in town, because he had created *Miami Vice* with Michael Mann, iconic hits like *Starsky & Hutch, Hill Street Blues.* He played great jazz, had excellent service and very attractive staff, including one woman who had caught Joe's eye and was apparently out in the garden tending bar for some private affair.

"Relax, Joe," Inge said. "You're at a nice dinner, surrounded by smart, beautiful women. Nobody cares about the waitress you were banging in the men's toilet last night."

"Forget about it, man," I agreed. "I got you a tequila."

Joe nodded his head and laughed that chug of his, but you could tell he was pissed. "Yeah, okay, tell 'em about the first time we got stoned."

"Stoned?" the third woman asked, a sitcom actress.

"With rocks," Joe explained. "Stoned as in stoned to death. Biblical shit. That's what they do over there. Go ahead, Whit, tell 'em."

"Wait, you got stoned? Where?"

"In a refugee camp. Tell her, Whit."

"So, wars all start the same way, basically," I said.

It was about eleven o'clock at that point, but I wasn't paying attention to time. We had a nice meal, and everyone was deep into aperitifs.

"Some politician who has never been punched in the face his whole life decides to invoke national security, invade a country, and blow up a bunch of whatever. In this case it was Bush, probably Cheney, who called the Pentagon, who called Minot Air Force Base, which sent B-52 bombers all the way from South Dakota to Kabul looking to fuck up a bunch of terrorists over September 11. Unfortunately, bin Laden was already hiding in a cave by the time we got there, and the Soviets had destroyed everything except a few farm animals and some mud huts, so Rumsfeld had to go back and tell his boss there was nothing left to target except a thousand miles of Stone Age. I mean, the whole place looks like a sepia photograph of Nod. Am I right, Joe?"

"Looks great on Tri-X."

"So, once the CIA paid the Northern Alliance to take Kabul, everybody moved south to Kandahar; we did, too. Me and Joe."

"What happened to Kashmir?" Inge asked. "Weren't you going to Kashmir?"

"Don't worry about it."

"Shush, Joe. Let him finish!"

"After a while, we headed back to Islamabad for a dead drop, then flew down to Quetta, which was the last real civilization before a border crossing near Spin Bolduc. While we were in Islamabad, I ate something that made me sick; I assume it was meat, because Joe was fine. But I got loopy flying down, from the fever. And by the time we got there, Joe had to hide us for a few days because of Taliban flowing into Quetta for medical treatment and supplies."

"Now we're getting somewhere," the other woman said. A movie actress.

"Where did you get stoned?"

"So, the second thing that always happens in war is collateral damage. No matter what the generals say on cable TV, bombs eventually go off-target and blow up a bunch of kids. Kill their parents and their grandparents and their goats and wreck their house, so they just start running around naked with blood pouring out their ears because of the concussion, until they get to the nearest person who gives a shit, which in this case was the UN; they had pitched a bunch of tents at the border. There were hundreds of them, right, Joe? Naked orphan kids wandering around whimpering for their mothers, but all the mothers were walking around in burkas, so you couldn't see their faces, and all the men were in beards looking the same, so there was no way for the border guards to know victim from deserter. The whole south of Afghanistan pouring into these PVC pipe corrals, then into this big favela of white tents with blue letters on the side."

"That's fucking horrible," Inge said. "Kids with blood pouring out their ears?"

"Plus, we were supposedly there to write a story, okay? So, I went to interview this Pakistani colonel in charge of the whole operation, and he had this office up on stilts that looked like a lifeguard tower on a huge beach with no ocean. You could see for miles in every direction, and it was desolation, smoke from brickmaker fires and diesel fumes from lorries. The locals were flying these red kites, small patches of bright blue sky. I asked the colonel what it was like to do his job, and he started crying. I mean sobbing. He said, 'I am not a Pakistani, not a Muslim, not an Afghan, not a bin Laden supporter. I am a human being.' Then he pointed out his window to the entire refugee crisis and said, 'This is a human being, too.'"

"Awful," the movie actress decided.

"I asked him about Taliban and al Qaeda fighters sneaking across with the survivors, and he cried even harder, choking on his words. He said, 'This is all happening because of one man. My people, they know everything, and they haven't seen him. Maybe you should go and look in the camps,' which we did. There was a guy at a sandbag checkpoint beneath a UN flag, which was ruffling in the breeze. He had a belt-fed machine gun, and he nodded as we walked by. A relief worker stopped us and said, 'You should not go in there. We don't want riots.' But we did, moving between these Pakistani soldiers on horseback with polo mallets."

"Polo mallets?"

"Yut, just regular polo mallets. Then these trucks rolled in full of blankets, because it was cold, and the mobs started gathering by the thousands. Aid workers started throwing stuff into the crowd, but people were desperate, so they started to riot, and the Pakistanis rode in, just wrecking people. Women screaming and yelling, kids stomped under the horses, a crowd going medieval, and Joe only had a fifty-millimeter lens, so he wants to get closer, but then I see a plop in the dirt, and I realize it's rocks. I told Joe we had to get out of there, but he didn't care, and then the whole camp is stoning us, charging us, screaming murder. It was nuts."

"Oh my god," Inge said.

"Get us another round," Joe told me. "I'll be right back."

I waved to the server, and we sat there for a while. Everyone needed time to think.

"So, where are you from, Whit?" the sitcom actress asked. "What brings you to L.A.?"

"I live in Virginia. We're going to a Christmas party at Meg Ryan's house."

"Oh, Meg's great! Sounds like a crazy life. What does your family think about all this?"

"They're used to it," I told her.

"Used to what?"

"Me being gone."

The waiter brought our drinks, and I was thinking how much fun I was having when Joe stormed back from the garden. I saw him coming, waving with his hand, livid.

"Whit, let's go!"

I stood up and started after him, and I could see the pretty-boy bouncer coming in from the side. He was Eastern European in a mob kind of way, wearing a nicely tailored suit, so big Joe had to jump up in the air like he was trying to dunk a basketball just to punch him in the face. The big guy ate the punch and was just about to take Joe's head off when I connected. We went to the floor, fists, feet, bloody this, bloody that, and we were just barely hanging in there, two on one, when I heard somebody yelling. I looked up, and it was Tony Yerkovich standing above us.

"Goddamn it, Joe!" he bellowed. The Buffalo Club has a small bar area at the front, and we had cleared it. "You can't fight in my restaurant! You're outta here! You're banned!"

"You can't ban me," Joe yelled back, completely baffled. "I built this place!"

"Banned for life! You didn't build shit!"

We got up and dusted ourselves off, and the Eastern European pretty boy said something flippant and walked off, and suddenly we were outside in the street.

"To hell with Tony," Joe said. "I was getting sick of his quinoa anyway."

There were three kids at Gitmo. I wanted to see them.

"These people don't have birth certificates," Major Smith told me. "I can confirm that JTF-Guantanamo Bay houses three male adolescents. We believe the youngest is thirteen."

I was wondering how long it took Rumsfeld to approve that disclosure when someone said, "Fair, firm, and impartial," and our CNBC crew stopped at a sign painted "Camp Iguana."

"We built this facility specifically for their care," Major Smith told us. I noticed a Warning No Photos placard flex-tied to the chain-link fence. "You will see that these detainees are well cared for. They receive age-appropriate education, therapy on a weekly basis."

"Do you interrogate them?" I asked.

"I have nothing further on that."

A guard opened the gate, and we walked to a small building. There were no people inside, no enemy combatants of any age, no sign of German shepherds. It was a simple air-conditioned space with carpeted floors, padded chairs, a jigsaw puzzle on a table near a dorm-size fridge.

"Are we allowed to shoot this?" Pohlman asked.

"Of course."

Joe laughed because of course we could shoot; that's why they had staged it. I stepped outside with the major, who seemed like a nice guy in a difficult job. I asked him about a twenty-foot gap in the green tarp, where one could look out onto waves, gulls hanging complacent over the deep blue sea. He told me General Miller thought it would provide hope for the boys to look homeward through the tranquility of the Caribbean. He hated to see young boys cry.

"Can you believe these people send teenagers to do their fighting?" Major Smith asked, with no sense of irony whatsoever. "That's what we're dealing with here. You understand?"

When we were done touring the tiny annex known as Camp Iguana, Major Smith put us on a boat for what he said was a little tour from the outside looking in. Our boat had a .50-caliber machine gun in the bow, which made for cool footage, and we got a good look at the forty-five square miles of rock that honored EPA rules regarding endangered species of birds and plants but fell outside Geneva Convention protections for men.

Just before dinner, we met General Miller in a parking lot on a hill overlooking McDonald's. This was the man who had dreamed up "fair, firm, and impartial," the father who had cut a peek hole in a razor wire fence, thinking the view would help thirteen-year-old prisoners stop crying. And before we even turned on the camera, I was thinking that I was a patriot, a tireless supporter of all those who had bravely served our nation. That it was my job to translate the hard parts of this place for a public who preferred simpler things. That despite my respect for the armed services, I found General Miller to be a pompous, sanctimonious prick. You might consider my assessment harsh, but I will note that after building Camp Delta, Gen. Geoffrey D. Miller was transferred back to Afghanistan, where he distinguished himself by being in command of people siccing dogs on naked, handcuffed men wearing soiled women's undergarments on their heads.

"Have you served?" he asked me after introductions, the general who built Abu Ghraib.

"Not exactly, sir. Though I did graduate Marine Corps Scout Sniper School."

"You? A marine?"

"No," I told him.

"I see."

We finished the interview, and I filed a three-part story when we got back to New Jersey. It was nominated for a Peabody Award. I could tell you more, but no. Guantánamo Bay is a part of my life I'd rather forget.

9

Nairobi, Kenya

[JANUARY 2006]

There's this awesome scene in the film *Black Hawk Down* where Somali khat mogul Osman Ali Atto is sitting in the Bakaara arms market reading *USA Today*. Eric Bana is lurking in the shadows pretending that Oakley Blades and a fly-fishing vest make him look less like a Delta Force operator. He's talking into a cuff mic because shit's about to go down, and then Mr. Atto stands up in his Montique walking suit, smoking a fat cigar. He climbs into the back seat of a Prado, and hauls ass out of Mogadishu, along this red dirt road through a cinder block village that looks like a lot of places I have been. It's just the Hollywood version of Africa, of course: blood diamonds and filth, child soldiers in rags posing with chain guns around generals who kill for sport.

"You guys want ice cream?" Rosie yelled, and everybody did. She had made a pie; you could smell it from the kitchen.

"I love this part," Jake said. "Dude's wearing a pinkie ring."

He and Mick and I were lying back in La-Z-Boys at the house in New Hampshire watching our favorite movie for the fourth or fifth time. Then that big UH-60 rolls up on Osman Ali Atto's SUV, and Medal of Honor recipient Gary Gordon tags the engine block with a .308 round, spraying oil all over the windshield.

"Will that really stop a car?" Mick asked. "He's got an M14, right?"

And I said no, a .308 round will not stop a car, but then that Task

Force 160 Little Bird swings around front with its flank-mounted M134 miniguns, and I said, "But those will."

The Black Hawk lands, and the Delta guys stroll up on George Harris, who is acting the hell out of that Atto role, cool as a cucumber with his fake Wayfarers and gold chains, talking into his flip phone behind a Bolivar Belicoso. One of the Bragg guys taps on the window with his knuckle, and Jake notices that HRT wears the same gear: Protec skateboard helmets with the gun-side ear sawed off and tanker goggles; sleeves rolled up, pilots' gloves with no index finger.

"'Night, Daddy!"

Chelsea came running in for a hug. Rosie behind her with dessert, then Collin in SpongeBob pajamas. They were six and five. Time for bed. Love-you kisses, all around.

"Listen up. This is my favorite scene," I told the boys when everybody else was gone. The pie was strawberry rhubarb, and it was awesome. Coffee ice cream, specifically not Ben and Jerry's. You could hear the wind howling outside, but it was toasty in there by the fire, Mick and Jake sprawled out in their chairs, tall for their age, athletic for their size.

"War ain't about guns," I told them. "It's the men behind the guns that matter. You've gotta read the book. Mark Bowden nails it."

And I hit the volume, because I wanted to hear the lines, the part where they've brought Osman Ali Atto in to see Sam Shepard, who is a complete badass playing General Garrison. It's just two guys wearing sunglasses in the dark, but the air is overloaded, and we all know what's gonna happen once the sunglasses come off.

"You've been here, what? Six weeks?" Atto asks. "Six weeks you have been trying to catch the general." Bunch of Arkansas white boys. "What is this, gunfight at the K.O. Corral?"

Sam Shepard laughs. "It's the O.K. Corral."

Atto says, "You shouldn't have come here. This is a civil war. This is our war, not yours."

Then General Garrison looks back and says, "Three hundred thousand dead and counting. That's not a war, Mr. Atto. That's genocide."

Which makes me want to clap, because what could be more American than standing up to a warlord spreading genocide in a Montique walking suit with a bunch of gold chains when all you're wearing is a T-shirt?

Right about then, Jake said, "Why do you like Africa, Dad?" and I realized I was there. I mean I am there, literally there, there in Africa, at that moment, thinking about my kids.

It's been thirty-one hours since Movie Night in New Hampshire, still January, but hot as hell in the lobby of the Six Eighty Hotel on Kenyatta Avenue, downtown Nairobi. I recount that scene in *Black Hawk Down* because the three guys coming up behind me are wearing walking suits, too. Short sleeves and epaulets, large men leaning backward, the way rich people carry weight.

I think back on what Jake had asked me about this place, how I should answer, because I do like Africa. I love it. I'm not talking about brochure Serengeti, strolling the savannahs late in a safari when the sun relents, your heart full, your mind pristine, ibex drifting off as a mirage. I'm not talking about Travel Channel Africa, which I bring home in the form of elephant tail bracelets or beads I robbed off Maasai. I'm talking about the birthplace-of-malice Africa, which has nothing to do with race, because the soul of Africa is Nature, and Nature will always be a contest between predator and prey. Fair does not matter to beasts.

Maybe that is my answer to Jake: that the lion appears out of grasses to grab a gazelle at the ass and work slowly toward the throat, indifferent to suffering, more interested in the hyenas circling and then the carrion birds prehistoric in size, the lilt of soft breezes as bugs carry off the remainder and the moon rises and the stars shine and tomorrow comes and you wake up to realize violence is a construct of man. Violence is man; there has always been war.

I mean, come on. How do you explain Africa to a sixteen-year-old? That it has sand dune deserts, a river running north, plains that bisect oceans, a mountain topped with snow? Africa is too big to describe with words, no matter how many times you have been there or how much you like to write.

How do you tell your son you love Africa because the greatest feeling in the world is knowing you are going to die, but surviving? That you miss war because death is an addiction and the more you get, the more you need; and the more you need, the harder it is to find? That toes over the edge of a high-rise in New York City is nothing compared to a whole continent full of opportunities to fall.

"I'll need your passport, sir," the desk clerk tells me.

So, I hand him one, and he checks me in to Room 603. Then I go to the internet room and sit down at the bank of worn-out keyboards to email Rosie, confirming my arrival. Up to my room for a spritz, then off to my first meeting with a man we will call Farrah.

Farrah is Somali. He's a handsome rascal, thirties, balding into that classic Hawiye forehead, sporting a mustache and a Western suit that fits.

"How was your flight?" he asks me.

"Great," I tell him. "Long, but I use the time to catch up on reading."

It is a bright, sunny day. We meet at an outdoor café popular with expats in a wealthy part of town know as Westlands.

"Did you come from D.C.?"

"No."

"Cool beans. It is nice to see you, man."

"You, too, brother."

Farrah is an unusual fellow. He has a BA in linguistics, speaks BBC English with an Indianapolis lilt. He is fluent in Swedish, due to his time at the University of Gothenburg; native Swahili; and various other dialects that require palatal clicks. His CV says he received his intelligence training from Muammar Gaddafi's Mukhabarat el-Jamahiriya in Libya during the eighties—which complicates our association, but only mildly, because he has plied that Libyan training on behalf of U.S. agencies as well. They find him useful because he knows Osman Ali Atto from his years working as a counterintelligence officer in the Somali National Army. Farrah worked with Aidid back in the day when Aidid was still a colonel, the genocide years leading up to what Joint Special Operations Command calls the Battle of Mogadishu. *Black Hawk Down.*

To make things even better, Farrah is a keen businessman with close personal relations to another former colonel, named Abdullahi Yusuf Ahmed. Yusuf has been appointed leader of a new Transitional Federal Government, which means the United Nations, at least for now, considers him the president of Somalia.

"Where are you staying?" Farrah asks me, as if he doesn't know.

"Six Eighty."

"Why do you stay at Six Eighty? We have nicer places."

"You know why, Farrah. Every spook in Africa stays at the Six Eighty Hotel. It helps me feel like I'm part of the club."

"You are a curious man."

"Takes one to know one."

We order flat whites and pastries with meat centers. I am looking around, as one might after just flying in from New Hampshire, when I think I hear somebody calling my name. I dismiss it at first as jet lag, but then I hear it again, louder.

"Whitcomb?" a man yells. "Whitcomb! What the frig?"

I see him coming across the esplanade, a large local-looking character wearing short shorts, a desert camo fanny pack, and his little sister's T-shirt stretched to bursting over approximately 265 pounds of steroid-enhanced muscle. He is all smiles and attitude, as if he has just out-benched me at the gym. Huge presence, effusive personality, everybody looking.

"What's up, my man?"

"Billy!" I say, like you do when your past appears out of nowhere and you want them to know you remember. "What the hell are you doing here?"

"Me? What are you doing here?"

Billy had made HRT a couple of years after me. He was a highly capable operator with party eyes, Chiclets teeth, skills not limited to guns. Everybody loves him.

"I live here, bro." He beams. "Well, part of the time. Cheryl and the kids live here when I'm on the job. Bought a house right over there. I love it. Gotta have security, but it's all good."

"Job?" He is an FBI agent. "What do you mean 'job'? Did you make Legat?"

"Nah, man. You didn't hear? I checked out of the Bu, went to work for Triple Canopy."

"Checked out? I thought you took a desk in Miami."

"Long story, but I'm here now. Which is cool. I'm a country head, stationed in Kabul. It's a great gig. A bunch of guys you know from back in the day, Six, Bragg, Ground Branch, a lot of marines. What about you? I heard you're out. Been meaning to read your book."

"Yeah. I've been out for a while now. Trying my hand at business."

"Business?" He looks at Farrah, then back at me. "Company business?"

"This is my friend John," I say to him, pointing at Farrah. "Sit down, bro. You want a coffee?"

"Nah. I'm heading back." He nods the way you do, pretending it will be great to catch up, but not in public. "Grabbing a couple things for the road. How long you in town?"

"Maybe a few weeks, maybe more."

"Anything I can help you with?"

"I'm good."

"I know the CT boss at the embassy, if that helps. She's the queen of Nairobi."

"I appreciate the offer, but I'm just here on layover. I'm going to Somalia."

Billy has this great laugh, and he just rolls right into it, life by the balls.

"Somalia? Bro, Somalia? What kinda business you in?"

"Chocolate!" I hear somebody yell, and there are two white guys walking straight at us. They are yoked also, wearing fanny packs unzipped over pistols with Pachmayr grips.

"Let's go, dude," the first man says. He is sporting a Big Johnson T-shirt and a Ping golf visor; covered in tattoos. "We're gonna be late."

"Who's your compadre, Chocolate?" the other one asks. His primary identifying characteristics are a porn star mustache and a lisp.

"This is my old buddy from HRT," Billy announces. "He writes books. Says he's going to Somalia."

"Good cover, good cover." Big Johnson nods. "Not that it's gonna matter over there. Look at yourself. I mean, what the fuck, bruh?"

"Chocolate?" I ask.

"That's my handle," Billy says. "Chocolate Thunder. I'm Chocolate Thunder over here."

Farrah nods, taking the whole thing in stride.

"This yer fixer?" the other guy asks. The lisp made it sound like "thixa."

It is a little awkward for a sec, but we are professionals. We all know the game.

"All right, my brother." Billy nods. My old HRT buddy. "I'll see ya when I see ya."

"Break a leg over there, pal." Big Johnson nods, and his buddy says, "Athalamu alaykum, motherthucker." And we all nod as they hurry off, and Farrah finishes his flat white, and I reach for my bottle of water.

"Small world, huh?"

"Sure is," I tell my Gaddafi-trained associate. "You never know."

Maybe this is how I will explain things to Jake. Africa is a large place full of small interactions among interesting people who never say "good luck" because they respect superstition and the oldest traditions of theater.

I was nine years old the first time I climbed into a plane. It was Uncle Harold's plane, a 1939 G-21 Grumman Goose painted white and a light shade of green. I remember riding to the Whitefield, New Hampshire, airstrip with my grandfather, who kept a pint bottle of vodka under the seat of his Buick. He was a quiet man who would steer with one hand and pinch the bottle between his knees, fold back the crinkly brown bag, unscrew the top, take a pull.

"Mmmm," he'd say.

Fred T., my father called him. He had married my grandmother after divorcing his first wife, who apparently went insane from syphilis. My grandmother bore five brothers in eight years and died at the age of forty-nine, before I turned one. Fred T. would mention her name sometimes, Loria. Then he'd cough, because he smoked Lucky Strike cigarettes with no filters. He'd have another drink, usually two swallows at a time, screw the top back on, close the bag, and reach back down between his feet. Sometimes he would nod, though not tell me why.

I asked him what it was one time, the bag, and he said, "Penance."

My uncle Mike called it a "frugal brugal" and had one of his own. My parents refused to discuss it.

Fred T. was not much of a talker, so I was looking out the window at Mount Washington, which towered over everything. Then, just past town, we drove by the entrance to the Mountain View Resort, which was the only reason there was an airport to begin with. A couple of miles later, we pulled into the gravel lot, and I saw Eric's mom parked beside the plane. She drove a late-model Country Squire with a chrome roof rack and a swing-out tailgate, which was open because the guys were unloading their bags.

It was the usual crew: Eric, Carl, and Grant.

"You're late, Whitcomb!" Eric yelled.

I was thinking it wasn't my fault when my grandfather said, "That's a nice plane. I'll see you next week."

My grandfather was a worldly man who might have accomplished more in life if not for being a drunk. He had come to New Hampshire from Riverside, California, in the 1920s. He kept a black-and-white photo on the wall of the kitchen that showed a Model T Ford stuck to its axels in caliche somewhere in Arizona. His father had abandoned the car, traveling cross-country, and put the family on a train. When summer came, and the road dried up, my grandfather took the train back to Arizona, got the car, and drove it cross-country, solo, despite a scarcity of maps and highways. He was fourteen.

"See ya," I said. Grabbed my bag. "Wouldn't wanna be ya!"

He laughed and called me "love," just like Eric's sister.

I remember everything about the plane: the smell of the leather seats, Eric showing me how the belts clipped backward, the roar of the propellers. The Grumman Goose is a twin-engine flying boat with side-retractable wheels that was developed specifically for millionaires who wanted to fly from New York City to the Hamptons, a water-to-water commute. That made sense, because Uncle Harold could use it flying from the Thirty-third Street Seaport to his houses on the Cape. Sometimes he would fly from the Cape to Whitefield. Sometimes he would use a jet.

The first time I ever flew, it was private, just four kids in a rich man's plane. The pilot's name was Patrick; he sat in the left seat with a headset, but no second officer. We would fly northeast over Maine, to a remote cluster of waters outside Eustis, a lake called King and Bartlett. I remember looking down for a runway, not understanding at first, because the shadows of clouds were so distracting. Then Patrick reached up for some levers over his head and did something that made a ratcheting noise, and Carl cracked a joke about crashing, just to scare me.

I remember the sound of the water as we skimmed the surface, the Grumman Goose a long, ribbed hull. We taxied up to a concrete ramp, revved the engines, and rolled to a stop in a patch of grass near four log cabins. ITT during Uncle Harold's reign owned a corporate retreat in the Rangeley Lakes, which we called the fishing camp. We each had our own guide, our own canoe, lobster for dinner with grenadine cocktails called Roy Rogers. My guide's name was Deb. He chewed Day's Work Tobacco and had a scar on his cheek where he had been bitten by a rat.

"More coffee, sir?" the waiter asks me.

And I realized I was daydreaming again, because I have loved aviation since that first flight from Whitefield. I admire the pioneers of airborne adventure, old planes, brave expeditions.

"No, thank you. Just the check," I tell him. "I have booked a charter. They're waiting."

It was easy to daydream in Nairobi, especially at the general aviation section of Wilson Airport, watching the fat-belly safari planes motor in and out to Tanzania, the fleet of King Airs back empty from their khat runs to Eritrea, the nomad lands of Djibouti. And here, my favorite spot to grab a Nescafé, the barrel bar of the Aero Club of East Africa, where one might later drink Tasker with pilots who will tell you the history of the continent as seen from the air.

I liked to think Hemingway had taken his coffee at one of those tables, his first trip to Kenya in 1933, on safari with Pauline. I know it's unlikely, because he arrived in Mombasa on a steamer and strayed to Nairobi, only for treatment of a fever. But his pilot, Fatty Pearson, certainly took his leisure at the Aero Club, and Mr. Pearson impressed Hemingway enough to become immortal as Compton in "The Snows of Kilimanjaro." So, maybe.

Either way, I was late for my own adventures, so I paid the check, grabbed my bag, and left for a Bluebird Aviation hangar, close by. There I met a Somali man in a blazer with gold buttons whom I will call Ebyan, because that is a common name among the Darod, and he asked me to use it. He was standing next to a white twin-engine Cessna 402B, talking with two men in pilot shirts.

The plane was a front-loader, just like the Grumman Goose, so I stowed my bag in the nose cone and shook a few hands. I had one of those small digital cameras whose lens pops up when you turn it on, and I took a bunch of pics, including the tail number, 5Y-UTD. I wanted pics because it was a charter that had been arranged by people I had never met, and I figured anything can happen in a situation like this. If things went south, maybe searchers would find the camera and get it back to Rose.

"We are ready, sir," one of the pilots told me after about twenty minutes, and I climbed inside. There were only two seats in the cabin because Somalia had no Avgas, and we were hauling fuel in plastic containers so the plane could fly a second leg. I sat behind the co-pilot, a professional-looking youngster of twenty-three who wore classic aviator shades and four gold stripes on each shoulder.

"Please wait," I heard a woman say. Then a man climbed in behind her with a video camera like they use for local news. The woman was wearing a hijab, and the man a U2 T-shirt. I looked at Ebyan, because this was supposed to be a private hire. He just shrugged, and I thought back on the HRT days, when you'd board a charter with a bunch of people you'd never met, trusting that everyone was there for a reason.

"Look," I heard the captain say as we climbed out of Wilson Airport. We had started in light rain, but the view splayed gorgeous once we passed through ten thousand feet. "Kilimanjaro."

The plane was so old, the black paint had flaked off the avionics panel and several dials appeared not to be moving. The engines were too loud for conversation, but it didn't matter because no one said a word until three hours later, when the twenty-three-year-old in the left seat said, "Shit."

He and the co-pilot were craning to look out their windows in all directions, searching for something on the ground. We had descended to two thousand feet, which was low for cruising but high enough to see that there was absolutely nothing man-made between our horizons.

"What's the problem?" I asked.

"The runway should be there," he answered. Then he tapped the fuel gauge, which was working but showed the left tank empty, the other on fumes.

Then, "Shit!" again, once they found the dirt strip, because upon final approach, a Dash 8 with a big blue "UN" on the tail pulled out in front of us, and the captain had to haul back the yoke. I was thinking about all the other crashes I had avoided in forty years of flying as we circled around for another attempt, and then we finally touched down on a bare patch of ground.

I saw a mound of rubble that might once have been a terminal, several other UN planes, and a dozen men hanging around a Toyota pickup truck with an NSV anti-aircraft gun mounted in the bed. Two of the men were wearing tiger stripe camo, the others lolling about in slacks. I homed in on the guy in raspberry flip-flops carrying a PKM across his shoulders like Jesus walking the Via Dolorosa. His buddy had belts of 7.62 hanging around his neck, because the PKM is a crew-served weapon, and every crew has an ammo bearer.

Nobody looked very excited about our arrival, but it was one hundred degrees in the shade, and there was no shade at all. It was 14:07, which meant the morning khat chew had settled into a mellow after-buzz, so the guys were just chilling. I did the math anyway: another King Air, a Caravan, and some kind of Fokker, all painted ceiling white with sky-blue markings. I counted twenty-two shooters distributed among three technicals, the crumbled remains of structures, tumbleweed, and silty dirt as far as the eye could see. I would describe the scene as mauve, ice pick stern.

Then the pilots shut down the engines, and I turned to other variables, including the names of people who might be wondering if I had landed. The obvious players included Rosie, an FBI agent in a midsize office, intelligence officers from two Five Eyes countries, and an Australian money man with a hyphenated name who might have been tied to a third. I was thinking about the propriety of paying seven thousand dollars for a one-way Cessna ride into Somalia wearing Aveda pomade and a blue striped suit. I was thinking about documents I had left with a bellman at the Six Eighty Hotel, instructions for Farrah should things go awry.

"Can you get the hatch, please?" I asked.

The girl in the hijab, who had slept the entire flight, turned the handle, pushed the hatch open, and climbed out without ever saying hello. Somebody outside said something I couldn't understand, and then Ebyan climbed out, too, and they all jabbered away with their hands clasped behind their backs.

And that's where it hits you. Where it hit me. The heat, the reality of my construct. Baidoa, Somalia, is 139 nautical miles from Mogadishu, which is the nearest civilization, a war-torn hellhole synonymous, for most Americans, with a fourteen-hour gunfight between Joint Special Operations Command heroes and a swarm of bad guys acting gangster with RPGs.

"That is our ride," Ebyan told me, pointing to a junker of a sedan.

I grabbed my bag out of the nose cone, bid the pilots goodbye. Then I checked to make sure nothing had been pilfered along the way:

a backup pair of jeans, a couple of T-shirts, and a medical kit comprising duct tape, iodine, and a handful of tampons. The biggest risk in gunfights is exsanguination, and trauma dressings don't take up much space in a bag, but I find Playtex Sport the go-to plug for arterial squirts.

"Pack 'em in, tape 'em down," as they say.

Oh, and I had a travel pack of U.S. dollars, of course, because there are no ATMs in Somalia, no credit cards or checks. Everything is expensive, especially the soldiers I'd have to hire; the politicians I would entertain; transportation, food, an indoor place to sleep.

"We must leave," Ebyan said, as everyone stared.

I thought back on the living room in New Hampshire with Mick and Jake in La-Z-Boys watching *Black Hawk Down,* enjoying Rosie's strawberry rhubarb pie. Collin in his SpongeBob pajamas, Chelsea's hugs, the cold wind outside. And then a couple of locals pulled jugs of Avgas out of the plane and climbed up on the wing to pour it in through a cheesecloth strainer. I saw Africa flat around me, baked earth in every direction, the birthplace of man devoid of smell except man's own odor. Then the pilots climbed into their seats, and the rotors turned, and my ride flew away.

"Why do you like Africa, Dad?" Jake had asked me.

"Penance," Fred T. might have answered, that first adventure involving a plane.

Maybe penance. Maybe no reason at all. Maybe just because it's Africa.

Osman Ali Atto looks nothing like George Harris. He wears suits I've seen at Harrods, silk ties, shoes my friends might admire. He does not smoke cigars, does not sport a pinkie ring, wears no gold chains at all. In fact, the real Osman Ali Atto looks like he works for the Royal Bank of Scotland, strikingly charismatic for a warlord who is said to have tortured and killed innocent people by the thousands.

I think back on the movie and decide it is entirely possible that Atto enjoys his *USA Today* in the Bakaara arms market, as depicted by Ridley Scott. He made his millions using guns to steal from the most impoverished souls on earth, so it makes sense that he would live rich among them. Men fear Osman Ali Atto because he controls East Africa's billion-dollar khat trade. Foreigners call him Monsieur Dozer because he owns construction companies that build roads for oil companies and NGOs. His trucks haul gasoline from Rwanda and Burundi. He owns telecommunications infrastructure used by the U.S. government in the global war on terror, controls illegal roadblocks with twelve-year-old sentries who can shut down commerce with a finger snap. He is the man who went to war with Delta Force protecting his buddy Farrah Aidid, then declared war on Aidid and killed him once the Black Hawks flew away.

Osman Ali Atto wears Aramis cologne, has a firm handshake, and displays well-aligned teeth. He's taller than I'd thought, heavier than his name suggests—"Atto" means "skinny" in Somali—and he's more or less average.

I know all this because he is standing beside me.

"Nice to meet you," I say. Monsieur Dozer.

There are lots of people around us, everyone shaking hands, so I offer mine, but an old man dressed in traditional macawiis and kufiyah walks between us. Ebyan pulls me away.

"You do not talk to this man," he cautions.

Ebyan is a pragmatic associate, an interpreter prone to efficiency with words. I trust him because he is well educated in things they don't teach in school, not even at Camp Peary. He cants his head a lot, seldom smiles. I trust him, which is good, because he's there to keep me alive.

"Please do not," he says. "I assure you."

I hold my camera at arm's length to snap a couple of selfies, gathering the famous warlord behind me so the boys will believe this part of the story. While I have the camera in my hand, I document the rest of our surroundings, which amount to a couple hundred Somali men ambling through the dimly lit interior of a whitewashed grain depot on the outskirts of town.

The building has a bunch of open windows and two steel doors for circulation but it's a sauna inside despite a half-dozen ceiling fans dangling twenty-five feet overhead from what passes for a scabbed together roof of corrugated tin. Someone has lined up rows of chairs like you might see at a timeshare presentation, chrome frames with black vinyl seats, shipping plastic still taped around the legs.

There is a stage of sorts at the front of the building, a speakers' dais with five high-backed thrones, a lectern with a microphone, a wood table for recorders. There is no address, because streets are not marked in Baidoa, but someone has hand-painted "Al Khalil Warehouse" in Western script.

"No photos," Ebyan tells me, but I ignore him.

There are several media crews along one wall, and I am standing in the VIP section with suits from the United Nations. I document faces near the stage, get the flag on the wall: two African leopards holding a blue shield with a white star. The rocker reads, "Somali Republic." Beneath the flag are three large portraits: Prime Minister Ali Moham-med Ghedi on the left, Speaker of the Parliament Sharif Hassan Sheikh Adan on the right, and President Abdullahi Yusuf Ahmed in the mid-dle.

My camera records time hacks, including the date, which is Febru-ary 28, 2006. It does not note the occasion, which is too big for any one camera: the birth of a nation. After two years in Nairobi, the Transitional Federal Government (TFG) of 275 regional strongmen is attempting a triumphant return. It is still too dangerous for them to set up shop in the capital of Mogadishu, so they have chosen Baidoa as their first seat of power. I would call their ambitions naïve.

I hear a drumroll. Then a man in shirtsleeves steps up to the lectern, says something over the makeshift PA. The crowd comes to order. Then an ensemble breaks into Sousa music. I look off to my right, at a marching band, though no one is marching, nineteen players all dressed in lime-green uniforms with yellow accents, white pants, shako-style hats.

Two of the men are holding tubas; four of them, trumpets or cor-nets; there is one trombone and a drum corps with a bass so old, it has skin on only one side. I assume the number they are playing is an an-them, because everyone is standing, including the diplomats beside me. I take pictures of the ramshackle band; pictures of the ministers, the media, the room. I note the wrinkled vinyl sheets rolled out to cover the packed-dirt floor.

And while the band is doing their best, I start to reflect on the fact that I'm standing in the newest country on earth. This Somali Repub-lic is a diaspora of bodega owners from Brixton, professors with wives in St. Paul. But they have a charter, and all charters list rules. Article 1 establishes Islam as the national religion and sharia as the law of the

land. Article 29 stipulates that 12 percent of the government will be
women, but that's just the UN talking, because there are two Somali
women in this warehouse, a patriarchy of clans. One of the women is
dressed in a red burka; the other, blue with a white star. Together they
remind me of a flag. Neither has any guns.

Eventually, the band stops playing, and the important people sit in
chairs. Various speakers say the usual things. There are four primary
players here: the Hawiye, Rahanweyn, Dir, and Darod. Then the
minor ethnicities, including the Tumal, the Reer Hamar. Governments, of course, need ministers, and those jobs go to power, so it's
easy to see who's who based on where they're seated. Osman Ali Atto
is minister of housing and public works, sitting near the front. I keep
an eye on him, because he is also head of the Alliance for the Restoration of Peace and Counter-Terrorism, which is funded by the CIA.
For now, I will admit that Osman Ali Atto and I share an objective:
money. He wants it, and I have some to trade.

After the speeches are over, everybody shakes hands, and the UN
flies away. I walk outside and stand among the watchers, who squat on
piles of rubble, the whole scene a landfill for people who have nothing
to discard. Ebyan and I are the only men in suits, standing in the dirt
lot as a yellow-and-white bus with Chinese writing chugs off, shuttling the last of the VIPs.

It's late in the afternoon, and I have not eaten since coffee at the
Aero Club; not a sip of water. I think about Joe in Paris, calling his
Black Card concierge for a nice plate of sprouts, maybe a top hotel
with percale sheets. I smile a little, until I realize there are no hotels
here, no plates of sprouts. It feels like last call at Fanelli, with Bob the
bartender sweeping up, pushing us out the door. And the guys all have
dates, but I'm on my own, that lonely feeling.

"We have to go," Ebyan tells me.

"Go where?"

"I do not know."

We walk for about thirty minutes, down a broken road that leads
into what were once buildings, now just cairns marking years of civil
war. We gather crowds of children around us as we stroll, most of
whom have never seen a white man, so they keep squealing as they
gather up their courage to run in and touch me, see if I am real. Happy
kids, just children.

"Sit here," Ebyan tells me when we come to what was once a piazza.

Three men with AK-47s have joined us somewhere amid the children, and when I sit on a concrete stoop, they stand around me. Ebyan walks away, the sun sinks lower, and a crowd begins to gather: old men and toddlers with moms in burkas or just hijab because they are too poor to buy fabric. Maybe forty people at first, then more, a hundred growing closer.

One woman walks up within a few feet, nervous smile, not a smile of humor. She has a small child, maybe three, and she is dragging the child toward me, the child crying, scared. Then she takes the child's hand so it can touch me, and I realize they think I am a ghost.

The child starts screaming, and the men at the back of the crowd are growing anxious, because they can see me but not what I am doing. I remember getting stoned in Pakistan, the way a crowd can turn, and then the three men with AKs feel it, too. One of them yanks the bolt of his rifle and points the front sight into the crowd, which scatters with terror, gone in a blink. I look up over my shoulder, and he shakes his head.

"Is not for you."

When Ebyan returns, we walk a short distance to a dirt lot inside a walled accommodation. Someone painted it before the war, a pastel shade of red, and you can follow the course of fighting from the scars on the walls. I read the Venn diagram of impacts, looping patterns of fully automatic 7.62, maybe some pistols. Then the chunks of wall break open to light where the turret guns have chopped away: piles of concrete from mortars, holes from RPGs that you can walk through.

"We will stay here," Ebyan tells me once I have joined him inside.

He is talking to the girl in the hijab from the plane, who has appeared out of nowhere. She is crying, so Ebyan puts me in a room beside hers, because she is scared. The rooms are open to the courtyard and have plank doors with cardboard in the windows. Someone has painted "ROOM NO 8" above my space, and I see that it has a cot, but hers has a coffin. A cheap pine box.

"Do not bother," Ebyan answers when I mention the girl's odd pallet.

So, I leave them and go to my room. I have nothing to eat, but I have a novel by a man named Jeffrey Lent, who went to Franconia

College and wrote *Lost Nation,* probing human frailty via plots set in New Hampshire. I think it might help me forget being hungry, so I read until the sun sets completely and the mosques' evening call to prayer erupts from loudspeakers across Baidoa.

Allahu akbar!

I lie there with my hands under my head until the stars come out, which I can see plainly through large holes in the ceiling. I lie there a long time wondering about Rosie and the kids, what they are up to. Dinner parties with my friends in New York. The smell of rhubarb.

Allahu akbar!

Eventually, I feel tired, and it has been a long day, so I want to sleep, but I know I can't sleep because of what might happen if I do. Maybe the night sweats will come, followed by dreams—not the soft slumbers of Africa but the haunts I've brought with me. So, I blink my eyes and pinch my skin to stay awake, like I used to on night pickets, jungle missions, desert operations near Huachuca.

Allahu akbar! Allahu akbar!

I lie there looking up at the stars as long as I can, because I know that if I fall asleep, I might wake up screaming, and that is not going to happen, because I don't want the girl in the coffin next door to think I'm scared, too.

10

Mogadishu, Somalia

[MARCH 2006]

Everything you imagine about this place is true, the contradictions of blinding sun and haunting night, earth tones and pastels, dust devils of scorched clay dancing listlessly in from nowhere. Nomad tribes of Dir and Gaalje'el drift across drought-starved grasses, the women reclused among domed huts made from thorny shrubs with hairy leaves, threadbare tarps. They call their homes *aqals,* and I notice the numbers growing, because this year is parchment dry, and clan leaders are walking their people to Baidoa by the thousands. They are starving.

"There." Ebyan points west.

The sky seems vast, ribbed silver-blue and lazy here on the outskirts of the city, where nomads have gathered herds of camels and goats. There are no trains or lorries, but planes sometimes appear out of nowhere carrying doctors and skids of clothes, and the tribes assemble around that hope. But there is no water, so the goats are dying and the camels fading; children breathe through their mouths, too thirsty to play. I stand there watching the giraffes, the agama lizards poking up their spiny heads, nature denuded, this shrubland of crumbling rock.

"Where?" I ask him.

"Just there."

The first thing you notice is the silence. Not an absence of sound, but an inability to gather it, some dying moan you feel in your gut knowing full well that its source and your understanding share no correlation. The sun is so hot it gives you chills. Then a breeze flits across, pregnant with shadows, and you realize there are men around you, dozens of them, and they are not a mirage. One of the men coughs, and you know it's probably tuberculosis, but that's the least of your problems, because there are four heavily armed gunships parked off to the right, à la carte armies you can hire for five hundred dollars a day.

"King Air," somebody calls out, one of the other crew commanders, and I hear the turbo prop whine. Then the truck engines come alive, and there's no more silence. Small puffs of exhaust, black if it's diesel; blue for the old gas V8s.

"Maybe today," I tell Ebyan, and he nods.

"Now, sir?" a teenager asks.

I say, "Let's go, boys," because my oldest soldier might be seventeen. "Degdeg, degdeg!"

I have a Toyota, too, a white relic with a chrome bumper, red and orange stripes. It has a 12.7 mm DShK heavy machine gun pipe-mounted in the bed, and a senior gunner who calls it sweetheart because *dushka* means "beloved" in Russian, and he speaks one word of English. We have an M60 with two cans of tracers, two PKMs in 7.62-by-54 mm, and five youngsters with AK-47s. Plus the driver, of course, who wears a Cubs hat and follows me everywhere I go.

"Wait until they unload the khat," Ebyan tells me.

"Yeah, I know."

We've been through this, three days running, standing at the airstrip with my thumb up my ass, waiting on a plane that is supposed to fly us to Djibouti. That's the plan, though nothing works like it's supposed to on the Horn of Africa. Every morning, Ebyan and I pack our bags, roust the crew, and ride out to the airstrip, where we wait for the khat flight from Nairobi. Every morning, we stop by a particular minister's house to say goodbye and reiterate our continued support for the TFG. Every morning, I count what's left of the cash, our original ten grand now short by half. It's all we have to pay our ten-man army; they are all we have to stay alive.

"Shit, boss." One of the kids winces. "Fuck Dick Cheney."

We've been waiting there in the sun for an hour, so I've been making the most of our time, teaching the guys obscenities and conducting a primitive sick call. One of the kids has a nasty gash on his hand that looks to be going septic. He calls himself Pimm.

"Hold still."

There's no need to waste a tampon, but the iodine might save his hand, and I have plenty, so I debride the pus as best I can, soak a Playtex, and have Ebyan tell him to swab it every couple of hours after we're gone. It's a nasty wound, and it hurts him when I touch it, so he is squirming around a little bit, and the others are needling him to toughen up.

"Bill Clinton," he swears. "Fuck Dick Cheney."

"Relax, man," I tell him. "This is serious."

"Not serious here," the driver says. "Show this boss."

He points to the guy with the M60, who reaches down and lifts one leg of his pants. He is wearing leather boots missing the laces, and I can see that there is no flesh at all from the top of the boot halfway to his knee. It's just the tibia and fibula, dry bone, kinda gray, and a strange-looking sleeve where the skin has healed like a cracked rubber band. It doesn't smell too bad. I hadn't even noticed him limping.

"Grenade." M60 nods. He is smiling proudly. "They want to be cutting it off. I say no. This leg and me, we be leaving this life together."

Then the driver yells for everyone to snap tight. M60 drops his pant leg and waves to a buddy in one of the other crews. Everybody starts to bristle, because it's not exactly a load of cocaine, but khat is still a drug, and these guys work for warlords. So, you never know.

"You have money?" Ebyan asks.

"Don't worry about what I've got."

Then I see it, one of those Bluebird King Air 200s from the hangar near the Aero Club in Nairobi. It's a flicker of a glint, at first, but then I can see it descending through two thousand feet on the same bearing of ninety-four degrees we tailed coming in. The King Air is the most popular dope ferry in the world because of its power-to-weight ratio, perfect for khat runs to remote airstrips, cubed out with bales of Baidoa's primary source of income.

The Bluebird deliveries roll in every morning like clockwork, and the four local shot callers roll in like clockwork to meet them. Khat is a leafy stem you chew and then hold in your cheek, kinda like Copenhagen mixed with bath salts. It turns your teeth Ozarky and loses potency within eight hours, but it makes life a whole lot more tolerable for people who have nothing else to think about except starvation.

"What did they tell you in Nairobi?" I ask Ebyan. He has the Nokia.

"They say today the plane will take us."

"That's what they tell you every day."

"They are your people," he argues. "Maybe you should call them."

The plane lines up its approach, and I remember our near miss coming in. Baidoa Airport is nothing but a worn strip of ground built by the Soviets in the eighties, which means it was never much to begin with. The runway has been bombed so many times it looks like a Twister sheet, but that's a good thing because its pattern of crudely patched holes is the only way to spot it in a thousand square miles of nowhere. There are other landmarks, but from the air, rubble is rubble.

"Degdeg!" somebody yells. "Degdeg!"

Then the plane lands and taxis to one hundred feet from where we're standing, and the pilot surveys the situation to make sure everything looks copacetic. I can read the tail number, 5Y-HHE; see the captain through the windshield, making up his mind. Then he gives the thumbs-up, and the technicals race toward the plane, escorting empty pickups for their share of the load.

The King Air rattles with the engines racing, and the door opens, and the pilot kicks out a big bale of khat, then another. The co-pilot sits inside with his hand on the throttles as the captain climbs out to do the deals. He has no gun, and it's a lot of money, all cash, and it's Somalia, but if things turn dirty, there will be no more khat, and everybody knows the rules.

"Thanks, boys!" I yell, after the khat guys race off, and some of them wave goodbye.

Ebyan and I start walking out toward the plane, and we get about halfway there when the captain yells, "Not today!"

And then I yell at him, and he yells at me, and he gives me the finger and says, "Fuck you," and I say, "Fuck you," but then he climbs up the steps and pulls the cabin door closed, and the plane flies away.

I stand there as the prop wash brushes my hair, the wind fades to the whine of engines as our only hope bounces down the runway, a glimmer of wings in the sky. Back to the silence of the nomads in their agal shebangs, who don't even notice because they've got problems of their own.

Ebyan and I wait quietly in our blue suits with our carry-on bags, camels standing ass to nose, chewing slow mouthfuls of cud, the goats all dead, dust devils of clay, wisps among the tussocks. I think about starving children waving sticks at flies, other kids too thirsty to bother, kids with machine guns, pastel-colored rubble, and acacia trees evergreen despite the drought.

"Maybe tomorrow," Ebyan decides. Somalia.

"Maybe tomorrow."

There's this sick feeling that comes over you—like when your connection is Cleveland, and you miss it, and the one bar at the airport is closed, and you realize you're not going to make it home for Christmas. The good news is that you still have $4,900 in your sock, but the bad news is your M60 gunner is walking around on bones for a leg because this is Somalia, and you're on your own, and there is no Google Maps or GPS painting the five-hundred-mile Darod trek back to Mombasa. There are no video blogs to rely upon for water holes, no verified Facebook explorers traveling with farm-to-table chefs, or culturally diverse security details to meet you for an evening Barolo among the prides of camera-friendly lions. There are no sat phones with Medjet helicopters standing by, rotors turning, in case somebody accidentally swallows gluten. So, no, it's not like getting stranded in Cleveland on Christmas Eve, but you get the idea.

"You have money?"

Ebyan waves to the technical, and they know the drill, so Pimm yells, "Fuck Bill Clinton," and smiles and waves back with his recently debrided hand.

"Yes," I tell Ebyan. "I have money."

I smile at the guys, because what else do you do? This is their home, so why would I want to leave it? They're happy I'm staying, happy to have shoes, happy for another day getting fed.

"I will call the minister," Ebyan tells me, and we start to walk.

One of the many great things I learned at HRT is that all threats are manageable if assessed properly and checked down in what we referred to as tactical order. First and foremost, HRT is a team, and every member of the team can shoot, but when you're in a gunfight and it's a big one, there is this odd moment when you realize it's an individual event of indeterminate duration and that no matter what the other guys are doing, you need to make some decisions. We called those situations "target-rich environments," and though my mind defaults to

maths, there is no time for equations in a gunfight, so, you keep things
simple, starting with the closest threat, because bullets miss with a
probability that is inversely square to distance. Today, the poet in me
defaults to metaphor, and I realize the closest threat is not a gun but
the risk of sleeping outdoors. We need to find a place to stay until we
can try again tomorrow.

"Let's get some lunch," I suggest. It's important to stay optimistic.

"Maca naa," Ebyan agrees. He dials the minister.

And it's almost noon, so we follow the donkey carts past the Col-
lecio Baidoa, now a bombed-out façade. We find a small building with
a sign reading "Macmacaanka Sare Aaran" and I have no clue what
that means, but they have pictures of fruit painted on the wall and
Fanta in small bottles that is warm but tasty. The floor is dirt, and they
use old motor oil to keep the dust down, so everything smells like
Midlothian. Ebyan orders some food, and we sit outside in plastic
chairs like you buy at Walmart. He has invited the minister, who rolls
up in the back of a Prado with his business manager and two guards in
a Corolla.

"You want camel milk?" the minister asks me once everyone is
seated. They all laugh like it's the funniest thing they've ever heard,
because fermented camel milk is a local drink that gives people from
Northern Virginia explosive diarrhea. It comes on hard and fast; it's
tough on suits in a city where there are no public toilets. You learn the
hard way.

"I'll pass."

We're sitting in a patch of oiled dirt, with the sun pounding away,
the minister's guards watching Pimm and M60 as they watch me from
the technical. People circle us, begging, selling cigarettes, cheap Chinese watches no one can afford, grateful for diversion. Another day.

"What about the meetings in Djibouti?" the minister asks. He has
lived most recently in a town called Longmont, near Denver. "Are
they waiting for you?"

"We need to get there as soon as possible." I shrug. "Which seems
to be a problem."

"What is the problem?"

"I do not know. Everything was moving nicely, but something has
changed."

"We do not want things to change."

"Perhaps you can talk to the prime minister," Ebyan suggests. "President Yusuf."

Then a man brings flatbread called muufo, camel tongue, and Top Ramen noodles. It's served in newspaper, *The Kenya Times,* which also serves as the napkin. You eat with your fingers, mixing everything from common plates, family style, three fingers and a thumb. You use your right hand because the left is reserved for cleaning your ass.

"The prime minister is too busy to worry about your changes. Where is Farrah?"

"Farrah is in Nairobi. He is trying."

"He should try harder."

It is impossible to overstate the complexity of this conversation: an American of my background and interests eating camel tongue in the impoverished capital of a week-old Somali Republic with a ministerial colleague of Osman Ali Atto's. We are surrounded by warlord khat dealers and nomad tribes, the minister's guards riding in a sedan, mine up on a Dushka.

"Things are already not what you promised," the minister tells me, annoyed.

"I didn't promise you anything."

"You say that now."

"This is business, the business of governments," I say. "No promises either way."

A girl in brightly colored wraps walks up with a couple of carved figurines, and one of the guards calls her "Midgaan" and shoos her away. The Midgaan are a caste of barbers and bonesetters, circumcisers condemned by relief organizations for genital mutilation. Ebyan has walked me through the Somali ladder of nomads, sitting outside at night watching the moon. There is another group he calls Yibir, which are spell weavers capable of magic. He once asked if I needed an amulet, and when I asked which one, he said, "What spell do you want to cast?"

"Maybe tomorrow," the minister says, chewing camel.

"Maybe tomorrow."

Later in the afternoon, Ebyan and I walk back to the small hostel where we have been staying. The proprietor is a cordial man in his forties who has survived the wars but suffered shrapnel wounds to his face. He has a kind smile but is tough to look at. He has painted the walls blue and yellow and green and pink. He calls it Carta Hotel, just three rooms.

I go inside to put my bag on the bed, change into jeans and a T-shirt, my only remaining clothes. Then I tell the guys in the technical to go home, and I walk the short distance to the remains of what was once a government building. It is three stories high, shattered to the rebar from heavy ordnance, probably tanks. I find stairs to the roof and look back toward town, ocher and flat except for cell towers, the minarets of mosques. You can see the thatched camps of sedentary clans to the south, sun setting over low hills west toward Kenya.

"Why do you like Africa, Dad?" I hear Jake saying.

There, the red-trance weight of an ancient people, immense beauty dulled by the chronic threat of violence. I think about Nature's indifference to any one species, the evolution of man. I think about Emily Dickinson at her window, how Conrad preferred rivers, what it must have felt like for Hemingway the second time he crashed into Africa, 1954. Then I walk over to the edge of the roof, climb up onto the parapet, and push my toes over, just thirty feet off the ground but the highest place I can find. I hold my hands out to my sides, close my eyes, breathe in the dry smells of the world.

I wait until the wind whispers *Chrisameechie.* My grandfather drinking penance. I think about Collin in SpongeBob pajamas, Chelsea saying "Daddy." I remember the first time I flew in that Grumman Goose up to Maine, skyscrapers in New York, leaning into bullets, the weightlessness of terror-infused dreams. I stand there a long time with my toes in space.

Maybe tomorrow, I think.

I used to feel something. There, I feel nothing at all.

By the end of the second week, things are degrading quickly. Each morning, Ebyan and I wake up, pack our bags, and go to the airstrip as usual, and each morning the line of people waiting to fly out grows longer. At first, it is a couple of new faces: men with black cases who claim to be advisers from UN-associated agencies. They have no guards, so they stand in the shade of my Dushka nodding and smiling like I'm their guy. I ignore them, daubing Pimm's hand with the last of the tampons, handing out cigarettes I've bought from the Midgaan girl in town.

Some days, the boys and I circle up in the shade of that big acacia tree and make fun of Ethiopians, practice new obscenities like "cock-sucker" and "Porter Goss." Then the King Air will appear as glint, and the technicals will fire up their engines, the co-pilot will park his hand on the throttles, the captain will gather his cash, and we'll yell insults at each other, and the plane will fly away without me.

"Maybe tomorrow," Ebyan will say, but then our guy in Nairobi stops answering our calls. Farrah is nowhere to be found. My stash of bills grows thinner.

The fifth day, it is wives of ministers, African dealmongers in embroidered topis who walk out in groups bigger than several planes can carry. The sixth day, it is ministers, too. The seventh day, there are so many people, the King Air circles three times but then never even lands.

Ebyan calls our minister for news, but the minister refuses to talk over the phone, so we drive out to meet him at his house. The government has installed sentries at his gate, and there are new faces inside, maybe a dozen people sitting with brightly colored suitcases, fidgeting over tea. A lesser-known minister tells us three aid workers have just been kidnapped from a relief station fifteen miles away.

There seems to be a bit of confusion over whether it was Oxfam or a Norwegian group. Then an argument breaks out concerning Al-Shabaab, which has tried to kill President Yusuf and Prime Minister Ghedi three times in the last year alone. It would be presumptuous to call the mood panic, but voices are rising, fingers pointing, dust a roil in shards of sun peeking through the tightly closed curtains. In the end, everyone agrees on one thing: The American has to go. Me.

"How?" I ask. "We've been trying."

It does not matter how, they aver. I am becoming a liability to the coalition, to President Yusuf's authority, to the government itself. Things are tenuous enough with the TFG trying to hold its own tribes together. Now the CIA is working four corners toward the middle, secret breakout sessions with the Ethiopians and old partners, including Osman Ali Atto, his Alliance for the Restoration of Peace and Counter-Terrorism. They blame me, but I argue that the business of building countries is complicated. Rome was not built in a day, I tell them, but they have no interest in Rome. One man waves his open palm and says Yusuf cannot hold his Mogadishu coalitions together if those coalitions are headed north to steal me for ransom.

"Interesting," I might have said, or maybe, "You gotta be fucking kidding me."

Either way, Ebyan and I go back to the Carta Hotel, where the innkeeper with the disfigured face has an idea. He walks me a short distance to the back wall of what he claims is a mosque, though it has no minaret, then behind it into a space between walls, where he points to a small redoubt. I say "small" because it is a remnant of corrugated tin suspended above a soldier course of concrete blocks. He has staged two bottles of water and a three-by-six-foot mkeka mat to keep me out of the dirt.

"No man finds you here," he tells me, trying to help. "All praise to Allah."

"In sha'Allah," I agree, there being no atheists in a foxhole.

I crawl in there, comfortable knowing rats will not be a problem, because there are no rats in Baidoa: no dogs or cats or anything with flesh, because they have all been eaten. I lie there a long time, trying to stay awake, but a man cannot stay awake forever, so sometime after dark, the noise of the city subsides, the Isha call to prayer erupts from a loudspeaker above my head, the moon rises a sliver and passes over the wall. My world falls still.

When I can blink no more, I fall deep into dreams, find myself sitting by a fire. It is a winter fire, a campsite at first, with spruce bows heavy above my head, but then there are people around me. I cannot tell who they are until the fire grows larger and I realize it is the Sunset Hill House, where I first learned trajectory, shagging golf balls as a caddy when I was twelve years old. The people in the dream include my father and my uncle Mike, who have set the blaze on behalf of the town for fire department training. They have red cans of gas and a box of matches. I watch them walk from room to room through that grand structure, dousing my youth and then burning it down.

I do not recognize the dream as a nightmare until I hear the tanks, the whine of turbines. There is a wind and a different flag, and I am in Texas, with a bunch of people called Branch Davidians, who, when they cannot kill me, decide to kill themselves. I see the razor flames of

Thermite tossed by ethnic Albanians into rooms full of neighbors, torch parades through the Alps of Kosovo, the rage of survivors. I see the bonfires of college football weekends, jamborees during Boy Scouts, quivering sheets of C-4 we would light to heat MREs during survival training in winter, embers of my father's pipe, pyrrhic conflagrations illuminating the dark corners of my subconscious.

"Allahu Akbar," a voice above me calls out, and I know it's a prayer from the mosque, but somehow I feel a monkey chained beside me. It's the monkey from Dir, the mullah's ape losing its shit as the riot grows, Joe working his Nikon as we race north against the night, those ISI agents from Special Branch making me sign their book.

"Allahu Akbar!"

Then, because dreams change without explanation, the monkey turns into a panel van, which pulls up beside me, and three men jump out wearing masks. They smell like Old Spice and malice. I feel the sun in my eyes, sadness knowing I will miss Mick's seventh birthday. Bag over my head, into the back of the van, pinned down against the floor by assailants who don't seem to care that I am one of the most highly trained killers on earth. I have been warned it was coming, SERE training, that I should not fight back because it's just a scenario, a way of preparing guys like me for capture by enemy forces. Something I have not seen coming.

"You ain't so tough now, are you?" One of Them prods, and some ill-defined time later, I find myself in a box made of Georgia-Pacific OSB, which I remember so well because that blue logo was all I had to look at for days. Klieg light, warehouse dust through air holes drilled into my ceiling. The taste of concrete. Naked with dark yellow piss all over my legs.

I'm tied up, head hanging over the edge of a stainless-steel table. Red towel over my face, being asked stupid questions about why a kid from New Hampshire would give up a career in theater to fly around the world doing renditions. Then carbonated water in my throat, convulsions, the what-the-fuck sensation that comes with thinking you know it all but are wrong.

Allahu Akbar!

It's the monkey, again, and he's getting louder. His voice grows coarse and threatening, a jet engine of angst. That little motherfucker is two feet from my face, barking in a man's voice, filthy with spite. He's swelling, dripping. I see tears forming in his monkey eyes.

Allahu Akbar!

You think some things will sustain you during torture: patriotism, resolve. But that's not true, not for me. Naked, cold, beaten, starved— your defenses start to fail, the way they do when you're surfing and you come off a wave, into a boil, the hydraulic holding you down. Deep down in a coral eddy, even after the violence ends. Everything empty. Still. And you can't breathe, but panic will kill you, so you relax, find peace in faith that what's next might be better.

Allahu Akbar!

I start to come around, waking up into that space at the edge of dreams where all the parts of life fit together in duplicitous ways. I think about Uncle Harold, how he lied about the CIA. Rosie, the kids. Things I have assumed about the world, things I have mistaken.

Allahu Akbar!

I blink my eyes, realize it is not me screaming. It is a holy man, a madrassa elder broadcasting Fajr, the morning call to prayer. I feel acutely aware that I am awake, and that I have not levitated into ready gun position, like those years after Waco. I'm not even sweating.

"In sha'Allah," I tell myself.

The monkey is gone.

There's nothing else to say.

K50 Airstrip is an abandoned Soviet air base about thirty miles south of Mogadishu. There is one prominent building with the roof blown off, several smaller structures that might have been barracks, a red dirt runway long enough to land UNICEF flights of baby formula and military cargo, and Fokkers shuttling men like Osman Ali Atto to meetings with spies. The main airport in town is closed due to fighting, but I don't care, because there is one flight out of Somalia today. The aircraft is bigger than a King Air 200, and I can see it from where I'm standing.

It's unusually hot this afternoon, a malaise of khat and despair that Africa likes to throw at you as if the filth and famine aren't enough. The scrubland around Mogadishu quivers in a mirage, a roiling montage of scorched sheet metal, desiccated tribes, chrome-sheen faces homogenous in their complete bafflement over my having found my way among them.

And that's the first thing we need to clear up, because getting here from Baidoa baffles me, too. Some might call it an escape or an evacuation, but both those things imply passage to something safer, and nobody would call this place safer. The U.S. military spent $1.7 billion and forty-three bravely uniformed lives fighting their way out of Mogadishu; I think it is entirely possible I'm the only American who ever fought his way in. I'm alive, but my toes are hanging over the edge of something taller than any cliff. My balls are tingling.

For those who have never been to Mogadishu, it's hard to describe. Ridley Scott did a nice job in his movie—all-day firefights near pink sandy beaches—but I would add murderous pirates in fishing skiffs, boys with machine guns who are not allowed to speak to girls selling cigarettes with their genitals trimmed off by old men using broken shards of glass. You can't forget missionaries pitching UNOSOM equality guidelines, potbellied children dying in scores, giraffes and camels, shamans shaking rattles and casting spells. And here I find myself among them, wearing a nice blue suit, wingtips, a loosely knotted tie.

The only shade lies off to my left, beneath an old tarp shebang that smells like ramen noodles and ass. I can see what appears to be a vintage 727 just like the one D. B. Cooper jumped out of in 1971. It's parked about one hundred yards north on what barely passes for a runway, even in Africa. There are no other planes at K50 today, none in Baidoa. I don't know who owns this relic, why it's here, where it is going, or from whence it came, but I gotta get on it.

"How much?" I ask Ebyan.

He has been talking to a local, standing among a bunch of women in burkas off to my left. Kids running around, looking oddly chipper. There is no terminal or baggage claim or customs. There are no buildings at all, just people selling shit I don't need, maybe twenty-five gangsters on cellphones, a 727 with stairs hanging out the back, a guy who claims he can get me up those stairs for some ill-defined fee.

"How much do you have?"

"Six hundred dollars."

"He will search you."

"Six hundred dollars."

"Give it to me. I will see if it is enough."

Everyone is staring and wondering the same thing: What is this guy doing here? And odd as it may seem, that one question is keeping me alive. In their minds, I am either a journalist or a spook—and I don't have a camera, so it's a loaded bet. Even rank-and-file shooters know the CIA is back with midnight flights and pallets stacked with dollars. Things have been dry for a decade, but things have changed: Deals are moving fast and furious between clans and Langley.

The only plausible explanation for my arrival would be that an agreement has been made with one of their bosses, and nobody knows which one. These guys are soldiers, and they know that kidnapping me without approval would exceed their pay grade. It might get them fired, might get them killed.

"This man does not believe you," Ebyan says, walking back over after about twenty minutes. "I told you they would search you."

The man is in his forties, humorless. He points to my pockets, which I empty; to my socks, which I show him. Then he rummages through my bag. He steals the duct tape.

"I've got nothing left." I shrug.

The man and Ebyan banter back and forth in Somali.

"He wants your passport," Ebyan says.

"Fuck him."

"I do not think so. It is the only choice."

"We don't know this guy, brother. My passport? You gotta be joking."

I look around, trying to do the math. It is hot. I am filthy. We are completely alone. I start crunching the numbers, counting barrels and scowls and distances in kilometers to happier locations. I try all the calculations, from third-grade addition to hard stuff used by people trying to prove the Riemann hypothesis, but I keep coming up with the number one, which is the number of planes in Mogadishu I can get on if I want to avoid months in a cage kneeling in front of a video camera with a knife to my throat.

"Does this guy have our money?" I ask.

"Yes."

"And he's not giving it back?"

"No."

I even regress to those overrated Venn diagrams, because my mind does surprising things in challenging situations, and I can see a lone-standing wall where the impact of bullets has documented proof of humanity's disregard for itself. There, in the middle, lies a coded subset of truths that remind me of the *Kryptos* sculpture at Langley, though easier to decipher. I have no money, no comms, no ride, no technical, no tin roof redoubt in an alley behind a mosque listening to a monkey screaming prayers five times a day. What good is a passport?

"Here," I say and hand the stranger my only remaining hope.

"You want water?" Ebyan asks.

"Thanks," I tell him.

I look out toward the plane, then at the men moving closer. I think about the choices that have led me here, to this place, choices I alone have made. I think about how I have needed a mission, and that I have mistaken my mission for theirs, the people with three watches and six-pack names who populate the world of money and guns. That Somalia needed a government, and the government needed GDP, and the United States needed to stop Somalia from becoming a haven for terrorists. How I know Somalia has the longest coastline in Africa, which means fish, and the Chinese want fish, but every time they move in, pirates try to steal their boats. If I can get the TFG to sign certain agreements, I can fly up to Djibouti for prearranged talks with the navy task force, which controls Bab Al-Mandeb, the straits of Yemen. Seemed like a plan.

"What will happen if your plan fails?" Farrah asked me back in Nairobi.

"It won't," I told him. "I saw the whole thing play out in a dream."

"A dream? That's what you want me to tell your children?"

Then Ebyan comes back with two bottles of water, and I drink mine, looking around at the squalor and the pods of men with guns staring through fake Ray-Bans at the lunatic in the suit. I think back on the events that led us to K50 in the first place. How earlier that morning, one of the ministers reported rumors of a plane in Mogadishu. No one cared a rat's ass how far it was to Mogadishu, what time the plane was leaving, whether the road was open, or if I could get a seat. Al-Shabaab was closing in, they said, and I was leaving Baidoa immediately. So, I did what any self-respecting businessman would do,

I whistled M60 up onto the Dushka, had Pimm load his belt-fed, climbed into yet another Corolla, and headed south.

It was hot, and desperate, and we were hauling ass through unfamiliar alleys, but I felt optimistic because no matter what, I was done sleeping in redoubts, next to coffins. But then traffic slowed, and the driver said, "Look away from this men. They are not be liking you white."

It was a checkpoint at the southern entrance to the city, with sandbags and a bunch of stacked-up tires and a drop gate you could not avoid. The driver rolled down his window, and there was banter back and forth, and he gave a guard some local scrip. I could see M60 right behind us, leaning over the cab of the Toyota, giving me the thumbs-up. Good to go.

"What was that?" I asked after we made it out of town.

"Many checkpoints here," Ebyan said. "Not all so professional."

It's easy to tell you what it was like for the next three and a half hours, because it was the same thing twenty-seven times in a row. The road was dirt, the shocks were useless. You'd get up to 122 kilometers per hour, which might not seem all that fast . . . until you come over the crest of a hill and there's a 105 mm howitzer crater ten feet deep, thirty feet around. The car bounces wildly as you lock up the brakes, swerving through the scrub brush. Then the driver stomps on the gas, because the road will kill you, but you don't know when the plane in Mog is leaving, if there is one at all, and you're dead if you miss it, so it's six of one, a half dozen of the other. It's Africa hot, but the windows are up because of the dust. Then the driver says, "Checkpoint," and you see a twelve-year-old in the middle of the road behind a burned-out deuce-and-a-half, and you slam on the brakes because he's waving a gun. You turn your head away, so he doesn't see you through the tinted windows and triple the price of the toll, and the driver screams something at him in Somali, and you wait for the technical to catch up, and Pimm yells, too, and it's a gunfight type of standoff until the twelve-year-old chooses life, waves you through. Giraffes amble along, a town here and there, you check your watch, Ebyan turning pale.

Read that paragraph again twenty-six times. I dare you.

Think about the odds of one of those twelve-year-olds shooting you in the head every time you come over a hill, because he's twelve years old and doesn't even have hair on his balls, but some guy who works for Osman Ali Atto will skin him if he finds out a car got through for free. Then you roll up on roadblock twenty-three, and the technical is nowhere to be seen, because it couldn't keep up with nine guys riding shotgun and a tired old engine. The driver yells at the twelve-year-old, like always, but this kid is having a bad day, so he shoots out the back window, and you're alive, but you're fucked, because you still have to drive through Mogadishu, and there's no tinted glass to hide your lily-white ass from Al-Shabaab, who want to carve it up and show the CIA who's boss.

"Pimp," Ebyan said once we finally pulled into K50. It was just past noon, but the day was already a shit show, and things were getting worse in a hurry.

"Pimp?" I asked.

"That's his name, the soldier with the infected hand. Not 'Pimm.' You misunderstand."

I just looked at him, trying to make sense of things that made no sense at all, this Friday afternoon in Mogadishu, no idea where exactly I was or how I was going to get out.

"These men have movies, American movies on DVD," Ebyan explained.

"What the fuck are you talking about?"

"He calls himself Pimp because of some famous thing, maybe Russell Crowe or Sylvester Stallone. I do not know."

I can explain my state of mind then simply, with no need for heavy-handed prose: I'm standing in a gravel lot in Mogadishu, Somalia, surrounded by men dressed in brightly colored kufiyahs and mirrored sunglasses, and wielding cellphones and belt-fed machine guns.

I have no technical, no money, no car, and I've just given up my passport.

If I don't get on that plane, I am dead.

This is Africa's simple truth.

Water

You bathe in shallows this
Penned rage swirling the
Birth of rhyme and its pace
An amble between us

Light pools distant deep
Ill-focused nod what life offers
When we look up to wonder
About what we have lost
Things at the bottom of the sea

There in haste we shuffle
Hollows broken frail
Built wisely not well of
Doubt because hope for love
And its gain bear no relation

You whisper to me from grasses
Those lines we dream but
Cannot muster awake
I reach to grasp
Reach out from suffering
Reach to hold you
Knowing the distance between
Might sustain us

11

K-38, Baja, Mexico

[JULY 1983]

The great pipe master Gerry Lopez used to say the best surfer in the water is the one having the most fun. And that might be true, but not in my case, because I've spent decades paddling into swell, and I still suck. Close friends say the ocean simply doesn't like me, that I have no business complaining, because I grew up at a ski area and never even saw a wave until my first year out of college. They tell me I should be grateful for Zen moments alone with my thoughts, because surfing is not a contest; it's a journey toward awakening. They tell me it doesn't matter how you get into the barrel; it's who you are while you're in there.

And I'll admit there are those days when the conditions are right and I find a little Zen in the whole life-fully-formed thing, because how else would you reconcile a man with my affinity for violence writing haikus about getting shacked in J Bay pits off Kouga?

Regardless, my search for the perfect wave started one fateful Monday at a Southern California beach break called the Wedge. A buddy, Mike Appleton, and I had decided to head west after college, seeking cross-country adventure via New Orleans. I wanted to be a rock star, and he was tired of winter, so we threw our bags into a 1968 Volkswagen bus full of guitars, amps, and Persian rugs, which would have served us well, except the bus caught fire and burned along I-10, outside Dripping Springs, Texas. The Highway Patrol gave us a ride to El Paso, where we jumped on a Greyhound bus and arrived in Costa

Mesa, California, on the Fourth of July with the hair burned off our legs. I had thirty-seven dollars in my pocket, a pair of flip-flops, and a T-shirt that said "Green."

I remember the moment I saw it, the Wedge, nature throwing a tantrum. We had heard about it from a skinny kid in a Baja serape, buying Zig-Zag papers at Ralph's. He had asked if we were paddling out, because the swell was kicking, and when I asked how to find the place, he canted his head like I was some kind of kook. He said it was right next to where Dick Dale lived with his two white tigers. I asked who Dick Dale was, and he started laughing.

"Bruh, you from Tustin?" he asked. "Dick Dale is king of the surf guitar."

Appy and I got up early the next morning, hopped on an OCTA bus to Balboa, walked toward the roar. A crowd of locals had gathered in the sand, holding those cool Makapuu fins bodysurfers wear. The skies were June-gloom misty with the sun filtering through. I watched that monster pop up and fold onto itself with a whoof. You could feel it in your knees.

"Bitchin'," Appy said to a couple of guys with Spicoli hair. "You fellas going in?"

We didn't know it at the time, but the Wedge is a local wave, world-famous for maiming tourists. We had no fins or sun-bleached hair, no tans at all. They just shook their heads.

"What do you think, man?" Appy asked.

"Are you kidding?" I said. "Look at that fucking thing."

There were only three guys in the water, which we thought was good, until we dove in and found out why. The Wedge rises off the rock jetty, a thirty-foot avulsion that looks kinda like a trapdoor to hell. It's got this little pocket in the middle, so you swim in there, and things happen fast. First, you think, *Oh shit,* and then the water sucks off the bottom, rag-dolls you, slams you headfirst onto the sand. I went dim that first landing, like when Big Bob hit me, but the undertow reached in and shook me awake. I remember trying to claw my way to the beach, and the guys with the fins shaking their heads at the goof about to die wearing chinos.

"You drowning, man?" I called out after about thirty seconds.

Appy was puking water, but still above the surface.

"Drowning?" he yelled. "I'm wicked stoked!"

Which brings us back to my love for surfing. During the past forty years, I have traveled the world in search of the perfect wave, everything from head-high rights in Puerto Rico to third-break kongs off the coast of Banyuwangi. I have floated soft-tops through off-season mush in Oahu, flown to black sites near Marrakesh where I could huck myself over the edge of shit so big I'd swear I was looking down into the fortress at Essaouira. In every session, I paddled out hopeful the ocean would accept me, and each time, I found it would not.

But who cares, right? Surfing is not about performance. It's about peeking up the skirts of Mother Nature; seeking mysteries in those warm, wet spaces; throwing yourself headlong into the poetry of local motion, the glimmer of a playful sun, maybe a couple of Foghat songs between drownings. I love the discovery inherent in those dawn patrol moments, when you're sitting there bobbing glassy and the breeze is offshore and you're talking nonsense with your buddies, sizing up the Samoan you'll have to fight if it's crowded and you're a haole.

That ease, that tension.

"Pi'i mai ka nalu," you say, and the bomb set arrives.

You feel an existential thrill, because this is about something that will exist only once in the history of the world, and you know surfing is not about what will happen if you catch the wave but how it will feel if you don't.

I love the lifestyle, too: acoustic guitars and drum circles around driftwood fires, beers with a half-moon rising. The way your skin feels, tanned, the afterglow of the day close around you. I love the craft of boards, plank Olos and mahogany Alaïas, scooters with side racks, those ugly bone knobs you get on your foot from lazy takeoffs. And surfing is a surface sport, but surfers seek deeper things, so sometime after that first beatdown at the Wedge, Appy and I found a new place on the water, at Thirty-third and Seashore, the Balboa Peninsula. Things were looking up, because I had my own room, my own bed, a tan, a job tending bar at a nice little place called Bilbo Baggins, off Harbor Boulevard at the Mesa Verde Center.

"Want a pitcher?" the bartender had asked after I'd spent a long day applying at 7-Elevens.

"Nah, I need a job."

It just so happened that the bartender was also the owner, a staid but charismatic native of Rancho Cucamonga named Jim Esposito. Jim looked me up and down, said I should have come by earlier, because he'd just filled an opening. But then we talked a minute, and I told him about dodging fiery death in Texas, losing all my worldly possessions. I told him about getting my ass kicked at the Wedge because I didn't have any fins, and how I lived naked on wash days because I didn't have a backup change of clothes. How I just wanted to be a rock star.

"Hang on, brother," Jim said. He picked up the phone, called the guy he had just hired, and fired him. I started the next morning, my first job out of college, scrubbing the Fry-o-Lator.

After that, things kinda fell into place. I was a high achiever, so I moved up to cooking burgers; then to the front door, checking IDs. The insurance money came through, so I bought a Les Paul, found a used board in *The Recycler*, a wetsuit at the Frog House, some Op corduroy shorts at Goodwill. And I worked at night, so I had all day in the waves, trying to learn what the cool kids were doing, ripping swell up and down the jetties.

My apprenticeship started out with one embarrassing wreck after another, but then, as often happens in life, you knock long enough on the same door, and it mysteriously opens. My very first ride was caught on film by another roommate, named Danny "Air Man" Ayer. Air Man was not a surfer, but he loved girls in bikinis, and he had a trust fund, so he often walked out with a camera in search of love.

"Whew hoo!" I could hear him yelling from the beach. "Yeah, man!"

I was digging life out there in the lineup, trying to act local on my six-foot, four-inch Mark Richards twin fin, which was cool but way too small for a beginner.

"That's bitchin'!" Air Man was yelling sarcastically. "You're the kind, bruh!"

The real reason for his excitement was a woman named Karen Witter, who lived across the street. She was super nice, and we had all seen her naked, because she'd been a *Playboy* Playmate of the Month. Air Man had grown tired of girls shooting Lemon Drops in their Dolphin shorts at the Blue Beet Café, so he was attempting to impress her. Love was his vocation.

"Go, Whit!" I heard Karen yell, so I paddled as hard as I could and somehow dropped into my first ride, feeling like Rabbit Bartholomew on the cover of *Surfer* magazine.

Until that moment, I had been a bookworm English major from a prominent eastern college, but now I was living a whole new dream: SoCal waterman, a legitimate shredder. I looked up from the bottom turn of that epic knee-high ride to where I could see Air Man snapping away with a *Playboy* Playmate of the Month waving, gorgeous in a French-cut bikini. I had a gig that night at the Red Onion, hair growing out in dreads, Jackson Browne tickets for a Friday performance at the Golden Bear. Don Henley was singing "The Boys of Summer" from a boom box nearby.

I remember riding the foam all the way into the sand and stepping off alive with enthusiasm for new excursions. The world was taking shape as I had dreamed it. If you ever saw Air Man's photograph, you would laugh at the smile on my face, which might be bigger than Kodachrome could capture. I keep that photo in a frame on a wall. Sometimes I still like to stare.

Somalia has surf, too, two thousand miles of tented third-reef barrels with nobody out. And as I learned during my years on HRT, life does not always line up in chronological order, so it is impossible to think about surfing without finding myself back in Mogadishu, racing along the coast toward K50 in the back of a Corolla. I remember staring out my window at those empty waves, thinking about how happy I would have been to wax up a board and paddle out.

"Pretty, huh?" I asked Ebyan, who ignored me. "See how it pops up the middle like an A-frame? You can take off either way, front side or back side, up to you."

There had been no checkpoints at all once we got south of Mogadishu, and the road was dirt but mostly intact, so we raced those last miles as fast as the car would go. That old Corolla looked used up in every way, but this was Africa, and we were alive, so no one complained.

"This almost there," the driver told us.

I was thinking about that scene in *Black Hawk Down* where they're riding helicopters along the coastline, everybody staring into that rolling beauty, the calm before the storm. I had seen those waves before, traveling Europe during spring break, my junior year in college. I was living in London at the time, but I had bought an Interrail pass so I could sleep on trains between hostels, five weeks on the Continent.

I stopped in Málaga at Easter to play guitar, busking for tips among the beggars near Castillo de Gibralfaro until I'd saved enough cash for a bus ride to Torremolinos. I loved a movie called *Hard Contract,* in which James Coburn plays an assassin grown tired of killing. He goes to Torremolinos to strangle a man, falls in love with Lee Remick—who looked a lot like Aunt Lois—a wealthy woman pretending to be a hooker because she is bored. There is a murder, and they all fly over to Morocco, my true objective.

I cannot tell you when I learned to overcome discomfort with imagination, perhaps while hiking the White Mountains as a kid, maybe during long nights in jungles and deserts, those years on HRT. Whenever it was, I sat there in the back of the Corolla as the sun beat down, my legs cramping, urging my mind to wander. I was smiling at the thought of being nineteen years old in Spain, how I had broken a B-string on my guitar, which made it hard to play Poco covers on the street corner for pesetas. I thought about what it felt like to go hungry, truly hungry for long periods of time; how I bought Bastos because cigarettes were cheaper than bread, masked the pangs.

I thought about finding my way to the Costa del Sol, where I dipped my toes into the Mediterranean for the first time. I remembered the warmth of those waters, not a ripple of surf but exciting, then up the long steps toward town, the walls of whitewashed stucco, ancient and tiered.

I remembered plodding along until I found Casa Suecia, where I rented a small room with a view of the sea but no glass in the windows, and the breezes would lull me to sleep while I was reading Hermann Hesse, as college kids do. I was too broke for food, but I met Swedish backpackers, a handsome man and his beautiful lover, who had just returned from Marrakesh. They would send me up into town with an empty Perrier bottle, which I would fill in the market with Basque red wine from Rioja. It was an "I buy, you fly" sort of arrangement.

At night, I would write poems while listening to feral cats fighting in the lot behind us, disco music lolling down from clubs. Sometimes

I would loiter, watching the beggar families hustling tourists, mothers breastfeeding toddlers while the fathers won scams involving shells and a pea.

Most sunsets, I would sit with the Swedish lovers, drinking out of olive jars as they told me about Morocco, the towns, the waves. I had saved enough for passage, because I was reading *Narcissus and Goldmund, Siddhartha,* so how could I not? Then the Swedish lovers moved away, and I went to Marrakesh, where I drank tea and walked out to the ocean, which looked like those beaches in *Black Hawk Down* because that's where Ridley Scott filmed them.

Then sun flickered through the window, and I was back in Somalia, back in the moment, because maybe life really is just a dream. Maybe it's all connected, reality. One grand illusion.

"K50," the driver said, and I snapped back into the moment.

There we were, Ebyan and the crazy American stranded at the second-best airport in Mogadishu, a long way from home. I remembered how, after a very long time, Ebyan walked back from somewhere and said, "We can go." Just like that. "We can go."

"To the plane?"

"Yes, to the plane."

He handed me what looked like a ticket, and I started to smile, because the best feeling in the world is knowing you're going to die and then surviving. But then I stopped smiling, because Somalia did not care about my stupid games. It is old and set in its ways, just as happy with death as with life and willing to spring either at you from the defilade of a rock pile or the shade of an acacia tree. And that's the rub, of course, because man is just another mammal here, high on the food chain but vulnerable to thirst, heatstroke, superstition, bullets, greed. The giraffes don't care about games; they just go about their day grazing the savannahs.

Somalia grows on you, an affectation, the way you learn to love cognac or Andrew Lloyd Webber. It rises out of the scrubland in the strangest transition, one moment earth, the next moment sea. It changes you, beguiles you, makes you want to dance to a song all its own, a truth written in a language that defies translation. This is the oldest part of the oldest part of the world, where we were all born of the same mother, and where that sorry bitch left us among the grasses to turn on ourselves and wonder why. Forever. Somalia lives alone among geographies, an illusion deeper than human understanding, wholly disinterested in anything more than the primal urges that drive all men to fuck and to kill.

"Wait here," a woman said when we got out to the plane. She was wearing a flight attendant uniform, standing at the bottom of the stairs.

"Nice work, brother," I told Ebyan. I could see into the belly of that 727, that darkness.

"We are not there yet," he cautioned, brave but pragmatic.

The men in sunglasses with AK-47s had followed us out and formed a shell around the dozen or so passengers. The sun beat relentless. We stood there in the shade of the wing for forty-eight minutes, until a man in a pilot's uniform walked down the stairs and checked our tickets. The bad guys were talking into their phones, cheeks full of khat, fingers on triggers. It felt so fucking heavy.

"Watch your head, sir," the flight attendant told me.

Then I stepped past her, up those stairs toward the interior, using my hands on the top of the seats until my eyes adjusted, and I found 4E, next to a window. The stairs came up, and the engines whined, and the captain said something about safety, and I took a photo of Ebyan giving me a high-five, which was the only time I had ever seen him smile. I felt my world soften, that adrenaline dump you get after a gunfight or your kid's soccer game or childbirth, when you've struggled bravely against consequence and escaped unscathed. But then the engines stopped. The pilot said something in Somali. The stairs opened, light flooded in.

I could hear voices yelling "fuck you," but this time those voices are from men with machine guns who have stopped us from leaving. They're coming up the stairs, then they're right behind me. I conjure Hemingway crashing that Cessna 180 on safari in 1954, thinking he'd been saved only to crash again. Emily Dickinson trapped in a slant of light.

In my mind I see M60 waving from the Toyota and Pimm beside him, swabbing his hand with a tampon, two bones for a leg. I hoped they'd made it home safely without me.

K-38 is a white concrete post on the side of the road in Oaxaca, Mexico. In 1983, it was common for Orange County surfers to stop there on the way through Rosarito to Ensenada for beer and tacos. Sometimes you and your buddy would grab a quick session at a reef called Theresa's, which in a decent winter swell can be the finest scooped right on the Baja Peninsula. Flat days, you would keep driving, find a room somewhere for twenty dollars a night, and just chill, reading books in the sand. Maybe dance with a pretty señorita.

I remember the first time I went there, with two buddies from Newport. They had a bag of reefer hidden behind the dash of a Ford Econoline van and they knew I didn't smoke, so they didn't tell me. I couldn't have cared less about my friends sparking up, but that region of Mexico was famous for corrupt cops who worked with thieves to break out your windows while you were in the water, steal your shit, and then shake you down once they found your stash. And they were good at it, which was a problem for me, because I did not want to spend the weekend in a Mexican jail with two surf rats over a bag of sticks and seeds. Settled it all for a hundred bucks.

I remember a different trip into Mexico, with a guy named Bob Venable. He had invited me down for the weekend, and he had a sister named Rose who ended up giving me four great kids, a wonderful life, and got me into the FBI. The Rose I was about to marry.

"So, tell me about these dreams," he said. Bob.

"Dreams?"

"Rose tells me you have all these dreams."

Bob was a slow talker, introspective, well educated, overtly mature. He was also a true waterman and looked the part. Hair to his shoulders, baby oil tan. He knew his way around the Wedge, had those cool blue-and-yellow fins, which meant he was a bodysurfer, which is a whole other thing. Bob was the oldest brother, so it fell on him to have that special talk with suitors.

We were sitting at a two-top by the front window of a dive bar called Hussong's Cantina. Hussong's was a famous spot back then, but only among day-drinking locals who drove their mother's car down to get shitfaced on change they'd found in the sofa. Hussong's had sawdust on the floor and tequila in jars with no label and a mariachi band that would play at your table if you happened to have a date.

They also had this guy who would come around with a cigar box full of D-cell batteries and a capacitor and two wires sticking out the side. For about fifty cents, the guy would hook you up by the fingers and more or less electrocute you while everybody laughed their ass off. Some kind of Mexican thing.

"She grew up on the beach, you know that," Bob said. "Do you really think she wants to move to Massachusetts?"

"Well, I have a job," I told him. "A respectable job. In the fall, I will be teaching English at a boarding school that costs almost as much as Harvard. The Berkshire School. I won't make a lot of money, but teaching is a respectable profession. It's a good place to start."

I mentioned Harvard because Bob was wearing a Harvard T-shirt and because Harvard had a way of popping up in my life. He had graduated Cal State Fullerton and had a master's degree in something, but I knew he liked to collect logos from prominent East Coast schools.

"It's in Massachusetts," Bob said. "Rose told me last year you bought a one-way ticket to Australia because you think you're a writer and need an adventure to write about."

"Well, I did." I shrugged. "Before I asked her to marry me."

"So, you're not going to Australia? You're going to give up that dream and be an English teacher for the rest of your life?" Bob loved his sister; he didn't know me. "In Massachusetts?"

"Well, probably not. Australia, I mean. Not now. But so?"

"So? You moved out here to be a rock star? How'd that turn out?"

I ordered another beer and a shot of that no-name tequila. "Well, at least I gave it a try," I told him. "There's nothing wrong with dreams."

"Not if you can fulfill them."

I waved at the guy with the box of batteries. It was going to be a long weekend. "You know, Bob," I said. "Your cousin Patty introduced me to a friend of hers at the *L.A. Times,* the city editor named Sharon Rosenbaum. She invited me to lunch."

The guy with the batteries came over, pulled out those two leads with their little Velcro attachments, and placed them on my fingers.

"She asked me what I wanted to accomplish with my life, and I told her I wanted to teach English a couple years, maybe teach creative writing, then go to work for a newspaper. Maybe her newspaper. Maybe the *Times.* And some people might think you don't just start at the top; you have to work your way up. But you know what she told me?"

"What?"

"She said, 'Chris, what you want to do is impossible, but it happens every day.'"

The guy with the batteries held out his hand, and I gave him some coins. He zapped me.

"That's great." Bob nodded, all mature and sarcastic. "It's nice to have dreams."

The waiter brought the tequila, which I threw back, with no salt or lime.

"But what are you gonna do with my sister when all your dreams fail?"

"Fail?" I asked him. "Are you kidding?"

I wanted to tell him that I remember what she was wearing the first time I saw her. It was a Saturday night, and I was working the door at Bilbo Baggins, things getting busy. A line of people had stacked up to pay the cover for a popular band called Listen, with my buddies Dave Witt on guitar, John Quetsch on bass. It was a lovely night, warm and optimistic.

"You get out today?" I asked a couple of buddies I surfed with.

"The kind, bruh. River jetty was pumping. How's the band?"

"Killer."

"Sweet, want a shooter?"

"Nah, I'm good."

I had come in around six because Jim Esposito let me eat for half price, which was cheaper than shopping. We started charging cover at seven, so things were just warming up, Don and Debbie behind the bar, Penny waiting tables. Jim walked out, saying hi to patrons.

"I see you ironed your shirt in a blender again." He laughed.

My wardrobe was limited to button-down oxfords and 501 jeans with rubber boat shoes from L.L.Bean, which you didn't often see in California. I stayed wrinkled.

"Keeping it casual, boss."

"Well, keep an eye on the big guy at table seven," Jim said. Jim was only about five foot six, but eight feet tall in terms of charisma. "Might need to eighty-six him."

"Gotcha." I nodded. Went back to checking IDs.

Then Air Man came over to help, because carding people was an easy way to meet women, and he knew all about Zodiac signs and stuff

I never really understood. The band started up, and the place was hopping. Then the ice-skating rink next door closed for the night, and more people came over, the terrace filling, everybody having a ball. Tommy Balch stopped in with a new girlfriend named Christie, and I waved them through. Shortly after that, I heard somebody yell.

"You asshole!" It was the guy at table seven.

"Come on, man. It's a party, relax," Jim told him, smiling. "Nobody wants trouble."

The guy finally sat down, and Jim put his arm around his shoulder, like he was being chummy, and before I could even walk over, Jim just started stroking, hard rights to the face. My buddy Cocaine Jeff jumped off the bar to take the wingman, and I loaded up on the stringer. John and Dave kept playing Billy Joel like it was nothing, people dancing, and us beating the attitude off those drunks. We threw them out through the courtyard, cleaned up the blood.

And then, at some point in the evening, I remember looking up, seeing her face coming around the corner: Rosie. She looked like the Beach Boys girl from all those records.

"Damn."

She was walking with her friend Nancy Witt, whose brother, Michael, had just pitched a perfect game for the California Angels. I don't know if it was the tan, or her eyes, or those Scott flip-flops found only in Hawaii, but I do know that it was love at first sight. A bolt of lightning.

"That's a nice shiner you got there, babe," she said when I asked for ID.

And I remember how I had been trying to think of a cool rejoinder when I heard Bob say, "Dreams," and I realized I was no longer at Bilbo Baggins. I was back at Hussong's Cantina.

"My dreams are real, man," I told him, motioning for more tequila. "In fact, I dreamed your sister long before we met. I love her. We'll take care of each other, no matter what."

Turned to the Mexican with the batteries. "Señor," I said, "gimme another dollar's worth of that box."

12

Darwin, Australia

[MARCH 2007]

"You're boiling oil, mate?" the big man said, talking into a cell-phone. "What do you mean you're boiling oil?"

It took me twenty-five years to use that ticket to Australia. It had nothing to do with surfing.

"Savages," Scotty told me. "It's a lovely country, Timor, but those cunts are vicious. They're spear chuckers, mate, love their machetes. Probably stoning Gil's place as we speak."

It was a Sunday afternoon at a hotel near the airport called the Mercure Resort, and I was lounging by the pool with a diesel mechanic named Scotty and a business partner we'll henceforth refer to as Knackers. Knackers is a six-pack name, of course, sufficiently generic for a man who is wildly complex. For now, imagine a six-foot-six second-row rugger with movie star looks and anchorman hair. He is Oxford articulate, drives a Porsche 996 Turbo S, which he parks at his waterside estate in Byron Bay. He has a beautiful wife and two gorgeous kids, sails ocean yacht races when he's not in Dubai, keeps a house in Managua, near his buddy Daniel Ortega. Knackers and I had met in New York, shortly after my escape from Somalia. We had a plan.

"Hang in there, brotha." He nodded into his phone. "We're keen to join you."

The three of us had flown up from Sydney with tickets on Airnorth TL508 into Dili, East Timor, but our flight had been delayed. For a week. Fortunately, the Mercure had rooms available and plenty of beer. The whole place had a day-drinking holiday kind of vibe, mostly steerage-class travelers headed for sex tours of Manila or snorkeling in the Phi Phi Islands. Darwin is a stopover hub, lots of oil workers and outback guides, a waystation for roofers.

· "There's five dead in Manufahi, mate." Knackers nodded. He took a drag, a swallow. "You haven't heard, Gillie? It's all Reinado's mob. He's back in the jungle, he's absconded."

"Who is he talking to?" I asked Scotty.

"Gil, mate. Gil Taylor."

Darwin looks enticing in brochures, a land of seascapes and natural wonders, but all I remember of that first trip is a limbo of tattoo parlors, karaoke bars, tourists biding their time, with gin served neat and too much sun.

"Xanana is calling for surrender, brotha." Knackers took a swill of beer.

"Gil Taylor?" I asked. "What does he have to do with this?"

"Aw, mate, he's a good fella," Scotty told me. "Knuckle hard. He's got the One More Bar. Best steaks in Dili, Chris, he's a butcher."

The air felt like a steam bath. Even the pool water was hot, the deck a scorcher. It had been fall weather in Sydney the week before, but Darwin is equatorial tropics, so it felt like the sky was sweating, that haze you get in monsoon. You could hear the sun crackling through.

"Guud, guud," Knackers was saying. "Fucksakes, Gil, guud on ya!"

Fortunately, the beer was cold, and there was plenty of distraction, including a large python sunning itself by the Jacuzzi and a bridal party in bikinis on their way to a hen do in Bali. The tiki bar was crowded with potbellied tradesmen in Speedos, leathery wives with front bums in straw hats smoking Winstons.

"There's nobody getting in or out today, mate," Knackers was saying. "The bloody SAS have closed the airport. Is there anything we can bring you?"

Scotty and I had been chilling while Knackers made his calls, checking with investors. Basically, we were just hanging out like you do on a layover—in this case, bound for a war-torn country known most recently as East Timor. I say "most recently" because it had been recognized by the United Nations only since 2002, following a war with

Indonesia that killed two hundred thousand people. Somalia had fallen back into chaos, making East Timor the newest country on earth.

"They've been coming up the stairs?" Knackers laughed. "Gil, you're legend!"

"Coming up the stairs?" I asked, trying not to eavesdrop. "Attacking the place?"

"I told you, brotha." Scotty shook his head, perfect elocution. "Savages."

As things often go during struggles for independence, East Timor had fallen into a vicious three-way. This one was among the military, the police, and a charismatic guerrilla leader named Alfredo Reinado. Fighting had broken out in the capital of Dili and spread throughout the country, displacing 150,000 people who were fleeing for their lives. Timor is an island, however, so they had nowhere to go, and to avert more ethnic slaughter, New Zealand and Australian defense forces had moved in with mechanized infantry. An International Security Force (ISF) had commandeered the country's only airport, closed the ports. There were tanks in the streets, fire teams patrolling villages, widespread hunger, typhus, dislocation. War.

"Stay in the fight, Gil!" Scotty yelled, sounding like he was rooting for a side in a footie match.

Knackers clicked off the Nokia, fired up another cigarette, then started dialing. He had a pocketful of SIM cards that he would change in and out with no explanation.

"Bloody Gil." He laughed. "He's got the chips cooker on boil. Complete legend."

"He'll be right," Scotty said. "Trust me, he's hard as."

Scotty looked happy as could be, wearing Blundstone boots with white socks, cargo shorts with a cellphone holster. He looked about thirty-five, stayed clean-shaven, never stopped smiling. He said he could fix anything but a broken heart, which is what my uncle Mike said, too.

"Hard as?" I asked him. "Hard as what?"

The server came around, and we had been drinking nonstop for days, so I ordered beers.

"Gerry!" I heard Knackers say. "How are you going, mate?" He stood up and walked off, a private conversation.

"Have you met him?" Scotty asked. "The Minister of All Black Fellas?"

"Gerry? Not yet. I hear he's quite a character."

"Character?" Scotty laughed. "Oh, mate, he's a full-on nutter. You're gonna love him."

I had, in fact, met Gerard Leslie Hand, former Labor Party minister of aboriginal and Torres Strait affairs, then Australia's representative at the UN High Commissioner for Refugees. At that point in his career, Gerry was also an influential Melbourne businessman and a primary reason I had just traveled halfway around the world. He had flown to Dili three weeks earlier and was now holed up south of the airport in a walled compound called Terra Santa. I did not know Gerry, except by reputation, but first impressions matter. He was smart, irrepressibly funny, tough as nails.

"They're going off," Knackers told us once he'd ended the call. "The boys have Reinado cornered outside Same. Comoro Road is choked with mobs. The port is a no-go."

"What about the IDP camps?" Scotty asked.

"What's an IDP camp?"

"Internally displaced persons," Knackers told me. "No worries. It's under control." With that, he disappeared.

"What's under control?" I asked Scotty. "It's a fucking war zone."

"Go ahead. Have your fun, mate," he said. "You two don't fool me."

And I was thinking that Scotty was easy to describe but that Knackers might take a little longer. Despite his upper-crust pedigree, he could be a fearless brawler. He smoked Nat Shermans in business settings, Marlboros at leisure. He drank Tooheys in Melbourne, Schlitz in New York. He did business, simultaneously, in cities around the world, scheduling his calls around GMT without wearing a watch. He had presidents on speed dial, magnates and maître d's; he knew tearooms in Istanbul, the best massage in Dar es Salaam. And though his name was a regular item in *The Sydney Morning Herald,* no one truly knew why. He'd made millions pioneering wireless communications, but Knackers's true interests were broader than wealth.

"What do you make of Oz, mate?" Scotty asked me after a while. "I hear you're a surfer."

"That would be exaggeration."

"Shit fer waves in Darwin, Chris. Best stay right here, poolside with your mate Scotty. Look at that one right there, the bridesmaid in the white swimmers. I'll warrant she's a gamer."

"I might go take a little walk," I told him. "Stretch the legs."

"A walk? Mate, have you lost yer nob?"

"We've been here a week. All I've seen is bars and this new tattoo."

"What else is there?" He shrugged. "Darwin is not known for its frills."

Then off through the open-air lobby, past the racks of croc farm brochures and maps to Alice Springs, straight out to a cab. I rode the cab to East Point, a patch of sand near the Darwin Rocksitters Club, where I could stand in the ocean gazing west. It felt a bit cooler there, with the terns and gulls circling above me, nature resplendent. I breathed in through my nose, imagining Darwin as Darwin had found it, a frontier outpost at the northern tip of something new.

As Scotty said, there was in fact no surf at all. There was no man-made skyline, either, because the whole place had been leveled by Cyclone Tracy in 1974, no harbor full of schooners like Perth, no fan-shaped opera house as in Sydney. But I had not gone there for touristy things. I had walked out to look off across the Timor Sea, past the Indian Ocean into what had not changed since the beginning of time, the part of the world that left me feeling stranded.

Africa.

What I had not told Scotty or Knackers or anyone else was that if the earth were flat, I could look across those waters all the way to Mogadishu. This was one year to the day after my escape from K50. I felt the moment as a hitch in time; the hitch was jagged.

Something deep and unhealed required me to revisit that moment, so I stared out past the horizon, looking inward for perspective. I wanted to know what it was that I missed so badly. And because I remembered the New Hampshire boy who had walked into swales seeking stars for reference, I closed my eyes, leaned back my head to imagine constellations. The borealis. I listened hard for breezes, which had always been truthful, but there were no breezes in Darwin.

All I could hear was men yelling in Somali, men coming up stairs. I could see Ebyan's face the moment he stopped smiling, all the passengers staring at me. I remembered standing up to fight, then gunmen reaching down behind me—and you can tell when someone knows it's the end, because they go limp. The poor bastards just whimpered as the gunmen dragged them away.

Chrisameechie.

I checked my watch, standing in those waters off Darwin, tide licking at my knees. I followed the second hand until the bigger hands paused at 1:14 P.M., which, with the time change, was the exact moment we lifted off from Mogadishu. One year to the minute.

After a while, I went back to the motel. The lobby was quiet, and the clerk said "Good day," and I looked up at the big departure board, which showed TL508 as "on time." Finally.

"How was your stroll, mate?" Scotty asked when I got back to the pool.

"Great," I told him. "Looks like we might be out of here tomorrow."

"I'll believe it when I see it."

Eventually, Knackers came back with his phone put away. He told us we were a go for our flight to Dili the next day, but the party would be at a place called Pub Bar with DJ Lurch. I was still thinking about Somalia, the energy of the world moving across oceans. I thought about waves filmed off Morocco, where I had gone as a thinker, reading Hermann Hesse with Swedes, drinking wine in bottles labeled Perrier. I thought about Osman Ali Atto, my aunt Lois in two strands of pearls, naked children bleeding from their ears as Rosie tucked ours into bed wearing SpongeBob pajamas. Uncle Harold, *The New York Times,* and the CIA, all those lies.

"Get yer gear off, Chris!" Scotty laughed. "Gonna get yer gear off tonight, mate!"

"You would know, buddy," I told him. "You're a legend."

"Legend, mate," Knackers corrected me. "Just legend. There are no articles in Oz."

Like I said, he is a complex fella.

"Dude, you have to stop acting like such a coward."

I must say, I was not used to men calling me a coward, especially not a man wearing a gorilla suit with a terry cloth headband, playing ping-pong in a bookstore recently used to film porn.

"If you want to commit suicide, do it like a man. Stop trying to find somebody else to pull the trigger for you. It's bad form."

Philip Fracassi is a novelist you might not know, though you should. And eQuator Books is a spot you will never know because it is gone forever, a casualty of amphetamine psychosis, left brain indifference to utility bills, and 2008. For five and a half magic years, however, eQuator Books was the arcade of scribes in Venice, California, home to some fascinating times.

"What are you talking about?"

Philip Fracassi was one of two owners, but I will focus on him here because he was the guy with the headband in the gorilla suit. His partner, Michael Deyermond, deserves an introduction of his own. But it is the shop that matters, at this point, because people ask me all the time about my favorite places in the world, and that was one.

"I'm talking about this death wish you keep farming out to oppressed peoples caught up in foreign wars," Philip said. "Hemingway already wrote that book. Get your own personality."

Then the door opened, and you could hear the party roaring outside.

"What's the score?"

L. Bellagio walked in with his girlfriend, E, whom I won't name because she had some issues at the time. I will note that she was best known as a spokesmodel for Chanel and from several blockbuster movies. I loved her as a kind yet tortured friend. Hollywood can be hard on women.

"I don't want to hear about your homoerotic fantasies of getting kidnapped by fourteen-year-olds with machine guns because you didn't get asked to the Sadie Hawkins Dance in seventh grade," Philip was saying. "This is a bookstore, man. You're employee of the month. Act it."

"What are you guys talking about?" L. Bellagio wanted to know.

"We're talking about Whip," Philip told him. He called me Whip. "This death fantasy."

"He's bipolar." L. Bellagio shrugged. "Don't waste your time."

"I'm not bipolar. I was an FBI agent, for Chrissakes. I've taken all the tests."

"You taught interrogation to the CIA," he said. "Tests don't fool you."

Places like eQuator Books are hard to create and just as hard to describe—kinda like Paris in 1929; Kay Barnes sipping absinthe with Sylvia Beach while Picasso drew on napkins for Djuna Barnes. One might call such a comparison prideful, except that those artists were just artists at the time; eQuator was no Shakespeare and Company, but it had poets, too. The bookstore attracted painters, Dogtown vets, preening actors, immodest intellectuals, rich people looking for signed copies of Gabriel García Márquez. There were drug dealers, rock stars sporting vintage leather jackets. At one party alone, I counted two Academy Award winners, the Pulitzer, a shitload of Grammys, and a child sitcom star trying to get laid off an Emmy.

"I've got winner," L. Bellagio announced.

Then Maria Bello said, "Are you going to serve or what?" She had just done a movie called *A History of Violence,* which seemed apropos.

"Four serving three," I said, because I was the linesman on duty. "Let's go."

In 2007, one of my favorite things in life was 1103 Abbot Kinney Boulevard in Venice, California. It was a beautiful single-story storefront with overhead doors that opened into birch shelves on concrete floors. It was bright and airy, with thousands of volumes, music by the Pixies. Venice was a gangland in those days, but you could get spinach quiche at Axe, chai latte at Abbot's Habit. My buddy Craig had opened the Otheroom nearby, and you could drink Red Stripe at the Brig, fistfight over games of pool. Hal's for dinner, jazz on Sundays.

"Nice shot," Maria said, then won the point.

Philip said, "This chick is good. Somebody get me a beer."

Like any decent clubhouse, eQuator was business up front, party in the back. For those in the know, there was a door with a punch lock behind the bathrooms, leading to the sanctum sanctorum, a shipping area decorated yard sale Bohemian with shag throw rugs, mahogany couches, upholstered chairs. There was a Marantz tuner from the seventies with Klipsch speakers playing Foghat, with the *Fool for the City* album cover on the desk next to a hand mirror with a pile of blow. There were about a hundred Hollywood posers outside, knocking on the door, trying to get in, but famous didn't get you shit at eQuator Books. Everyone was famous.

"Have you finished shooting your new show, Whit?" E asked.

"Yep. We wrapped yesterday," I told her. "First episode premieres next week."

"What's it called?"

"*Identity*. Thursdays at eight, on NBC. Have you met Penn Gillette?"

L. Bellagio said, "I got winner," and E said, "Is that cocaine?"

"Great guy. Penn, I mean. Brilliant, curious about everything. Teller, too, who speaks, by the way. Mile a minute. They want to start a security company with me, using magic."

"How's that work?" L. Bellagio asked.

"I'm not too sure, but it sounds compelling."

Then the door opened again, and it was Joe with an armload of Miller High Life.

"Who needs one?" he asked. Then: "Isn't that where they filmed the money shot?"

Maria said, "What money shot? What are you talking about?"

"The guys hired out the shop as a porn set," he explained. "They told the director that Whit was the landlord, had to be here during filming due to insurance regulations. Liability."

"Liability?" L. Bellagio asked. "What kinda liability you find on a porn set?"

"This table?" Maria asked. "They used this table?"

"It was weird," I decided. "A porn shoot. Not erotic at all, just acting. The director is a famous guy named Paul Thomas who played Peter in *Jesus Christ Superstar*, the movie."

"Yeah, he's real famous." Joe laughed, that infectious chug.

"The main guy, Tommy Gunn, went two hours nonstop, took a twenty-minute break for lunch, then went off on command right in front of the Nabokovs. Told me he just bought a boat."

"A boat?" L. Bellagio laughed. "A boat?"

Then Joe said, "Come on, Whit. There's somebody I want you to meet."

And Philip said, "Hey, Whip, there's an envelope on the desk. It's for you. I want you to look at it later, when you get home. I wrote something for you."

So, I got the envelope and put it in my pocket and hugged E and grabbed a High Life and followed Joe back out to the party, which was crowded, optimistic. There was a glass showcase on the right where they displayed their most valuable books, first editions of *The Catcher in the Rye, Huckleberry Finn*. I noticed that someone had placed my books in there, too, with a handwritten card reading "Signed by the author," twenty-five cents apiece.

Joe said, "I see your stuff is catching on," as we walked down into the party, which was rocking, with the overhead doors open and vain people spilling out into the street.

And I remember thinking about *Identity,* my first network gig after five years on cable. I thought about projects with David Mamet, and with Sir Frederick Forsyth, who told me to call him Freddy. I thought about Rose in New Hampshire, Jake in college, Mick in high school, Chelsea and Collin at the Bodhi Tree Montessori. Joe had a new baby boy with a recent fling, and L. Bellagio had a toddler. I thought about work in New York, missions in Africa, visits to Langley. The cocksure shine of eQuator books, all my famous friends. It was a heady time.

But pride, as they say, cometh before the fall, and in 2007, we were all flying a little too close to the sun. It was Kabuki theater in those days, riding private jets around the world, disguised in colorful masks, one six-pack name after another. Actors and spies, a collaboration.

"Whit, this is my friend Owen," Joe said.

"Nice to meet you, man," I said to one of my favorite comedic actors.

Then other people came up, and we all laughed and drank and told stories, and I walked around looking at the volumes, thousands of books people had taken lifetimes to write and pitch and sell. Then, later that night, once the party had faded, Joe and I got into his ragtop and drove back to his house, where I stayed off and on for years, and we let his dog out and had a nightcap of twelve-year-old Macallan.

After a while, Joe called it a night, but my mind was still racing, and I remembered the envelope Philip had given me, so I pulled it out and read the contents sitting on the cracked leather cushion of an original Stuckey chair. It was a one-page note, neatly typed, titled "Sainthood."

"The brave drive themselves forward," Philip wrote, part of a longer letter.

> Because success is not given, you realize when you are the older demographic, victory in life is not akin to victory in chess, because there is no clear-cut win, there is no clear-cut loss.
>
> There are friends. There are lovers. There are consequences and fate and children and luck and a face you see in

a moment, just a moment, that is a face you've never seen and will never see again, and you realize, fuck yes, fuck yes, then okay, then let's go, then let's drive this train forward and you put your weight behind it, and you push, and you drive, and you hope.

And, sometimes, you sit alone at night and wonder as if in a deep sleep about the faces and the touches and the embraces of so many of what's out there, and you configure the equation of your success and debate the merits of completion versus journey and your wonder embraces you, but also tears at you, beats at you, makes you doubt a road once narrow, now broad.

Makes you wonder about love, makes you think about fate, about legacy, about completion.

Philip was right: I did need to stop acting like a coward. I had escaped from Somalia, but I needed that feeling again, of taunting death but surviving. I needed war, but I needed a war I could manage. As it turned out, I knew just the place.

We flew in from the south, up the mouth of a broad gray river. There was a small village near the ocean, black sand beaches, one long row of waves. Then up that river to where it grew dry and split at a confluence of slides and disappeared into palm forests, hand-cut flats full of rich green grasses. The whole thing appeared out of nowhere in the starboard window of an Embraer EMB 120 Brasilia. One moment sea, the next moment ground.

"That's coffee growing down there, Chris," Scotty said without even looking. "Manufahi district, best there is. Timor is known for it."

"How can you tell?"

He was stuffed in beside me, Knackers across the aisle. They'd both been napping.

"Aw, I been here heaps, mate. Always the same route. You can tell by the engines."

He opened his eyes, leaned over, and looked out my window. We were only a couple thousand feet off the ground, descending. Timor was 450 miles from Darwin, a two-hour hop.

"That village down there is Same, brotha, where the SAS boys had Reinado cornered. I reckon they'll be busy humping up into the mountains now that he's got away."

"Looks pretty average to me," I told him. "I don't see any mountains."

"Wait for it."

He leaned back in his seat and closed his eyes again.

"Wait for what?"

"Just about . . . now," he said, and as if on cue, we hit a patch of updraft turbulence.

Scotty smiled as the plane bounced over a long spine of peaks that rose out of the jungle with no preamble. He closed his eyes and leaned his head back as we descended, so low I could see men walking ridgelines where there was no trace of cars or roads. It was all thatched-roof huts and naked dirt squares where people had burned holes in the jungle for communal living.

"How's that for mountains, mate? Feels like Jurassic Park down there, I'll tell ya."

And Timor is only sixty miles wide, so the next thing I noticed was a giant statue of Jesus on a hill with his hands in the air bestowing blessings on a harbor, like in Rio. The plane banked hard over ocean, then hard again, and lined up our final approach along a coastal road, which was marked with piles of rubble that had been buildings, prettier than Baidoa, though just as sad.

"Welcome to Dili, mate," Scotty said once we had landed. Knackers yawned.

There was no one else on the plane because Australia had issued a travel ban due to the fighting. And it was hot when we climbed out onto the tarmac, not as hot as Darwin but hot enough for me. I could see a line of UH-60 Black Hawks parked along the runway, two C-130s, armored personnel carriers, and GP Medium tents. I saw a bunch of civilians queued with bags outside a building that looked rough but intact, so I headed that way. Then, under a steel awning, past some Australian Army guys behind sandbags with an American M2 .50 cal., to a small window and a man in a blue uniform, who said, "Boa tarde."

"Boa tarde." Scotty smiled, then: "Obrigado," once we got our passports stamped.

We picked up our bags curbside, walked out to a RAV4 in the

gravel lot where a tiny Timorese woman wearing a stylish blue dress was standing with a phone to her ear. The first thing I noticed was her bright red lipstick, then the high heels way too big for her feet.

"How're ya going, love?" Scotty hugged her. "Cesarina, say gudday to Chris."

"Fuck me running," she said. "You're a big fella."

"Ga'day, love." Knackers laughed. "How's my best girl?"

"There's a war on, boss," she said. "Have you heard?"

The parking lot had no other cars, so we packed ourselves into the RAV4 and rode out the access road until we came to what had once been a traffic circle but now looked like a slum. All you could see were sheets of rusted tin, sun-bleached tarps, women with plastic pails, skinny kids running around with sticks. Men sat in packs, trying to look tough. Maybe three thousand people.

"Watch yerself, mate," Scotty told me. "These blokes will stone their mums."

"Fuck me, Jesus," Cesarina said. She hit the horn and the gas, yelled, "Dizzy knobs!"

We turned right just past the IDP camp, drove the coastal road west about a mile, and stopped at a twelve-foot wall with the name "Terra Santa Resort" in paint. There was a gate with two guards in brown polyester, whom Cesarina dressed down for looking slack, then a long driveway to a U-shaped cluster of single-story buildings. The east wing looked new, the rest under construction.

"Home sweet home, brotha," Knackers announced, and we all piled out. I saw an older gentleman wearing Coke-bottle glasses. "Ga'day Gerry!"

"Oh, get off it, mate," Gerry said. Gerry Hand. "I've been on crackers for a bloody week, while you're singing karaoke." He reached out his hand. "Who's this bloke, and what have you brought me?"

13

Dili, Timor-Leste

[MARCH 2007]

I rose early that first morning at Terra Santa thinking I'd have a look
around before things got busy. Gerry was already up when I walked
outside, drinking Nescafé at a white garden table beneath a bright yellow umbrella. The proprietors had done their best to dress up the
place with an open-air breakfast patio, and Gerry looked quite at
home wearing an open-collar shirt beneath a seersucker blazer while
hunched over day-old papers.

"Bloody whiners," he mumbled, the former Minister of All Black
Fellas. "What is it about the Australian Labor Party that makes them
shill to punters?"

It seemed obvious that he was not talking to me, so I walked over
to where workers were building a courtyard pool, then looked up at
the surrounding mountains, which someone had lit on fire.

The Terra Santa Resort looked anachronistic, vaguely European,
with brightly colored tiles and shrubs in planters, a breakfast patio,
steam trays with bangers and eggs. I thought about how exciting it felt
to wake up at war in the newest country on earth, safe behind masonry walls, enjoying a nice breakfast with a well-known government
minister, a money-minded spook, and a diesel mechanic who loved
karaoke. Then the breeze shifted offshore, and the smoke from the
jungle fires drifted down among us, and Knackers emerged, talking
into one of his phones.

"How'd you sleep, mate?" Scotty asked me a few minutes later.

"Brilliant," I said, then we all spritzed up, and I grabbed my camera and climbed into the RAV4 for a long drive in the country.

As luck would have it, the road from the airport was the only road into town, so we had to pass back through the IDP camp, which seemed to have grown overnight. The shanties and blue tarp shebangs crowded the road, funneling traffic into a chokepoint that seemed strategically designed. And because this was not my first war, I tried to keep my eyes peeled, get the lay of the land. Refugee camps are more tragic than dangerous, but starvation makes people do odd things.

"Ema halo, ema halo!" I heard someone yelling.

It was a boy, maybe fifteen years old, squatting at the side of the road in a used-up truck tire. He was pointing at me, hollering, "Ema halo!" and then he stood up and a bunch of his buddies noticed, maybe a dozen boys, and they started hollering, too.

"Malae, malae! Ema halo!"

I was sitting in the left front seat of the RAV4 with the window down because it was early but already hot, and the AC was broken.

"Ema halo!" the kid in the tire kept yelling.

He started walking toward us, and his voice stood out, because there isn't much going on in an IDP camp at eight o'clock in the morning, no coffee shops or showers or schools.

"Ema halo, ema halo!"

I rode along, imagining how much it must suck for people who have spent their entire lives hunting and gathering in the jungle to be trapped with rival clans in a filthy city bombed flat by unknown invaders. Every day is a challenge—going to sleep hungry, waking up in despair—then, all of a sudden, a C-130 roars overhead, full of soldiers, and you've never even seen a plane.

"Watch him, mate," Scotty said. "He'll knife ya."

I watched my mirror as the kid walked up behind us, all swagger. Then he stepped alongside me, got right in my face. I was watching his hands for weapons, but I was thinking about how this particular camp impressed me, so new the NGOs hadn't arrived with their decent-looking tents and their doctors without borders.

There were none of the shiny SUVs you see hauling aid workers from UNICEF countries, no trucks full of blankets. I saw no Red Cross or Catholic Charities, no missionaries from Assemblies of God distributing pallets stacked with Bibles and donated clothes. I saw no trace of any aide organizations, no police, not a single robin's egg beret. I didn't even see any flags, which was odd, because flags are the first thing you see in camps, political parties staking their claims.

"Ema halo," the kid was saying, close now, almost a whisper. "Ema halo."

"What is he going on about?" I asked Knackers, who had put down his phone.

"Fuck if I know, brotha." He laughed. "I'll wager it's not hello."

"*Malae* means 'white fella,'" Scotty told me. He was in the back, holding a VB traveler in a neoprene cozy. "Step on it, mate. They'll be stoning us."

But Knackers did not seem to mind the sudden agitation. He smiled at the kid and idled along as if we were out for a sail off Perth.

"What is that language?" I asked. "Indonesian?"

"Nah, it's Tetum, brotha," Knackers told me. His hair looked perfect. "Bahasa Tetum, the native tongue, is still used in the districts. Most of these families come from the east."

The kid reached out to touch my arm and whispered, "Ema halo."

Something bounced off the door with a loud thud. I couldn't tell what had hit us, but a group had gathered on the left flank, looking all mean. I flashed back to the parking lot in Dir, expecting Knackers to hit the gas, but he drove casually along, happy as could be.

"This is Comoro Road, Chris," Scotty told me. "The main road east."

It didn't look like the main road east or anywhere else for that matter, because it was mostly dirt lined with banana groves, the burned-out shells of cars. You could see signs that money was trickling in, charities and entrepreneurs. Money follows war. Everybody has a logo.

"Mind the tank, brotha." Scotty pointed. It was coming right at us. "Bloody Kiwis."

"Portuguese is the official language," Knackers told me, swerving in and out of traffic. "You'll hear Indo in Dili, Tetum in the districts, bits and pieces of English in the camps."

Half a mile from the camp, we bridged a dry riverbed, three hundred yards across. Scotty said it raged in torrents during rainy season, a wall of water that came out of the mountains, washing people away. He said the Timorese had different names for it, because the island had started as a crocodile and the whole place was alive with spirits in various forms.

"Wait, what?" I asked. "What kind of spirits? I thought Timor was Catholic."

"Oh, they love their magic, mate." Scotty nodded. "They queue up Sunday for hymns, but they'll be casting spells for supper. Trust me, I'll show you totems."

The road was shit, everything grew tight around us, donkey carts and open-back trucks. Mostly it was Timorese dodging Australian soldiers, the whole mood contentious.

"Look at that one, Chris," Scotty said. He pointed to an old woman chewing betel nut, her mouth the color of beets. She was wearing a T-shirt that read, "I HEART MY BUTT."

Then things got busy, grass fires in the hills to our right, blue ocean to our left, that contradiction of filth and beauty you find in developing countries. I was sweating profusely.

"That's one of the mobs you'll be looking to take on, mate," Scotty said at one point.

He pointed toward a hand-painted sign that read, "Seprosetil Security." There were three single-story buildings, a couple of trucks parked askew, three guards in a patch of dirt.

"That will be Alcino and his bunch," Knackers told me, always the man in the know. "He holds about a third of the market, mostly thugs who will burn you down and have your women if you don't pay protection. Maubere is the primary competitor, bigger than the army."

I wanted to comment on the amateur appearance of the place, but I kept my mouth shut. All I knew about Timor, at that point, was that they had a war, and I needed a war I could manage. Knackers represented an international group of emerging markets investors who followed conflict looking for profit. My job, if I decided to take it, would be to stay behind and build a security component large enough to protect assets and personnel. Timor presented a rare opportunity for profit. I felt like I could find some.

"A-N-Zed," he said, pointing to a bank. "We'll use them to send our transfers across."

We drove past the Hotel Timor, which looked like the place to be, then went around a corner . . . and everything mysteriously ended at a stream full of garbage with a one-lane bridge. The garbage spilled into a harbor with naked kids jumping off an old fishing boat made of tar patches over wood. The hull—red-yellow stripes painted like a flag—was grounded in sand.

"That's the Cristo Rei on the hill," Scotty said, guiding from the back seat.

"Impressive." I nodded. "Looks like Rio."

"Aw, mate, the Catholics love their Jesus."

The statue towered over everything, high on a hill looking out to sea, Christ the King in long sculpted robes with his hands open to heaven, that traditional pose. I had thought we'd get a closer look, but Knackers pulled the wheel right, and we turned up into the mountains, past what he told me was the home of a man named José Ramos-Horta. He said Ramos-Horta had won the Nobel Peace Prize in 1996 due to his efforts during the conflict. Both Scotty and Knackers thought highly of Ramos-Horta, who looked Australian, and of President Xanana Gusmão, who did not.

We drove high over a ridge, leaving the smoky filth of the city behind us, then down into what struck me almost immediately as revelation, a seascape of breathtaking beauty. Australians called it Backside Beach because the Cristo Rei statue presents its backside to it. It is a broad cove surrounded by lush peaks, unspoiled vegetation. I saw a small cluster of huts, less than a village, two dugout canoes.

"Holy shit," I said, absolutely stunned. "It doesn't even look real."

But we were not there for sightseeing, so Knackers raced up the coastal road to a place called Hera, where he and Gerry had leased a harbor with a dock for use for organic farming.

"Hera has suitable access by road and the only private seaport on this side of the island," Knackers said as we passed through a small traditional village. "We'll stop on our way back."

"On our way back from what?" I asked.

"Aw, mate," Scotty said. "The east. You'll lose your nob. It's another world entirely."

And it was. We stopped once for water and a nice lunch of fish, passing through Lautém district on our way to land that had no name on any map. First it was fields for miles, Kansas-flat expanses of dirt that looked unpolluted since the beginning of time. Organic food was all the rage in 2007, and Gerry had developed markets throughout Asia.

"Well, mate, what do you think?"

After three hours of driving, Knackers stopped in the middle of a stunning landscape: tall mountains, primeval forests spilling pristine waters, brightly colored birds. *Jumanji.*

"This is crazy," I said. "Beautiful. Is this why we're here?"

We all got out of the car, and Knackers called Timor the brass ring of Asia. He pointed to broad plateaus of untapped resources; jungles full of needy populations who checked every box on post-conflict recovery charters at the Asian Development Bank. Timor had genocide, IDP camps full of malnourished children, a population of indigenous peoples who had been culturally subjugated by patriarchal oppressors. As one of the world's poorest nations, it boasted illiteracy, gender inequality, five hundred years of colonial exploitation. Timor had 95 percent unemployment; pervasive disease, including tuberculosis, dengue, and one of the last known leprosy segregations in Asia.

After a while, Knackers said, "Climb in, mate, I'll show you why we're here."

We drove a short distance to where the road disappeared into triple-canopy jungle. He parked at the entrance to a gravel pit that looked like any gravel pit, except that this one was on fire.

I said, "What the hell?"

"Methane, brotha." Scotty laughed. "God's own barbie."

The pit was maybe one hundred yards wide, fifty feet tall, a broad erosion, one massive garden of multi-colored flames. I could not believe my eyes: the rocks were burning.

"This is why the world is coming to Timor, mate." Knackers nodded. "Follow me."

We walked another fifty yards, through a lush jungle full of cockatoos to what looked like a small pond, except this pond was black, a pool of oil bubbling right out of the ground.

"Largest known fields in Asia," Knackers said. "Estimates are eighty billion dollars of readily accessible crude, halfway between China and Oz."

"Can you believe it, Chris?" Scotty said. "They're filthy with the stuff."

In fact, I could not believe it, all the way back to Hera, which turned out to be a man-made port Knackers had acquired for shipping. I thought about all the things I did not know about Knackers and Timor as Scotty showed me around saltwater tanks in a warehouse built for aquaculture, clearly a ruse. I thought about what I should have learned in Somalia, working the shadows between money and guns, the confusing world to which Uncle Harold had introduced me.

Then Scotty announced that it was time to head back to Dili.

"Guud, guud, brotha," Knackers said. "Let's get the spare car. I'll ride the RAV back with Chris, meet you at the One More. I'm keen to catch up with Gil, introduce you."

"What about the curfew?" I asked. Dili closed at dusk. "Will we make it?"

"Ah, mate. That's for tourists." Scotty laughed. "The Moon Bar will be raging."

"Moon Bar?"

"It's a knock shop, mate. Chinese girls and karaoke. Better than Darwin!" He walked over to a sedan sunken to the axles in caliche. "Look at this, the wankers."

Without explanation, he stormed off toward a group of locals squatting against a fence. Everyone started yelling. Then Scotty pulled out a dollar bill, and two of the locals stood up.

"They do this on purpose," he groused. "They spent two hours burying the thing in mud so I'd pay 'em a dollar to spend two hours digging it out. For a dollar, mate. A dollar."

"Where's the shovels?" I asked him. "I'll help. How do you say 'shovel' in Tetum?"

"They don't have a word for 'shovel,' mate. They call 'em spoons, big spoons."

I stood there watching as the two men labored over the car, thinking about dodging rocks after breakfast in an IDP camp full of hungry children, only to discover eighty billion's worth of oil bubbling out of the jungles full of birds and brightly colored flames.

I thought about a Nobel Peace Prize winner named Ramos-Horta, nameless places on maps, humanitarians rolling in on C-130s full of cash, a woman wearing a shirt that reads, "I HEART MY BUTT."

I thought about waking up in a war zone on the far side of the world, what it might take to build a security company for a diesel mechanic and an investor called Knackers.

"Spoons." I laughed, shaking my head. I was back to sorting spoons.

.   .   .

"Mate, it's on!" Scotty was yelling.

The Moon Bar was crowded with drunken expats, and he had his shirt off with a microphone in one hand and a VB in the other. He was reading karaoke lyrics off a flat-screen monitor, trying to follow "Sexbomb," by Tom Jones, with two Sri Lankans in MC Hammer pants singing backup.

"What did I tell ya!"

"Get some, Scotty!" I yelled back. Party time. "Get it, brother!"

Knackers and I were doing shots at the bar with a large Black man from French Guiana who spoke just enough English to work for the UN. Everybody burning off a little steam.

"Spy on me baby, you a satellite," Scotty was singing, tone-deaf in the key of G.

I said something about loving Africa, but the guy told me he didn't care, because French Guiana is in South America, a whole other continent. Knackers tried to bail me out, saying I was drunk from the One More and that Americans couldn't drink to begin with.

I called him a sod, because whiskey is hard on idiom. Then a smaller man walked over claiming to be a Cuban doctor, and we all toasted the Timorese flag with cans of counterfeit Budweiser from Beijing.

"Get yer gear off!" Scotty yelled, then stripped down to his tighty-whities.

The Moon Bar was a knock shop, after all, so the mama-san with black lipstick was hustling drinks to the VIP room, where they had a pole. Every once in a while, I'd see some guy disappear with a hospitality girl, emerge ten minutes later looking sheepish.

"Do you love it?" Knackers was laughing. "Best spot in Bairro dos Grilos!"

The Moon Bar could have been in Barcelona, for all I knew. Gil had insisted on shots and beers at the One More Bar, once we got back from Hera. The rest had been a drunken blur.

"Sexbomb, sexbomb," the crowd was singing, and Scotty was dancing around in his Jocks, with a war zone cast of characters, which always looks the same.

It's easy to spot the Kellogg Brown and Root types because they're builders. The UN guys are easy, too, because they are from places like French Guiana, fun though reserved because they send their salaries home. You've got the GNR, Portugal's National Republican Guard, who mostly pump iron and sunbathe, an American or two, and a handful of Five Eyes spooks who look just odd enough to fit in. Unlike the Chinese.

"Come on, Scotty," Knackers said after a while, because even knock shops have last call and the mama-san was pushing us to the door. "We're off to Terra Santa. Big day tomorrow."

The lights came on, and the Moon Bar emptied out, and there are no rules about drunk driving in war zones, so Scotty climbed into the Corolla, and we raced each other, shitfaced, laughing.

Somebody had nicked Scotty's clothes, so he was naked behind the wheel, waving his arm out the open window, and we were neck and neck most of the way, those dirt streets dark under a slit of moon, not a single light in town. Knackers could drive like a pro because of his Porsche twin-turbo, and the RAV4 was faster than the Corolla, so we pulled ahead.

"You got him, brother." I laughed, looking back over my shoulder as Scotty lost ground, but then Knackers yelled, "Lord!" and I turned around to see a tank parked in the middle of Comoro Road. It had a giant klieg spot, and somebody was waving a Maglite to slow us down.

"Shit," I said. "What do we do now?"

"No worries, mate. Watch this." Knackers slammed on the brakes, and we stopped right next to a soldier with two gold bars on his collar, a Steyr AUG at ready gun.

"There's a madman behind us, Captain!" Knackers yelled. I remember thinking how credible he seemed, because he was six foot six with movie star looks and his hair was perfect. "He's naked as, Captain, and he's got a pistol. We're running for our lives!"

With that, he stomped on the gas, and we didn't stop until we got back to Terra Santa. Gerry was asleep when we drove in, but the guards were awake, so I walked over and asked if they spoke English. One of the two guards held his fingers up to show that he spoke a little.

"Ema halo," I said. It had been bugging me all day. "What does it mean? Ema halo."

He looked at me with no expression and said, "Make Timor people forget, malae."

"Forget what?"

"Forget to live," he told me. He was trembling. "You ema halo."

14

Bali, Indonesia

[MAY 2007]

A lot of dads would not invite their teenage sons to war, but we were an adventurous bunch, and I needed a hand. Jake and Mick were coming up on summer break from college and had spent time building Project HOPE houses in Nicaragua, meaning they had their shots and passports. So, about a week after Scotty's command performance at the Moon Bar, I flew back to the States, packed a suitcase full of cash, and told Rosie I'd be home for Christmas.

I met the boys in Bali.

"Bracelet, statue, sarong," a woman was mumbling in pidgin English. We were sitting on a nicely groomed beach in chaise longues with men in uniform bringing us drinks.

There were only two ways into Timor in May 2007, the Airnorth flight from Darwin and a flight on a regional carrier called Merpati, which flew Tuesdays and Thursdays from Denpasar International. I had seen more than enough Darwin, so once I got back to Dili, I found a house and a car, and Rose booked the boys on flights via L.A. through Tokyo.

Gerry and the fellas had flown back to Oz, but Cesarina was on the payroll, so she looked after things in town and set us up with suites at a nice Kuta Beach resort called Kumala Pantai.

"How much for the carved elephant?" I asked the local beach vendor, a rookie mistake.

"Oh, *bule,* very good price for you."

Then her daughter walked over, her sister, her uncle, several by-standers. It was on.

"Wristwatch, bracelet? Massage?"

"How much for those?" Jake asked, pointing to counterfeit Ray-Bans.

Mick said, "Offer him half." He was good with money.

I smiled as the boys negotiated deals, and I bought trinkets, thinking about Christmas. Though I sought war, I loved my family in traditional ways, so it was always a difficult choice, being home or being gone. Rosie told Collin and Chelsea I would bring shark teeth for presents, which helped a little, and she was training for a marathon while finishing her doctorate, so having three fewer men around the house did not strike anyone as a hardship.

"Hey, Dad, this is great," Jake told me, after the vendors had moved on to other tourists. "I thought you said there was going to be a war. I love it here; it's awesome."

"This is Bali, bud," I said. "Enjoy it while you can."

He was right, of course. Bali is awesome. *Eat Pray Love* hadn't happened yet, so crowds were light, and we had the place to ourselves, an umbrella, and a little table where you could put your lotion, the new Baldacci. It was mostly sunburned tourists and kids building castles.

We sat there for a couple of hours, because the boys were tired after twenty-four hours of flying, then we took a swim in the pool, rented scooters, and rode down the Bukit to Uluatu, which I had seen in movies. A monkey stole Jake's hat because they are trained to rob you, an age-old scam.

"Wow," Mick said the first time we hiked out to the cliffs above temples, looking down on famous breaks. It was a big swell, and you could watch surfers carving white trails across sparkling blue faces. We climbed down into the cave, the one you paddle out of, then later in the day, we rode back to the hotel, showered up, and went out for a nice dinner. We saw a tourist show with beautiful women in grass skirts dancing to gamelan tunes. The next day, we walked Kuta, bought T-shirts that read, "Where's My Foreskin?" and "Get a Foot Up Your Moot."

We stopped at a tattoo shop, though nobody got ink, and we rode all over Denpasar, sharing a classic father-son experience until Tuesday afternoon, when we packed up and headed to the airport for our Merpati flight home to Dili. We had three seats together.

"This kinda reminds me of Nicaragua," Mick said, looking out his window as we flew in from the west. All he could see was the coastline and the mountains. But then we landed, and he saw the military presence and the IDP camp, now five thousand strong. Desperate people, the squalor.

"Well, maybe not Nicaragua," I told them as we were driving back to the house.

Jake pointed out his window and said, "Is that guy wearing face paint?"

And then we turned off Comoro Road, and I slowed down at the entrance to a walled compound Cesarina had found us, one of the nicest in town. It was about a mile from the airport, in an area called Bemora, and once we got there, Jake said, "Holy shit, Dad. Is that a moat?"

And it was a moat, just like you might see around a castle, about twenty feet wide and ten feet deep, with a concrete bridge. The outer walls were made of cinder blocks, poorly stuccoed, with heavy steel doors and a padlock you'd open with a combination, not a key. There were no street signs or addresses, but every operator on HRT had a call sign, so I painted my identity on the wall, a way for friends to find us at 28 Surik Mas.

"Why is everything burning?" Jake asked. That constant smoke.

"The Timorese are not big fans of plants and animals," I said. "Not in Dili, at least. It's a slash-and-burn kinda mentality."

"Can we take these helmets off now?" Mick asked.

There was a roar as an APC rolled by, huge cloud of dirt, a guy waving from the turret.

"Holy shit, Dad. Was that a tank?"

I should point out that we were all wearing full-face crash helmets because our main source of transportation was a rough-looking Corolla with the windows broken out from stonings. Most people welded steel grates over the windows, like you see on golf carts at ranges, but I hadn't had time. The helmets were kind of goofy, yet effective.

"Hey, this isn't bad," Jake said once we got inside the gate. "I call dibs on rooms."

The compound was good-sized, with a dirt yard and a house in the middle that looked vaguely Mediterranean. There were two portico entrances, main doors leading into an open floor plan with a dining room to the right and a rudimentary kitchen. There were four bedrooms with en suite baths. Each room had its own AC, which was great, a big water tank on stilts for showers, and wood-frame windows, almost everything concrete or tile.

"Stow your gear, boys," I told them. "They'll be coming soon."

Jake toured the rooms and staked his claim, then Mick put away his clothes and they met me outside near a bunch of empty liter-size bottles of Bintang, a popular beer.

"Who's coming?" Jake asked.

"You'll see. Grab that can of gas."

I lined up the Bintang bottles on the ground, showed them how to hold the funnel so the gasoline wouldn't spill on their sneakers, filled everything about two-thirds full.

"Are these Molotov cocktails?" Mick said. "Is that what we're making?"

I showed them how to mix in some Downy Snow, and when Mick asked why, Jake said, "So the gas will stick to them while it's burning."

We got everything just right, and then we staged the bottles around the perimeter. I took one of the bottles and lit the fuse and showed them how to throw it. They got to see the flames.

Once we were all set, Mick got infielder gloves and a baseball, and we went out into the yard to play catch. It was hot, and we worked up a sweat, tossing around a ball, but the sun started to set at about six thirty, like it did every day, so I told them we'd better get some dinner. The only food you could find those first months was canned, boxed, or frozen, everything imported from China. You could buy greens in the street markets, but the Timorese fertilized their crops with human excrement, so we settled for macaroni and cheese.

"You hear that?" Mick asked just after we had finished. It was dark in the house and hot because there was no electricity, so we had walked outside, and you could hear things changing.

"Yeah, I hear it." I nodded. "They're coming."

It always started the same way, with the city falling quiet. The night was a sliver of moon, stars aglimmer. Then an eerie clanking din, low and then louder, impossible to pinpoint in terms of location. The din would rise, pots and pans against poles, bamboo against houses, a low moan like a drumbeat, though I could never figure out the rhythm. Then you would hear the tracked vehicles in other parts of town, the call and answer of voices in a language that made no sense to me, gunfire, screams of pain and rejoicing.

"Who is coming?" Jake asked me. "What the heck is going on?"

I showed them how to hold the spears, long sections of rebar sharpened at the end, so you could impale anyone coming over the walls. I stationed Jake out back, Mick beside me.

"Use the Bintang bottles first," I told them. "You got your lighters?"

They did. And we stood our posts maybe forty-five minutes before the fighting spilled into Surik Mas and you could hear the Australians rolling in with fire teams and armored vehicles.

The din became a roar, the roar a tumult, then it was fucking on. You could feel them banging against the walls, reports of ancient weapons and modern guns, screaming in Tetum, myths and incantations.

"Light 'em up, Jake!" I yelled, because it was worst where he was posted.

"Over there, Dad!" Mick yelled, and they were pounding on the gate, so we put the rebar spears down and lit the Bintang wicks, tossed the bottles over the wall. You could hear the whoosh and smell it, the petrol smoke, diesel exhaust from the APCs. Then, all of a sudden, there was this strange quivering glare, and I looked up at phosphorus illumination flares on tiny parachutes descending.

"Watch that shit. It will burn you!" I yelled to the boys. "White star clusters!"

"Call the embassy, Dad!" Jake yelled several times, but the embassy didn't care. There was no 911 in Timor, we were on our own, there was no one coming.

And Mick is a scrapper, so he tried using a hose to keep the house from burning down, but there was no water because there was no electricity, so he went back to tossing bottles, just working away. It went on like that until 03:40, when everything kinda petered out.

"Think it's over?" Mick asked. He was eighteen years old. "I could use a drink of water."

"Yeah. I think we're good," I told them. "You boys get some rest. Busy day tomorrow."

"It is tomorrow, Dad," Mick told me.

"Good point," I agreed. Then we sat there a minute, letting the whole thing sink in. "By the way, I don't see any reason why your mom needs to know about any of this, do you?"

"Nah," Jake said. "This really isn't her kind of thing."

We called it the Hash.

Every expat in Dili would tell you the Hash House Harriers were a drinking club with a running problem, basically a hangover and a sweat. The Harriers, known locally as the Puddle Jumpers, is the only organization I ever joined that left me beaten, disillusioned, and grateful for the privilege. It is an exclusive club where everyone has a six-pack name, though there are very few secrets. Virtually everyone fails at the Hash because failure, as it turns out, is the objective.

"On, on . . ." is their motto. I could hear Big Tony yelling it about fifty yards ahead of me. "Big Tony," to be clear, was the Christian name of a mysterious twenty-seven-year-old Australian who had been Hash-tagged "Full Press Body" for obvious reasons. I was a good runner, but Big Tony looked like the spokesmodel for *International Male,* so I was having a little trouble keeping up.

"On, on!" Job in the Gob started yelling right behind him.

Then Stain called out from the middle of the pack, where he was running with Grand Master Daisy and Two Lights, the fastest woman. She was known for prominent nipples.

I called out, "On, on!" then stopped dead in the middle of a shanty village called Baire Pite, turned around, and took off running in the opposite direction. Mick and Jake were trying to stay with me, but they had been in town only three days and seemed slightly rattled.

"What's that mean, Dad?" Mick asked me. " 'On, on'? Why are we stopping?"

"It means we're in the lead, dude. Suck it up. We've got to win this thing."

And that was the beauty of the Hash. One minute you were racing your ass off through the streets of some Micronesian village, playing Hare and Hounds with a bunch of expats sporting irreverent names like Two Shits, Whoremonica, and Priscilla Queen of Desserts. The next minute, you were standing in a circle drinking beer with a spiritual adviser named Shamcock who had a pewter beer mug inscribed "Prick of the Week" and an eighteen-inch multi-colored dildo carved out of wood. The Hash is a race, and you want to win, but the rules are stacked against you, so you persevere.

"Watch that pig!" Jake yelled, because we were running through a cluster of huts, and the people who lived there had a huge bull shoat roaming loose. Some of the locals had never seen a white person, let alone thirty-five of them running through their yards, yelling at one another in English.

"Malae, malae!" all the kids were hollering, running along. "Malae, malae!"

"What the fuck?" Mick called out, trying to navigate the chaos.

"On, on, boys," I told them. "That pig won't bother you."

We raced around a corner and right into a patrol of Kiwi soldiers trying to keep everybody safe. I waved hello to one of them, but he ignored me, because it was ninety-seven degrees, and he was wearing a helmet.

"Over there," Mick called out, pointing at a white chalk mark on a tree. "I see the trail!"

He turned right, down a footpath, across a dry riverbed, then over a stick fence and into a corral of goats. We were way ahead of the pack, which got the boys all fired up, because they were competitive, and this was their first Hash. But just when the boys were starting to gloat, Jake, pointing at blue marks on a wall, said, "Shit. Does that mean we went the wrong way?"

I called, "On, on!" resilient in knowing we had just gone from first place to last.

And that, of course, is the whole point of the Hash. It is a race started by Victorian Brits who knew well that the faster one races through life, the quicker one fails. So, you just keep trying.

"How do we know when this thing is over?" Jake asked, checking his watch after about fifty-five minutes of misery. He and his brother were good at sports, though mostly tennis and golf.

"You'll see," I told him. "On, on!"

And just like that, we turned left onto a larger road, and you could see it up ahead, the open gates of a construction outfit called Ant Eater. They specialized in sanitation, which meant pumping sewage out of holding tanks for the United Nations and dumping it into the ocean.

"Loser buys!" Mick announced, and we sprinted the final one hundred yards.

Half the pack was already done by the time we rocked up, but there are no losers in a Hash, just five big Igloo coolers on a flatbed truck, four of them full of beer.

"How'd you go, boys?" Grand Master Daisy asked once everybody had started to catch their breath. The last of the runners were trickling in.

"On, on," Mick said, toasting the effort with a can of Tuborg. Now the veteran.

The man named Shamcock called, "Circle up!" and everybody gathered in a large formation around him. I counted thirty-seven Hashers, all covered in sweat and filth, everyone smiling.

"First order of business is news and announcements," Grand Master Daisy called out. Every club has officers, and he ruled the roost. "Any newbies today?"

Mick and Jake raised their hands, along with four or five others.

"Here, here!" everyone yelled. Those British roots.

"Do we have anyone who has completed their fourth run, therefore presenting themselves for inclusion on the H-Three Wall of Shame?"

Everybody started laughing. This was my fourth Hash, and I knew what was coming.

"This oughta be good," Jake said.

"Yeah." Mick was laughing, "Get in there, Dad."

So, I walked out to the middle of the circle, as you do. All I could think about was Black Thursday during HRT selection, surrounded by gawkers, filthy, tired people trying to name me.

"Does anyone know this worthless bloke?" Daisy asked.

That's the way it worked, joining the Hash House Harriers. After four successful runs, you'd walk into the middle of the circle and smile steadily as a bunch of drunken strangers humiliated you with scandalous rumors. Once everyone had taken their best shot, they'd call out suggestions, and then the Grand Master would put you on your knees in front of the spiritual adviser, second in charge, who would raise a Tommy Lee–size phallus above your head.

"Anyone at all?" the Grand Master called out that evening, smiling. "Someone tell us a story."

I looked around the circle hoping to find a port in the storm. I knew Brewer's Droop, a coffee grower from Mumbai whose wife complained that he drank too much at the Hash and couldn't get it up. His daughter was there, an eighteen-year-old called Miracle because of her father's performance issues and because she was so beautiful that nobody believed he'd sired her. There was Flogger, Full Press Body, and Two Shits, the president of ANZ Bank, who was best known for wearing a black leather biker's vest and playing Sting covers on acoustic guitar.

I saw Mudflap, U-Bend, Mini-Dickus, Scab Lifter, Cavity Kid, Rocks Off, and Toe Rag. There was The First Lady right next to Rotten Ovaries, an unfortunate juxtaposition. Then Wee Willie, Tax Avoider, Sadistic Countess, and Butt Sniffer closed out the ranks.

"I understand there was a party last night," Shamcock called out. He wore knee-high soccer socks, one green, one red, oversize glasses, undersize Jocks.

"Matter of fact, there was," a man said. His name was Bob Down, and I forgot to mention him because he was usually quite reserved. "Would you like to hear a story?"

"Oh, yes, we would." Daisy laughed. "Proceed, Bob Down. Please, proceed."

It all started at the One More Bar. It was Friday night, just after seven o'clock, when we rolled up to Gil's place wearing polo shirts and those full-face helmets. Things had settled down in Surik Mas after "the Battle of White Star Clusters," but you would still get ambushed all over town, mobs appearing out of the banana groves with rocks and clubs.

"This is the guy I was telling you about," I told the boys. "Gil is the arm-wrestling champion of Timor, so don't even try. He's the one boiling oil while we were stuck in Darwin."

"I don't blame him," Jake decided, still fresh from the attack.

The parking lot was full by the time we got there, so I pulled across the street to where a bunch of kids had gathered on the beach to watch foreigners drink to excess. Dili is a small city built around a harbor, and the whole place was dark because the Indonesians had blown up the power grid and nobody had figured out how to rebuild it. All you could see were the green and red running lights of ships offshore and the One More, an open-air oasis near Cristo Rei.

"Gimme dollar, malae," one of the local kids demanded as I parked. I told Mick not to encourage them, but he is generous to a fault and started handing out singles.

"Dollar, dollar, dollar!" They all started laughing, trying to get inside our pockets.

"Come on, man. You know better than that," I told him. "You'll start a riot."

"Lighten up, Dad," Mick said. "It's just a bunch of kids."

We locked our helmets in the trunk because you don't want to walk into a Hash party with a motorcycle helmet when everyone knows you drive a Corolla. Then upstairs to the bar, which was crowded with expats, mostly Australians. I knew everyone, so I introduced Mick and Jake around the room, found a table near the front where there was a hint of a breeze.

"What the hell is this place?" Jake asked, newly revived. "It's awesome!"

And it was. Every person at the One More had a story to tell because only crazy people go to war without a gun, and crazy people tell the best stories. These were adventurers by trade, bold souls addicted to conflict, because life is short and what's the point in boredom?

"Who's this, then?" I heard someone say. I turned around to see Miracle there with an umbrella drink and three hot friends. They were wearing dresses, earrings, tans. Glowing.

"Hey," I told her. "These are my sons, Mick and Jake. Boys, this is Miracle."

"No shit," Jake said. "Where did you come from?"

And I knew the drill, so I left the boys to the girls and walked over to the bar, ordered drinks. Everybody was in a great mood because curfew had been moved back to eleven and there were fewer soldiers in the streets. I was happy because the house still reeked of gasoline.

"How's business, mate?" Daisy wanted to know while I was waiting to order.

"We're getting there, brother," I told him. "Slow and steady wins the race."

"Who's next?" I heard a man call out in a foghorn growl. It was Gil, sitting at a high-top, surrounded by admirers. The arm-wrestling champion of Timor was taking all comers.

I knew better than to start something with a butcher, so I waved hello and spent the next hour or so buying everybody dinner. And I will stipulate that Australian aid workers don't like tequila shots, but American frat boys do, so after a couple of hours, everyone was feeling no pain. I started thinking about how I was a pretty stout wrestler myself, so I decided to give it a try.

"Mind if I have a go, big fella?" I asked Gil. He knew me but didn't care.

"Suit yerself, Yank." He nodded.

I sat down, and we set our grips, and I pulled, and he pulled, and I beat him.

"I wasn't ready," he told me. "Go again."

I beat him again. Then his buddy Kieran noticed and stepped closer, said I cheated.

"Careful who you call a cheater, mate," I told him. I won a third time.

Then word spread about what was going on out back, and people crowded around, and Gil said he was worn out from previous matches, so we switched hands, and I whooped him lefty. At that point, somebody bowed up and somebody said, "Asshole," and somebody threw a punch, and it was on like you see in movies, thirty drunken Aussies just getting some. Chairs were flying.

As happens in a brawl, sometimes you take a shot and end up on the floor. I remember looking up to where Mick and Jake were sitting with Miracle and her friends at the other side of the bar. And I will state for the record that Jake was an excellent amateur boxer, about six foot six with a wicked left hook, and Mick was a brawler, but I had put them through enough, so I got to my feet and whisked the boys out to the car, ruining all hope of their getting lucky.

Which brings us back to the Hash, Bob Down's story.

"He's a bully!" Bob Down started yelling as I stood there in the circle. "What kind of father would start a row while his boys were chatting up our dear Miracle? He's a nob!"

Then Two Shits yelled, "Wanker!" And the rest of them joined in: Two Lights, Flogger, Full Press Body. "Sod him, the bloke's a nob!"

"He's the prick of the week!" Jake hollered, my own son fanning the flames.

Everybody started to wave their beers, laughing me naked in a dirt lot surrounded by septic tank pumpers. Once everyone had had their fill of the abuse, Daisy raised his hand.

"This man is a sinner," he said. "He's a wanker, a sloth, a usurper of joy, corrupter of teenage lads. He is a coward of the lowest and most despicable order. What shall we name him?"

"Cock Blocker!" Miracle yelled, which made everyone howl.

"You know what? I need no help declaring this bloke the Prick of the Week!"

It was my fourth Hash, so I understood that Prick of the Week meant I'd be given a tin mug with a UN lanyard and two rules. Rule number one stated I could not let the tin mug out of my sight until the next Hash. Rule two required me to drink absolutely anything poured into it.

"On your knees!" Daisy commanded.

I knelt in the dirt as Shamcock lifted the brightly painted phallus above my head.

"From this day forward, you will be known as Cold Spoon!"

At which point they all cheered and toasted and chugged beer from cups glued to a ceremonial oar called the On Down. After a while, I went up to Two Shits, the president of ANZ Bank and an excellent guitarist. I told him I had never heard the term *cold spoon.*

"Aw, mate," he said. "It's what the nurses do in hospital when they're giving you a sponge bath and you pop a rod. They tap that offender a couple times with a cold spoon, and down goes your stiffy. Easy as."

He poured red wine into the Prick of the Week mug hanging around my neck. Someone had tossed a cigarette butt into the mix, and I remember standing in that filthy lot surrounded by Ant Eater outhouses as Mick and Jake went back to hitting on Miracle.

I took a long drink, thinking about how I had given up a wonderful life writing books and appearing on television to travel the world in search of war. That I had taught my teenage sons to mix napalm, risked their lives fighting destitute peoples in what we would forever call the Battle of White Star Clusters. That I had promised sharks' teeth to a first-grader on the odd chance I would make it home for Christmas. That I somehow found the whole thing normal.

"Cold Spoon!" Two Shits called out to the Hash, and they cheered my shortcomings.

Cold Spoon indeed.

15

Dili, Timor-Leste

[FEBRUARY 2008]

A s it turns out, starting a security company in a war zone is not all shits and giggles.

The first barrier to success, of course, is violence. By the time I moved to Surik Mas, Timor had lost 200,000 men, women, and children in the fight for independence, with another 150,000 driven from their homes during the 2006 crisis. The United Nations had flown in 1,600 police to secure an Integrated Mission in Timor (UNMIT), but lawless IDP camps controlled the airport, the harbor, the road to the east. The rebel leader Alfredo Reinado was still out in the jungle with 120 guerrillas despite the ANZAC Battle Group, comprised of 2,000 soldiers, 33 armored vehicles, 12 Black Hawk helicopters, three C-130 cargo planes, and a dozen naval vessels, including a guided-missile frigate called the HMAS *Adelaide*. The Malaysians had deployed troops; the Kiwis, too; and the Portuguese had billeted a special operations component called the National Republican Guard (GNR). The whole country lived under martial law.

Despite the international show of force, however, Timor's political parties had squared off in murderous riots leading up to the presidential elections in May 2007. The Nobel laureate and former prime minister José Ramos-Horta handily defeated Fretilin leader Francisco Guterres about six weeks after I arrived, but then came parliamentary elections, which were even worse.

Former president, poet, and war hero Xanana Gusmão eventually won the government, but not until district rallies blew up in violence, including a Viqueque event at which a candidate called Alfonso "Kuda Lay" Guterres was shot and killed by a hit squad of plainclothes cops. Other attacks and assassinations occurred daily, including a gang fight in Dili where somebody lobbed a grenade into a crowd of bystanders.

I'm not complaining about the violence. Don't get me wrong. I went there to build a security company, and nobody needs a security company when the whole population is cuddled up in a soapy shower singing "Kumbaya."

I'm just trying to explain what it was like that first year in-country, the differences between launching a Starbucks in Toledo and building a private army in an animist jungle full of machete-wielding orphans. At the end of the day, I was a "see one, do one, teach one" kinda guy, and I had traveled halfway around the world to find a war I could manage. I'd accomplished tougher things.

And in the interest of full disclosure, I will admit that Philip Fracassi was correct: my fourth-grade obsession with Ernest Hemingway was based on fictional representations of Conrad's search for Wolfe's homeward-looking angels. Lives may turn into books, but they don't start that way, and despite my obsession with death, I fully realized the difference between metaphor and deed. Timor seemed like an opportunity, a world outside the world I had failed.

Hemingway aside, most things don't always go according to plan. Sometimes growth is not about healing; it's about working fourteen hours a day seven days a week for nine months without a breather, trying to turn CIA cash you earned in Somalia into a private army that whispers "ema halo" because they think you have the power to kill with a glance. So, you work your ass off building market share throwing Molotov cocktails with your kids, drinking more and more because vodka worked for your gramps. The business grows. People prosper. On, on . . .

And then you wake up one Monday morning to a coup d'état.

"Sir, I regret to inform you that the president has been shot."

I remember those words, precisely, because the man on the phone was Nito Gusmão, APAC Security's VP of operations, and the prime minister's oldest son. He never called me sir.

"Nito?" I asked. "What are you talking about?"

"The government is under attack, sir. Reinado has come down with the rebels."

I checked my watch because I had worked late the night before, and I felt confused. It was 0842, February 11, 2008. You don't forget a moment like that, your first insurrection.

"Buddy, who is under attack? Where? Right now?"

"President Ramos-Horta has been shot. From what I understand, Reinado has sympathizers from the F-FDTL, generals and weapons, moving toward the Parliament building."

Nito spoke native English in measured tones. He was smart, brave, a patriot like his dad.

"Ramos-Horta has been shot? Holy shit, Nito. Is he dead?"

"We don't know. The president was coming back from his walk near the Cristo Rei, and they were waiting for him when he got there. Reinado's men shot him down in the middle of the street. There was a battle with his protection detail. It was an ambush."

"What about the GNR, the ISF? Are they responding? The PNTL?" I asked.

"I think they are not taking sides."

"Have you talked to your dad? Is he okay?"

"The rebels went to the house. His vehicle has been located. He is missing."

"Where are you?"

"On my way to the office."

"All right. Call everybody in, lock it down," I told him. "I'll be right there."

Which brings us to the second barrier to success: personnel. It was difficult to find executives in Timor, those years, because the Indonesians had killed them all off during the revolution. Hiring the PM's eldest son is always a good move, and Mick and Jake will forever remain enshrined as founding fathers of APAC Security, but the company would never have gotten off the ground without Cesarina, the first person I called after Nito hung up the phone.

"Fuck me running, boss," she said, then something about wankers and nobs.

I will note that Cesarina stood five feet tall in six-inch heels and weighed seventy-eight pounds with a rock in each hand, but she was intrepid, focused, bold. I have worked with executives at Goldman Sachs who had nothing on her. Within a week of my arrival, she had found a way to register APAC as an expat vendor, despite the government's being steered by mobs throwing grenades. She found us a walled compound with a moat in a city reduced to tents, reliable transportation (albeit a Corolla). She taught us Indonesian, scheduled meetings with government leaders, sniped lucrative accounts. Cesarina negotiated pacts with gangs, navigated riots, walked me through the country's 13 districts, 442 village *sucos,* and 2,336 smaller *aldeias.*

"I need information," I told her.

She said, "I'll call you back," and I knew that would be enough.

Cesarina had better intelligence than any agency in town. She knew the "Our Father" in Latin, the spirit names of every ghost on the island. When I asked her about "ema halo" during our first private conversation, she told me to buy three bags of rice and drew a crude map to a remote village in Manatuto District. When I drove out there, I found a man who was naked except for cotton gym shorts and two smudges of paint on taut black skin.

He had bright blue eyes, which confused me, and did not speak English, but he seemed to understand why I was there. After I handed two women the three bags of rice, he walked me down a path to an animist burial ground of totems made from cow skulls, black and gray horns. We stood there for the longest time, and I had no idea what the hell was going on, but then he put his hand on my chest, where my heart should have been, and said, "Ema halo." He spoke no other words.

You might think I digress here, but these are the things that flow through one's mind during a coup d'état, when widespread violence sweeps down from the jungles, and no one trusts the army; at least that is what flowed through my mind. And because things can be difficult to understand in a life fully formed, I need to explain that APAC had become one of Timor's largest employers by the time. We had hundreds of employees, including Nito and three extraordinary Timorese in the executive suite, but the company would not have gotten off its feet without a handful of expats who fully embraced the business of black magic, spies, and guns.

Allow me to introduce them.

·   ·   ·

Remember when I said nobody ever really gets recruited to the intelligence community? Well, that's not entirely true, and I cannot introduce my second in command without a little background.

Every once in a while, you meet someone who stands out for specific reasons, someone with unusual talents that could prove useful in broader applications. Sometimes people turn up in a life fully formed for reasons that are not immediately obvious, but you're a patriot, so you decide to get involved.

"What are you thinking, brotha?" Knackers asked me. We were in New York City, having drinks at a popular new Mexican place in SoHo called La Esquina. The room was getting loud.

"I love it," I told him. "It sounds like a great plan all around. When do we go?"

It was a Friday night in October 2006, still early, with Manhattan unwinding with happy hour margaritas, that kind of buzz. I almost always went home to New Hampshire on weekends, but Knackers had flown in from Hong Kong to say hello, so I stayed to hang.

"We need to set up accounts in Singapore, mate," Knackers told me. "Gerry has the particulars, but we'll deposit fifty thousand a month for expenses."

I was doing the math when some Wall Street goof elbowed between us. I was about to knee him in the nuts, but Knackers said, "You're good, mate," because he's that kind of guy.

And remember how I said there are two ways into the George Bush Center for Intelligence at the Route 123 entrance, that the left lane is badge access for CIA employees, contractors, and cleared associates? Well, that's not entirely true, either. Sometimes the best way into the CIA is not through Langley at all. Sometimes you get there through the back door of a corner delicatessen near the intersection of Kenmare and Cleveland Place in Manhattan. In October 2006, people in the know would go there as if they were looking for chalupas.

"What are you thinking in terms of time line?" I asked him. "I've got commitments through the holidays, but I'm free after the first of the year."

"Guud, guud." He nodded. "I've got London on Tuesday, Tel Aviv Thursday, back to Managua for the weekend, then home for a fundraiser in Sydney. There's some bits and pieces regarding incorporation of the shell entity, then on to Dili. Maybe right after the New Year?"

"Brilliant." I nodded. We toasted the plan with shots. "How's the family, brother?"

"Guud, guud, Chris. They'll be keen to see you."

And then we asked for menus, thinking we'd order tapas, but another person stepped in, waving for a bartender. This time it was a woman, so small we barely noticed her.

"Do you mind?" she asked. Heavy Russian accent.

"No worries." Knackers smiled. He cleared space, and she fit right through.

"Australian?" she asked him, waiting on an order of six Palomas.

"Yes, darling," he said, the charmer. "You must be Russian."

"American," she told him, polite though stern. "I'm American."

Then she was gone, and we had a nice dinner at the bar, talking inconsequential things. After nine o'clock, people moved off to other places, but Knackers liked La Esquina, so we moved to a corner for aperitifs. We had been comparing adventures, and he was telling me about the tragic Sydney-to-Hobart yacht race in 1998, when six competitors drowned in a monstrous storm. Knackers's boat had capsized in the freak seas, and he'd thought he was a goner, but the navy rescued him by helicopter after six perilous hours in the water.

"Makes you appreciate what you've got, mate. Death. It's a specter."

He was just getting to the penultimate moment in his story, talking about how he was a strong swimmer, but that hypothermia was setting in and he was thinking about saying goodbye to his family, when I heard a voice. It was a smaller voice, a woman's voice, the Russian.

"Were you not even going to come talk to us?" she said.

"Oh, hello, love," Knackers told her, but she was looking at me.

"I'm sorry. Do we know each other?" I asked. I was by no means a celebrity, but I had been on TV for years as an FBI sniper. New Yorkers pay attention. I got the occasional notice.

"No," she said. "Not really."

Then she handed me a business card with her name and title. She asked for mine, and I could tell she knew about my FBI days, because she said something about the *Today* show, which I had done that morning. For reasons all my own, I used a white card with a red .308-caliber dot in the middle, my name above it, "assignments worldwide" in the lower-right corner. There was no phone number, but if I liked you, I would write something on the back.

"Best way to contact me," I said, offering a spare AOL address.

She said something about the KGB becoming the GNU, then laughed and walked away.

"What was that all about?" Knackers asked once she was gone.

"New York." I shrugged. "You never know."

I did not think much more about it until Sunday afternoon, when I was sitting around my apartment, playing guitar. My BlackBerry pinged, and I checked messages. It was her. The note read, "I'm on the Upper East Side with three Tahitian women. If you can find me, I will walk across the park with you to my next engagement. Udacha, Ay."

And I remember sitting there, trying to figure out where a Russian claiming to be an American would have found three Tahitian women on the Upper East Side of Manhattan. As luck would have it, I knew there was a new Gaugin exhibition at the Met, which of course would include Tahitian women, and it sounded intriguing, so I headed that way. I could not remember exactly what she looked like, but there was only one woman in the crowd wearing a white Cossack hat, knee-high boots, and St. Petersburg fashions; it was an easy guess.

"You're late" was the first and only thing she said when I got there.

And she was no conversationalist. We walked halfway across Central Park before she told me she had grown up Soviet, one of two daughters to a famous violinist who had traveled the world performing Stravinsky. She said the family had immigrated when she was seventeen, via Montreal, settled near Boston, where her dad taught lessons. She had attended a Soviet conservatory, then applied to Harvard, but did not get in because she spoke no English. Boston College had accepted her for the same reason, but now she was in New York, working on a resident visa. She and her boyfriend were leaving for Argentina in December. She did not have much time.

And so, six weeks later, just before Christmas, after doing appropriate due diligence, I met her at Penn Station, took the 9:15 Amtrak to D.C., where we got in a black SUV and rode seventeen miles west to the George Bush Center for Intelligence at the Route 123 entrance.

"Do you have an American passport?" the lady asked on our way in. The CIA clerk.

"Nyet."

I was about to explain things, when a man in a suit showed up, and we all parted ways. The Russian went left, and I went right, down the odd geometric hallway to where Sue sat at her desk with the bottle of anthrax and her bobblehead Jesus.

In the cafeteria having a cup of coffee with me, she said, "You just walked a Russian national in the front door of the Central Intelligence Agency. Wearing a Cossack hat. She looks like Pola Ivanova, for Chrissakes. Maybe I'm getting old, Whitcomb, but what the hell?"

"I can use that in my next game of Two Truths and a Lie," I told her. "Who'd believe it?"

"What should I call her?" Sue asked me. "Just in case."

"I don't know." I shrugged. "She told me to call her Ay. Let's go with that."

Which brings us back to my dinner with Knackers at La Esquina, where we had laid the foundations for our security efforts in Timor. As luck would have it, the CIA had no immediate use for a Russian national in a Cossack hat, but APAC did. I hired her about six months in.

"What we got, Ay?" I asked, my first call after Cesarina.

"What do we got? We've got a frigging coup d'état."

She was chief operating officer at that point, second in command of the entire operation. Ay had become a powerful member of the business community, an associate of President Ramos-Horta, chummy with the biggest names in town. She was an extraordinary leader.

"It's a shit show," she told me. "But we're good."

"Are you at the office?"

"Yep, with Alex. Ano and Jacinto are here, too."

"I'm on my way. Hold what you got."

My third call was to APAC's twenty-three-year-old chief financial officer, a fraternity buddy of Mick's who had called looking for adventure. He had a degree in architecture, a capable mind.

"Are you fucking kidding?" He laughed when I asked about news from the embassy.

"Fair enough. Any word on Ramos-Horta?" I asked. The CFO's name was Brett. "Is he dead?"

"They're flying him to Oz," Brett told me. "Reinado is dead with a bunch of his rebels. Xanana is missing, and there are reports of other attacks, but it's all still rumors."

"Well, the phones are working, so they haven't seized comms," I told him. "I'm driving past Parliament right now, and it's mobbed with Aussies. See if the airport is open. I want to get you guys out till things settle down. Alex will stay for now, maybe get him on a boat."

"Fuck that." Brett laughed. "We're not going anywhere."

And that brings us to the third and final barrier to success: insurmountable odds. Nobody even thought about failure that day. Not Nito, not Ay, not Cesarina, not Brett.

It's important to note that by February 11, 2008, APAC Security had twenty-nine clients in eight districts from Dili to Tutuala. We had bought Seprosetil, moved into a larger compound, established a dispatch center, and offered all guards professional training. We secured Timor Telecom, the power grid, the Australian Federal Police. People depended on us.

"How we doing, Colonel?" I asked the man guarding the gate when I got to our office.

His name was Alex, and he was a former Spetsnaz officer who liked to wear shorts so you could see the gnarly scar where he had been shot fighting mujahideen in Afghanistan during the eighties. He chain-smoked, nodded a lot, got along well with the locals. I asked him one time if he had ever crossed the Khojak Pass. He had nodded his head, smiled nostalgic, then said, "Nyet."

"Is day in paradise," the colonel told me as I arrived. Deadpan. "Cum see, cum sauce."

Alex was a hard man of few words who often got them wrong.

Once APAC survived the coup, it was time to start a band.

"The sound of gunfire off in the distance"—I was singing "Life During Wartime" by the Talking Heads.

We called ourselves Ugly Early, and that was an excellent name because crowds in war zones tend to go that way. People flocked to our shows all over town, mostly bars, the occasional private function. Critics raved that we were the best band in the whole country, but we were the only band in the whole country, so we had rock star egos, though only onstage.

It was a Saturday night, and we were rocking a new beach spot called Caz Bar near Cristo Rei. I was the front man with a Stratocaster, Two Shits in his black leather biker's vest, working a pointy blue Ibanez. We had Ay on violin and a Timorese rhythm section that sounded like Muscle Shoals. This particular show, we had a Manitoba Hydro executive named Spam on congas, which worked beautifully, because our slogan was "Classic Rock Timor Style."

"This ain't no party, this ain't no disco," the whole crowd singing along.

And the joint was packed. I mean it was happening. We were half-way through the third set, and it was a big turnout, because everyone had showered up after the Hash, and Dili was thick with expats now that President Ramos-Horta had survived being shot and Prime Minister Gusmão had emerged from the jungle unscathed. APAC Security was thriving. All I had to think about that night was three chords and a prayer. Music is the great healer; I was making progress.

I remember stepping in for a solo, my head back like you often see with guitar gods. I was feeling the true meaning of "Life During Wartime" among people who lived it every day. And then there is this moment when you're a musician and you're onstage with a killer band and the whole place is balls deep in the pocket and you're all moving as one, an old energy that transcends things picayune. You feel hope for the human race because you've been to war but can play guitar.

Two Shits was yelling into his mic because he was having the time of his life, and the crowd was yelling back, and Ay was bowing some Tchaikovsky licks on an expensive violin, and Spam was ringing the shit out of a triangle with the wrecking crew sharing the groove.

You could feel the dirt floor bouncing in your gut, and I was looking out at the crowd of revelers, thinking about how playing in a rock band might be the best thing about being alive. I was thinking about how lucky I was to have played live almost continuously since that open mic at the Franconia Inn, the high school band with Stu Hamm before he became an icon, Dr. Neptune and the Rare Orchids in college with Herb Lockwood, the great Misha Cooney on bass.

I thought about crazy gigs I had played, including one at a bar on the Upper West Side of Manhattan called Prohibition. We were covering this very same song when David Byrne, the man who co-wrote it, walked right in front of the stage but didn't even wink. I thought about playing frat house battles of the bands, weddings, biker events, birthday celebrations. I remembered Scandies Winebar in London, busking for deutsche marks at the Marienplatz, running out of strings in Torremolinos. I thought about a guest appearance upstairs at the Irish Brigade with Elephant Boy and the remarkable Andrew Hellier fronting Rotoglow.

"Trouble in transit, got through the roadblock . . ."

The place was rocking, and we got to the part in the song when the volume quiets, and everybody changes their dancing, mostly bass and drums.

And in that moment, I heard something loud at the other side of the bar. It was a man's voice, getting aggressive in Tetum, he was not singing along.

Then the band swelled louder, and everybody went back to big-move dancing with their hands over their heads, and the booze was flowing, and we were just having a blast. I thought about one time, playing Merle Haggard on a flatbed trailer at a stock car race in Oxford, Maine. My uncle Mike was there, and he was hammered and looking for a fight, so he broke a guy's teeth out with the barrel of his pistol. I remember the guy on his knees, bleeding all over his T-shirt while I was trying to cover telecaster licks with a Peavey T-60.

I remembered the USS *Cole* bombing in 2000, when I flew into Yemen on a C-5 Galaxy with HRT riding shotgun, two hundred fully armed colleagues from the FBI. We had set up a command post at the Aden Hotel, but the Yemeni Army surrounded us with belt-fed machine guns and would not let us out. All we could do was drink naqe'e al zabib and work out—until one night, when the manager told us about a disco we did not know existed. They had a full band playing Yemeni tunes and an extra guitar, so I asked if I could sit in. They thought that would be great.

And I remember standing there on the stage wearing Royal Robbins cargo pants with a fully automatic rifle slung over my back and an electric guitar in front, playing "Proud Mary," thinking this would really be a fun story to tell the kids.

But then the front man looked at me and said in phonetic English, "Hotel California," and we got to the big solo, which I just happened to know, and these two Romanian belly dancers walked out onstage, and I was thinking you just can't make this shit up. But then the show ended, and we took the elevator up to the sixth floor, where we were "hot racking" in eight-hour shifts, three guys to a bed. There was a Marine Corps Fleet Anti-terrorism Security Team just outside the elevator, behind sandbags, with an M60 just like my boy had in Somalia. And I was laughing at what a great jam we'd had when this guy from the U.S. Defense Intelligence Agency handed me a piece of paper that said the guys who blew up the USS *Cole* were going to blow up the Aden Hotel. We were all going to die.

Two Shits and I sang harmony on the chorus, then finished with a big swell. Everybody clapped, and you don't want to lose the momentum, so we went right into "Sympathy for the Devil," which is always a crowd-pleaser. But in that brief lull, I saw the Timorese guy who had been making all the noise in back. He had moved up, to right in front of the stage, and I could see that he was shitfaced, which is unusual for people who can't afford food, let alone beer.

"I rode a tank, held a general's rank . . ."

I saw the guy walk up behind a twenty-four-year-old aid worker who had just finished her master's in conflict resolution at William and Mary. He reached up under her skirt and went wrist-deep into her no-no square.

She screamed and a couple of GNR men saw what was going on, intervened. A half-dozen plainclothes Timorese emerged out of nowhere with police batons, everybody started yelling, and as bar fights go, this one went fucking big really fucking fast. It was an Altamont Speedway kinda rumble, which was weird, because that one had been during "Sympathy for the Devil," too.

We kept playing through the first chorus, but by the third "woo, woo," the bartenders had split and villagers had started flowing in from outside. The Caz Bar was open-air, so the first thing I noticed were the rocks. Then they broke all the bottles of booze, then the furniture, then the walls, the roof. Three hundred fifty people screaming and running into the night, shit flying in, bamboo spears and beer bottles, people bleeding and lying on the ground, and then it went full melee.

The band was still onstage with instruments, of course, and Ay had a very expensive violin, but I had a Klon Centaur and a '61 Strat, which people who know gear would hate to see destroyed. But we all knew the drill, so Spam grabbed a bottle of Jack Daniels, and we ducked into the corner, because corners are the best place to be when a building comes down.

"Ugly Early!" Spam was yelling, the conga player in bell-bottoms. "Ugly Early!"

Then Two Shits handed me a towel, because I was sweating my ass off, and Ay handed around the Jack, and the rhythm section said, "Boa tarde, Chris" and disappeared out the back.

I sat there thinking how I loved to play guitar in bands, that this might be my craziest gig.

"Hand me that bottle, Ay," I said as they tore the place to the ground.

Sometimes it sneaks up on you, insanity. You don't even see it coming.

16

Santa Cruz Cemetery, Bairo Pite

[NOVEMBER 2010]

B y the end of our third year, APAC Security was the largest employer in the country. We had survived a coup d'état, the counterfeit economy, dengue fever, malaria, motorcycle wrecks, endemic corruption, endless riots, and the myriad ethnic and cultural challenges inherent in managing remote outposts among tribesmen who still hunt with bows. By Christmas 2010, we had grown a murky financial instrument into a multimillion-dollar enterprise, navigating complex interactions one might expect with corporations mining eighty billion dollars' worth of oil along the nuclear highway between Five Eyes interests and China.

When the UN Mission in Timor (UNMIT) went to tender in 2010 with a contract for protective services, we bid and beat all competitors. This meant APAC won domain over UNMIT headquarters at Obrigado Barracks and all housing, offices, physical assets, and employees in Dili, all thirteen districts. We guarded the airport, the hospital, BNUs and ANZs, NGOs ranging from Catholic Charities to the Norwegian Children's Fund. We moved millions of dollars in cash throughout the country and provided bodyguards for visiting executives, a subscription-based security bulletin, medivac, and other helicopter operations.

By the beginning of the third year, APAC had also stolen Maubere's clients, seizing 90 percent of market share and fighting off both a local start-up called Gardamor and G4S, one of the largest security companies in the world. We had stations in every district, guards at hundreds of locations. We paid the highest monthly salary on the island, provided each employee with forty hours of internationally certified training.

We built a formidable intelligence network with agents in government bureaus, with regulatory agencies, international corporations, and martial arts gangs, including Zero-Zero-One and Seven-Seven, the most dangerous offenders. We built concrete blast walls around the prime minister's house, installed cameras and microphones at sensitive locations, and offered round-the-clock surveillance. We stole power.

And they say, nothing succeeds like success, but success came at a cost.

"Got a mouthguard, mate?" asked Kieran, the guy from the Hash fight at the One More.

"Nah, I'm good."

"Here," he, now one of my closest friends, told me. "I've got an extra. You'll need it."

In November 2010, you could not live or do business in Timor-Leste without hiring APAC Security. If you did not pay us for protection, the locals would burn you out.

"How about another helmet?" I asked. "This one is too small."

"Over there, mate. In that bin. Should be plenty to choose from."

And before you call APAC's business model extortion, understand that your Western aversion to colonization implies fairness. I would argue that it is easy to say that when visiting Croatia, where you can find a nice villa and feel welcomed by the neighbors. There were no villas in Dili, which is a problem when a Schlumberger exec moves to town and decides to park his Range Rover where your hut used to be. He barbecues steaks while your kids starve, runs his AC all night while your family tries to sleep in the dirt under a tree. APAC succeeded because Timorese had no qualms about murdering oil execs who told them a shit sandwich was cake.

"You want a beer?" I asked Kieran. He chain-smoked cigarettes and stayed half lit.

"Nah, mate. I'm good."

"How's this work? Where do you want me?"

"We go second row," Kieran said. "Let the GNR take the first volley. Then it's whatever."

"No rules, right?"

"No rules." He smiled, buckling up his helmet. "Get yer yayas out."

Which brings us to the true cost of success: hubris. When violence is your business, violence sometimes becomes your recreation, too, and whatever progress President Ramos-Horta and Prime Minister Gusmão brought following Reinado's attempt at a coup, my demons raged. Though I had moved to Timor hoping to find a war I could manage, war had seized me.

"To your positions!" a man called out. I knew him as a United Nations Police commander.

"If you go down, stay there, mate," Kieran told me. "We're in this to have fun, not prove a point. If it's just bones or stitches, we go to the Cubans. Anything serious, they'll lug you to the Aussie docs at the airport. They're suited for trauma."

"You sure nobody knows who I am?"

"Fuck, mate. Everybody knows who you are. But once you pull that visor down, you're just a bloke in riot gear. Another anonymous male."

He was right. Dili was a small city where everyone knew my face, though my identity varied. To business types and government officials, I was "APAC CEO" or "sir." Everyone at the office called me "boss," except for Ay, who called me "C," and guards, who called me "Kita Buang" because I wielded the power of *fekit*. In English, I was "the main ghost" (more about that later).

I said, "On, on," and Kieran put in his mouthguard, grabbed a baton.

"Steady!" I heard a large African yell. He had a whistle and a club. "Steady!"

I remember lining up. There were about thirty of us in helmets and shields, with those shin guards that catchers wear behind the plate, ballistic vests, and hickory clubs.

"Steady . . ."

I remember thinking about the Battle of White Star Clusters, the times I had been ambushed and stoned. I thought about the hundreds of disaffected youths who banded together in predatory style to roam the streets with impunity.

"Steady . . ."

The streets of Dili were dark at night, so crime ran unchecked. Few Timorese had guns, but they made arrows out of rebar, threw stars cut from sheet metal, clever sorts of blades. They spread claims of immortality, using terror to render peace tenuous.

"Steady . . ."

It was still early when they came out of the banana trees, mostly shadows and taunts. This was my first fight in UNPOL gear, and I thought back to that first kickoff when playing college football, everyone looking forward to full-speed hits. And I knew most firearms had been recovered following Reinado's death, so it was Stone Age combat between grown-ups and half-naked kids. But I will note that I have seen, made, or cleaned up a shitload of dead people in my life, and I can honestly say that rocks and knives kill just as effectively as things that go bang.

"Oh, hell yeah, brother," I told Kieran, but he was focused.

And then the African yelled, "Now!" and blew his whistle, and I noticed two things almost immediately. First, the kids coming out of the jungle appeared to have no interest in us at all. They sprinted in scrums at one another, met with surprising force, and they had machetes and crossbows instead of rocks. Second, none of the UNPOL men around me seemed to have the slightest interest in joining the ruckus. They just stood there, ambivalent.

But then Kieran started running, and I started running after him. We crossed a flat stretch of dirt that could have been a soccer pitch, though it had no goals. And at first it felt like all the other fights of my life had blended together, somehow playing out in my mind the way a song flows through me when I'm playing guitar onstage, the crowd one roar, because we're all connected through energy, wave states that make us human, part of a larger game.

"Malae! Malae!" somebody yelled, more from surprise than anything, but he did not engage me, and I realized that I was laughing and calling out names of my own, which included "Kieran!" because he was laying people out; his skills were impressive.

"Malae, malae!"

I heard somebody coming up behind me and turned just in time to see the steel pipe in his hand arcing toward my head, and in that instant, I remembered climbing into the ring with Big Bob, my first time sparring at Finley's. I saw white light, felt a sudden sadness, then nothing.

"Whitcomb," I heard someone say. "What's up with this D.C. sniper?"

It was a dream, and I knew it was a dream even when I was in it.

The first thing I noticed was Al Roker, back when he was the roly-poly weatherman at the *Today* show, backstage at 30 Rockefeller Center. I had just walked out of the greenroom to get made up, and he was standing next to the lady who presses your jacket while you're waiting. Matt Lauer was sitting in front of a mirror, getting his hair done, reading *The New York Times.*

"Morning, Al," I said. "What do you want to know, brother?"

"Are we going to get this jerk or what?"

"Oh, we'll get him," I said. And I was smiling, because Al Roker is one of the nicest guys you'll ever meet and because he used to keep a tablespoon of peanut butter in his suit coat pocket, back when he was losing all that weight. He would pull out that spoon, and the peanut butter would have lint all over it, but he'd take a bite and then go right back to doing the weather.

"Do you think it's one guy or two?" Matt asked me. Matt Lauer.

"I think it's just one."

It was right in the middle of the news cycle when someone was going around shooting people at gas stations. A national story; perhaps you remember.

"I saw a guy on MSNBC thinks it's more than one," Al said.

"Clint Van Zandt." I nodded. "I used to work with him in Quantico. He thinks people should run around in zigzag patterns while they're gassing up their cars. Kinda weird."

Then a producer said, "You're up in three, Chris," and the makeup artist dusted my nose; the lady who steamed the jackets handed me my blazer.

"Break a leg, pal," Matt told me.

And I had just done *Imus in the Morning* at Don Imus's studio in Queens, so I already knew what I was going to say. I walked out to the library set where Katie Couric was sitting, in one of those overstuffed chairs. Ann Curry said hi, then Natalie Morales, and then Katie said hi, and the stage manager counted down the hit, and we got serious, because people were getting killed. I remember saying the word *varmint* in reference to flat trajectory rifles and wishing I had used a less colloquial term, but everything else went well. And it was a two-segment hit, so when we went to the commercial break, Katie said her skin was dry and asked for some lotion.

"I hear you're going down there for on-scene analysis," she said, just being friendly. The D.C. sniper story was the biggest story in the country, and NBC wanted me local in case it happened again.

"Yep, shuttling down this afternoon."

"Delta?"

"USAir."

A production assistant tossed Katie a bottle of lotion, and she squirted some into her hand. And we were just chatting, because Katie Couric is every bit as smart as she seems on TV. But then she started rubbing lotion on her thighs, then the insides of her thighs. Then she spread it onto her legs, and I was sitting approximately twenty-seven inches from America's Sweetheart on the library set of the *Today* show staring unambiguously at a full-on crotch shot. Bright yellow panties.

And just when I was lost in the wilderness of that moment, thinking it might be the oddest thing that had ever happened in my life, I heard the director count us out of the commercial, and Katie tossed the lotion, and we went right back to talking about snipers killing people in Washington, D.C. Like it was nothing, another day on TV.

Then someone yelled "Whitcomb" again, and I was looking up at Kieran standing above me wearing a blue UNPOL helmet with a fogged-up shield. Dreams change without notice.

"Fuck, mate," he said. "You right?"

I got up to my feet, and the first thing I thought was that I had a glass jaw and needed to be a little more careful, because I had been knocked senseless way too many times.

"Am I bleeding?"

"Not that I can see."

I was checking my head where it hurt in back, looking around to see what I had missed while I was out. The soccer pitch was empty except for a few bodies, all Timorese. And my vision started to clear to the point where I saw a kid lying on the ground with his eyes open.

"Is that an arrow?" I asked.

I walked closer, because the kid had about four inches of steel sticking out of his chest with a white paper plum on top, which you could not miss because his skin was unusually dark.

"Looks like he's dead."

"Come on, mate," Kieran told me. "It'll be on at the One More. Let's get pissed."

I leaned down and pulled out that arrow, which had glanced off a rib and burrowed under the kid's skin, barely a drop of blood.

"Hang on, brother."

Maybe it was getting knocked dizzy or because I had been drunk for months in a war zone sprinkled with animist totems built by shamans with blue eyes who, without a single word, taught me the meaning of *ema halo* for three bags of rice.

I don't know why I pulled the arrow.

"You gonna keep that thing?" Kieran asked.

"Yut."

And I know what you're thinking: that a dream sequence involving Katie Couric on the *Today* show just doesn't make any sense during a gang fight in Timor. But I will lean back here to remind you that a life fully formed does not always make sense in the moment, that the mind does funny things. That there is purpose in dreams. They cleanse us; they keep us real.

"That was a corker," I told Kieran as we walked away.

"You sure you're okay, mate?"

"Never better."

I kept the arrow as a macabre memento mori. I'm looking at it as I write this.

I cannot tell you exactly when I broke, but I will admit that I did.

Maybe it was working around the clock for years, trying to impose order on chaos. Maybe it was the bottle of vodka Fred T. taught me to keep under the seat of the Corolla. Maybe it was the weight of *ema halo,* which I wielded without mercy but never fully understood. Hell, maybe I brought the end with me, some flaw of psyche or resolve I had not tamed in tamer places.

Whatever it was, I was sitting on a couch at Surik Mas watching MotoGP the first time I felt the end coming. It was a Sunday, and I was hungover from an Ugly Early gig. It was still morning, so I'd had a little hair of the dog but was not yet hammered. Valentino Rossi held the lead on a Yamaha, but I was a fan of Casey Stoner on a Ducati. And it was an exciting race, the Malaysian Grand Prix at Sepang. Great circuit; I've been there.

My phone rang.

"Gudday, Chris," a man said when I answered. "Sorry to ruin your weekend."

"Colonel?" I asked.

"Yes. I need you to come over as quickly as possible. We have a problem."

Everything is a problem in the security business, especially in a place like East Timor, where your clients are used to boiling oil to keep half-naked men from surging up their stairs.

"What's the problem, sir? What's going on?"

"I don't know," he told me. "That's why I'm calling. We have twenty men inside the compound walls, and they seem highly agitated. You'll need to see this for yourself."

I was used to client calls for help, but this one seemed particularly disconcerting, because the man on the line was Col. Grant Edwards, in-country commander of the Australian Federal Police. In addition to holding senior rank as security adviser to Timor's secretary of state, Edwards had immediate access to soldiers with guns. Why would he need me?

"Are you at the office now?" I asked him.

"Yes."

"I'll be right there."

Nito Gusmão was there waiting when I arrived.

"What's up, brother?" I said to him.

The AFP headquarters was a walled compound with a staff of seven APAC guards working eight-hour shifts twenty-four hours a day. Nito, as you may recall, was the prime minister's son and APAC's director of operations. He was a remarkable man in innumerable ways.

"We have a problem," Nito told me.

"Yes, I can see that. Why do we have twenty men here on a Sunday?"

"One of the guards discovered a security threat and called for backup. But you should not have been called. You should not have come."

"Why not?"

"This is a Timorese problem."

"This is an APAC problem."

"Do not mistake the two."

Then the uniformed supervisor walked over and said, "Boss, fuck-sakes, it's a shocker."

Most supervisors were multilingual; this one spoke Australian.

"So I hear. What's going on?"

"The lads found a ghost in the well."

"Ghost in the well?"

"Yes, powerful *buang,* very angry. I call dispatch for backup, but they call *jefe aldeia* and *jefe aldeia* say call you. This spirit only listen to main ghost. Need *fekit.*"

"A spell?" I asked. The *jefe aldeia* was like the mayor; we rarely called him.

"Ema halo, boss. Ema halo."

Which brings us to the question we've all been asking. What the fuck is *ema halo,* why did the Timorese call me "Kita Buang," and what made them believe my *fekit* allowed me to kill strongmen by tossing a kernel of corn?

"All right," I said. "Show me what you got."

Which he did. The AFP compound had a large paved courtyard with a dug well at the far end, so we walked over to where a pack of men stood around the deep, dark hole.

"I see what you mean," I told him, peering down at nothing. I will admit that verifying a ghost in a well is not as easy as one might suspect, so you fake it. "How can I help?"

"We need to make offering," the supervisor said. "*Buang* very angry, you can see."

"Roosters?" I asked. It was not my first rodeo. "Black roosters? How many you thinking?"

"Yes, of course, boss. Maybe two, maybe three."

"How much do you need?"

"Thirty dollars."

"Here. Bring me a young dog, too, just in case. A female. Not in heat."

"Stand by."

Crisis resolution is all about managing variability, crafting solutions.

At that point in life, I had chased terrorists across continents, escaped Mogadishu, wrangled publication deadlines with Little, Brown and *The New York Times*. I had offered sworn testimony to the U.S. Senate, taught high school English. I had been trained by the best, from Gunny John Wayne Johnson at the Marine Corps Scout Sniper School to a CIA driving instructor called Sha Na Na.

"Stand back," I told the crew once the supervisor showed up with the animals. Then: "Hic et ubique!" because curses sound cool in Tetum, but all I knew was Latin.

"Kita buang," somebody whispered, and I slit two rooster throats.

"Malae buang," someone announced proudly, then "bagus, malae."

And I stood there for a long moment holding a dead bird in each hand with a young dog shaking between my feet. I do not claim to be a shaman, but I figured something had to die in a sacrificial offering if I wanted to chase an angry spirit out of a well.

"Here," I said, handing the roosters to a senior guard. "Only Timorese man can appease this Timorese spirit. You spray the blood."

You have to think quickly when you're the boss, offering sangfroid when the chips are down. No corporation is going to pay extortion when the CEO of a security company can't even deal with a ghost.

"Well done, mate," Colonel Edwards told me once we were finished. "Did they teach you that at the FBI Academy?"

I laughed and joked that it was more a CIA sort of thing.

"How long before we can wash the blood off the walls?" he asked.

"Might give it a couple days."

"Cheers. I appreciate you stopping over."

"Anything else I can help you with?"

"Nah, it's leg day. I'm off to the gym."

And the first thing I will tell you is that I have no idea why the Timorese believed my magic trumped darker forces. Sometimes I think it easier to explain how a ski racer from New Hampshire escaped a roomful of Taliban, only to settle on an island in the middle of the Pacific driving a busted-up Corolla. Via Mogadishu and four years with NBC. After a career in the FBI. Playing guitar.

The second thing I'll say is: Who cares? In the end, it does not matter why they called me "Kita Buang"; it helped us survive. And here is where I try to make sense of a moment in life we all experience though seldom understand, a crisis of faith best discussed in books and songs. It was not the ghost in the well that broke me that Sunday, not the hangover or the interruption of the MotoGP. It was not the sacrifice of a couple of roosters, spraying blood all over a wall.

What broke me, I realize all these years later, was that I loved it.

All of it.

I loved that an entire culture believed me omniscient, omnipotent, malign. That they feared me. They depended upon me not just to feed their four thousand families, but also to keep those families safe from a spirit world of vapors that would fly in on the full moon as shadows of goats to lay waste among people they loved.

"Kita Buang," they called me. The main ghost.

That Sunday was the first time I believed them.

Air

We age alone vapor
Things children dream
Breathing heaves
As they run through mountains
Voices just echo
Skies marbled clouds
Horizons listing indifferent to
Men who falter believing
Faith will prevail

At the bottom of the ocean
Rhythms fail us
The scope of our lives
No more than wisp
Some days the silence of drowning
Rings hopeful
Death wrote in stanzas
An early peace

Think of me as the Coming
Breath and its absence
A wheel of toil
Truths you believe
No more than chance
What we sip at the end is
Air lent briefly
Because one life
Might be the whole life
One God our only

17

Bali, Indonesia

[DECEMBER 2012]

There is a point in every wave where placement and resolve meet at takeoff. Sometimes you think *damn,* and the wave passes unridden because you're too deep in the lineup or not deep enough, the entire session a series of closed-out faces, ill-formed mush. Those days, you laugh and paddle after the next one knowing it's all just the pull of the moon, water moving inchoate, the skies your chimera. And surfing is as much metaphor as sport, so you seek the spirit of the moment, each ride an opportunity to learn, one calculation in a larger equation.

At least that's what I got out of surfing, the skier used to snow.

Sometimes it's a big day, ten feet at seventeen seconds, which is waterman code for steep drops, triple overhead, the breeze offshore, tides diurnal. Those days, it feels like the whole world is pumping, and maybe you get things right, so the wave lets you in, the beginning and the end a package you hold precious to unwrap later. Big swells start nascent, a node on the horizon, more spirit than hump. And it's your home break, so you see it before anybody else, though everybody is watching. You lean onto your board, paddle around a little bit trying to judge the peak, but then everybody starts scratching because they're caught inside, and that ain't good.

Whew, you whisper as it rises up, a Goliath, and you want to get it before it gets you, so you sprint out to sea, energized by the consequences of failure, the power of the thing. Your mind is screaming, but there's no point in swearing. You're scared shitless; that's the objective.

Bomb sets rise out of the ocean incarnate, a feathered spline of ribs. One minute you're horizontal, the next inverted, poling yourself down some glassy slope like it's race day at Killington, only this is no mountain; it's liquid, a moment in time. Your mind screams that it's going to kill you, because the wave is bigger than your house, and it feels like you're lying in the bathtub trying to ride the whole third floor. But the best surfer in the water is the one having the most fun, so you huck yourself over the edge, drop fluid into a bottom turn, pick a line, and Nature curls around you, your knees bent into the hollows, body mind and soul one focus, big life mortgaged small. It feels like provenance, getting barreled, an unpayable debt.

"Hu! Kai ko'o Loa," I used to chant, sitting out there in the lineup.

I would be the loner farthest out, hands cupping the waters as I sat my board, waiting for the one in a thousand, the rapture many people hope for but only the faithful gain. Sometimes I would close my eyes and listen for premonitions, truths of the human condition offered as whispers, birds hanging on sifted air. Those days, I could make out the echoes of places I had been, the cries of wounded hearts, youth at war, youth at play.

Sometimes I'd hear nothing at all because Bali is an island in an ocean that sits apart from the dry regions of the world, a whispered dimension, though mostly in my head. And because I love maths, I would use those moments to think about science, the magic of Copenhagen in 1929, Heisenberg arguing his uncertainty principle with Niels Bohr, using pencils to calculate the stochastic nature of time. I loved to bob in breezes disassembling Bohm's theories of consciousness, sieving them through what I understood of Camus. Slow days could be like that, surfing a point cloud of choices, paths distinct, life yours to fathom.

And I will admit that Bali is known for magic mushrooms, but this was all before I discovered two-bag shakes at the Galaxy Bar, Friday nights after we had showered up, the pre-game before band gigs on Eat Street or Kuta, where we'd hit the clubs. Perhaps I had been knocked silly too many times, but my mind tended to wander those afternoons, not with the help of psilocybin, but through darker hallucinations. I had grown tired in ways I could no longer describe, too tired to make sense of things, too tired to dream.

"Hu! Kai ko'o Loa."

Surfing gave me a chance to unwind from Timor, those pressures. I could sit out there in currents reminding myself that all choices are human, that it's okay to fail, though not forever. And though my youth was spent in mountains, the world is mostly water, so I would imagine ways it might cleanse me, the slow lick of streams, rain quenching fire. I would think back on Whitman and Thoreau, what I had read about ponds and rivers, then saltier spans crossing the Med from Gibraltar to Tangier.

I thought about what Melville had found in eddies, the older scribes of Alexandria stealing knowledge from ships seeking port, those pirates. And because most days are average, I would sit in flat waters thinking about air, because air sustains us, one endless sky. How we are all just vibration.

"Kai ko'o Loa."

Then, that day in 2012, the one I remember.

It was a stunner, low tide, the afternoon session, my second year in Bali. Every surfer has a home break, and mine was called Pantai Berawa, where I held a sixty-year lease on two hectares of beachfront rice fields between the Canggu Club and the house where Roman Polanski supposedly stayed, though I never saw him. My place was called Villa Komodo, a sprawl of gardens and stone manses built around a pool in an expat enclave, Umalas II. I had a shop called Half King Surf Collective at 177X Jalan Oberoi, in Seminyak, a wooden longboard brand called Volant, an event space where I hosted parties with my Bali band, Shotgun Slim.

"Go, son," I heard Alex say. He spoke in a calm voice, because he was short in stature but knew big things about life, our philosopher king, Alex the Australian.

"Fucking tourists," Peter Smith grumped, the other American.

I turned my head to watch some Brazilian kid disappear over my shoulder as the set rolled through, but that whole commotion was behind us, because locals chased great while visitors settled for good.

Then my buddy Tai paddled up, said, "You playing tonight?"

I said, "Hell, yeah, man. Deus. Eight o'clock. You coming out?"

"Aw, yeah, bruh," he said. "Maybe cover some Stones. I'm feeling it."

Tai Graham was two things, the best surfer on the island and a prominent drummer in a band called Pandora. Tai had a pop-up nightspot, too, which was open only Thursdays, one of those places you had to know somebody to find. It was called Black Dog. Tai was the shit.

"Say some of that Hawaiian stuff," Peter Smith told me. "I want a big one."

Darren said, "Lighten up, Yank. It's only waves."

I was known to chant between sets because I had watched all the old Bruce Brown movies about Big Waimea, how pioneers charged hard on massive guns. And it's everyone for themselves out there on big days, our wolf pack and well-known pros.

"Hu! Kai ko'o Loa," I said. Then my buddy Kenny Cole pulled up. We called him Lingus.

"Watch the boil, mate," he told me, because he'd just caught the bombie.

Boil is Aussie for hold-down, a place where the bombie dumps you after the ride, a chasm between rocks at the bottom, where air goes away. You can see it bubbling on the surface after the wave has passed, some reef hydraulic, foreboding.

"Thanks," I told him, because he knew where I was headed.

"It's a proper hold-down, mate. Look after yourself. The channel is closed."

"I believe you."

All breaks are local, so my guys knew the best locations, using features of the land for reference, because everything looks the same at sea and because waves have minds of their own. It got dark early because Bali is equatorial like Timor, and it rains a lot in December, so the skies were gray. And surfing is the highlight of every outing, but beer was important, too. A woman named Ibu Made ran a *warung* on the beach with Bintangs for a dollar. We were all getting thirsty.

I said, "It's getting late, boys. Bintang thirty. Maybe one more set."

But then Darren yelled, "Outside!" and I didn't even look, I just started scratching.

The swell appeared out of nowhere, deeper than I had previously seen. The light had gone flat, and there are shadows at sea, but it was hard to read them. It looked the way nausea feels.

Holy shit, I thought. *Is that real?*

And waves come at you in series, the third often the biggest. I made it up over the top of the first wall and felt relief . . . until I saw what was behind it.

There's a technique for tunneling under faces you cannot pull into, and it's called duck diving, but my board was too big, and the wave was too big, and I knew that my only hope was to paddle faster. I saw a guy called Frog yoking himself up the face of the second wave, Darren and Leo and Alex in various places, and it looked like everyone was going to make it, but then I saw Tai Graham, who had found the apex and was already up on his feet, dropping into the gnarliest thing I had ever been part of.

Things happen quickly in a set like that. The top of the wave is vertical, gossamer thin, the evening breezes just a mist as you pass through, thrilled to have escaped. You can't see well until you're down the other side because the spray is blinding.

"Put your back into it, mate!" Lingus was yelling, ahead of me, trying to help.

I saw the third wave coming, and it was huge, and I knew I was not going to make it, but Leo was yelling something I couldn't understand, and Darren was busy with issues of his own. Alex was trying to decide if he was going left or right; then he was just getting barreled.

And I don't know about better surfers, but my ready action drill came down to a short list of unfavorable outcomes. Tactics seem pointless when the entire horizon is rising up to kick your ass. I felt like I was walking into a gunfight waving a note from my mother.

"Paddle, mate!" Lingus called out. "Don't be a wanker!"

That's when I realized that even in a life fully formed, you have to be careful what you wish for. Most of these guys had surfed before they could walk, cut their teeth on famous drops. I had caught my first wave at the age of twenty-two, floating ankle biters off 33rd Street in Newport Beach, trying to impress a *Playboy* Playmate of the Month.

Yes, I had survived bigger drops, but only bodysurfing in chinos, which does not count. And yes, I had enjoyed sessions in famous locations, but there was no YouTube in those days, no widespread knowledge of Mavericks; freak shows like Nazaré, Todos Santos, Teahupo'o. This was not Don Henley singing "The Boys of Summer"; it was more like Wagner played backward with the oboes out of tune.

Then it had me.

I remember looking up and not seeing sky. I couldn't see the sun or the moon or Ibu Made serving Bintangs on the stairs, nothing whatsoever in terms of birds or physics or maths. The wave sucked me up the face, steeper and steeper as I tried to wish it away, fully aware that I was headed for a flogging and that the flogging would be rude.

I rolled off my board, tried to kick it free, but there was nowhere to go. The wave sucked me backward, out onto the lip, where I could turn my head and see that I was floating not in water but on air. This kind of thing happens in big waves, going over the falls, and I probably thought of myself as a tough guy at that point in life, but nobody is tough fighting Mother Nature. I remember the fall, first the loss of reference, then a long pause before I hit the surface, a blue skin of ocean parting white, stars behind my eyes.

It all happened so fast, I did not brace for impact—but that would not have mattered, because the hit came hard, knocking out the last of my wind, and then it was an intersection of worlds, everything going down, down, down.

I remember pretending it wasn't so bad, no worse than other beatings, a tumble and a wash. My arms had not dislocated, my head never hit the reef, and you may recall the first thing they teach you at SERE training is to conduct an inventory of injuries that might hinder escape. I felt unusually cold because the wave had torn off my rash guard, but even in the worst part of the beatdown, I felt myself laughing because I had been there for the big one.

Down, down, down toward the bottom of the sea.

Colder and darker, violent still. But then I felt the reef jagged against my skin and knew it was over. I felt the roil diminish, everything a froth, some kind of deepwater moan. There was this strange sense of exhilaration as I lay there, because the best feeling in the world is knowing you are going to die and then surviving. I felt safe, thinking, *Yes,* I had taunted God, but maybe God admired my resolve, maybe the whole point in chasing death was to get a sneak peek of His realm.

Right? I mean I loved the edge because I was mortal, and mortals seek revelation, the way origin story heroes live didactic arcs, chase chthonic truths, men like Icarus and Faust, women all the way back to Eve. Gunfights and high-rise buildings are no different from bombies; it's all about the view.

Chrisameechie.

The first thing I noticed once the water quieted down was that my ears hurt, so I realized I was deep. My lungs were starting to burn be-cause I was already out of air when I went under, but I had been the breath-hold champion of the Franconia College Pool, so I had that going for me. And I was used to bad situations, trained for crisis, im-mune to panic. I assured myself everything would be fine once I made it to the surface, just another swim, so I reached down to grab my leash, because boards float, and it was too dark to see, and I needed to know which way was up. Then I gathered my legs beneath me, pushed like you do coming off the bottom of a pool after a high dive, headed toward the light. I might have been smiling; it was time for a beer.

God disagreed.

At least, I think it was God, because something invisible slammed me down hard, stuffed my body flat into a hollow within the reef. It made no sense, because the water had stilled, the wave had passed.

What in hell was that? I thought.

I was running out of consciousness and didn't have a lot of time to fuck around, so I reached out my hands to feel the walls around me, crawled to my feet again and pushed again, and God slammed me down again, just like before.

And I swear I had this moment when I realized there is a place at the bottom of the ocean that is dark and cold for a reason, that this was not a dream, no hallucination, that my life fully formed had brought me here on purpose. I thought about the chain mail of arrogance that had saved me in similar situations, realized chain mail is no advantage when you're drowning.

Kita Buang, I heard somebody say, a different voice, mocking. *You ema halo?*

I felt earth beneath me, water all around, fire in my lungs, not a breath of air. I understood that my life, up to that moment in time, had been a gift, a gift that I had squandered. My spirit dimmed. My thoughts became clear. This is what I saw.

"Shit, boss, do you remember that time you stabbed me?" Brett asked.

It was a Friday, payroll, APAC's toughest day of any month. My last day in Timor.

"I never stabbed you, dude."

"The fuck you didn't."

Brett and I were the first to arrive at the eight o'clock meeting. Anyone who has ever made payroll understands the complexities of matching money coming in with money going out and we had four thousand employees at that point, all over the island. We would get together early to map out the day, the Timorese operations staff and all five expat bosses.

"What do you call that?" Brett pulled up his shirt to show where he'd taken stitches for two separate wounds.

"You stabbed Brett?" G2 asked. He was the third to arrive, a twenty-four-year-old CFO who had been in-country about a year. He looked like Howdy Doody, only shorter.

"We were arm wrestling, and I beat him," Brett claimed. "The fucker shivved me."

"Oh, I shivved you? Couple years in the jungle, and you think you're a gangster? You're a frigging architecture major from a flyover state, tough guy. Grow up. I barely broke the skin."

I kinda laughed, because Brett was an outstanding young talent, irreverent, creative, hard. We had gone through a whole cast of hopefuls those first years, searching for stars like Ay. My leadership style was to fly them in, tee them up for success, and crush them when they failed. I'm all about perseverance, because everybody gets knocked down. It's what you do when you get up.

"What about that time you bit the guard's nose off?"

"I did not bite it off."

Ay arrived for the meeting in a dress soaked with sweat. Alex strolled in, smoking. "I was there," Ay said. "You definitely bit him."

"The son-of-a-bitch stole a Rolex," I said. "I have a reputation to protect."

"Oh, sure you do, boss." Brett nodded. "Mr. Ema Halo. Ooooooo, I'm shaking."

Timor was a hard place to fit in. The local butcher would walk a cow down the street, slit its throat, gut it, and carve fillets like it was the meat counter at Piggly Wiggly. I once saw a guy with a bald eagle on a leash, and I said, "Nobody keeps a bald eagle on a leash," and I bought it for sixty bucks to set it free. But they had clipped its wings, so I had to give it back, and I was feeling violent . . . until I turned around and this Timorese had his pants down around his ankles and was having a go at himself in front of the bank. Then an Aussie tank rolled by, clouding everything with filth, so I stepped into an alley . . . where I saw a squid on a clothesline, but it was not calamari: It was a human placenta; families get together after childbirth and eat it.

"What about that time my body man got his head chopped off? At the office."

"It was two guys," Brett nodded. "Not one."

I had been sitting at my desk doing paperwork when I heard this noise, so I looked over at my best guy, Joao, who was standing outside my window, tough as can be. I was thinking he'd take care of things, but another guard walked up and chopped his head right off.

"Fuck, man," Brett said. "It was a lot of blood."

Which brings us back to drowning. What I saw at the bottom of the sea.

APAC was a "work hard, play hard" kinda place. Being CEO required indiscriminate brutality, intuition, bawdy humor, the ability to stay drunk for months at a time. And don't get me wrong, the team performed like Goldman Sachs guys in public, but you don't waste profits on sensitivity training when the employees are chopping each other's heads off every time somebody finds a ghost down a well. We had no DEI, no EAP, no HR at all.

"Quit dicking around," I told them. "It's payroll. What do we got?"

"I need one-point-two million dollars, pronto," Ay said. "The wankers are already lining up at the gate."

Nito arrived, calm as could be. Nothing fazed him.

"The UN is holding up Bemori payments pending complaint," he said.

"Why?"

"Some employee named Graham Cook went to get in his car yesterday morning and noticed something hanging out of his dog's rectum. He asked our guard to dislodge the item, and to much disgust, he realized it was a condom. He is demanding investigation."

"You can't be serious," I said.

"Got the email right here."

"What about BNU?" I asked.

"Already doing disbursements," G2 advised. "We're good, even without Bemori."

"Colonel? Anything from your shop?"

"Another day in paradise. Cum see, cum sauce."

In a rare moment of something approximating happiness, I might actually have smiled.

"Wow," I said. "Is this really happening? After forty-three payrolls, one finally works?"

"Don't jinx it, C," Ay told me. "Take the win."

But there were no wins in Timor. In that moment, I heard the boom of a transformer blowing, some screaming, and when I ran out to see what had happened, I found a man lying dead inside our walls. He had been building the second story of a house around a power line and had accidentally leaned too close. Electrocution had popped him like a cat in a microwave.

We had several hundred guards lining up for cash wages, so I had a couple of guys drag out the body. Then I walked over to shake a few hands, because I was Kita Buang, and greeting the troops is good for morale. Unfortunately, two rival groups got jealous, started a squabble, and I was fully into the whole *ema halo* thing, so I just flashed blind with rage. I was six foot four with 237 pounds of muscle at that point, because I had cut back on vodka but started shooting steroids, which you could buy over the counter. And just as I was about to go hands-on with a vocal offender, Brett ran up to tell me Maubere had kidnapped two of our mobile supervisors, stolen their scooters.

"Maybe we pay small ransom," Janni advised.

But I said, "Fuck ransom, Janni. I'm going to crush those fools."

Before my posse could assemble, I jumped into an SUV and raced two miles to a walled enclave of ancient Portuguese homes. The place reminded me of the piazza my first day in Somalia, crowded to bursting with men, women, and children, dead silent in the beating sun.

"Malae, malae!" I heard a woman yelling, then a man said, "APAC no good!"

I jumped out, blind with rage, turned to my left, where a group of thugs stood waiting.

"Where's my men, you motherfuckers?" I yelled.

Nobody said a word. The Timorese were like that: stolid, brave. They did not fear a fifty-year-old white man wearing khakis. This was an ambush.

"*Malae* no good!"

I heard the thud of rocks denting sheet metal, then the sound of breaking glass as they stoned my car. I felt a rock whisk past my head, then another. And as if on command, the kids moved behind their mothers, the mothers stepped behind their men, and the men reached down to piles of bricks they had staged to kill me. The courtyard was small, maybe thirty feet to the nearest local, and I was standing in the front yard of a house full of gangsters, no hope of escape.

"APAC no good to Timor!" a couple of bystanders were yelling. "Tidak buang kita!"

I didn't give a shit about escape. I had dyed my goatee black, wore skull rings on my fingers just for breaking heads. I was hitting three hundred milligrams of testosterone a week, benching 320 for six, had a bottle of vodka-flavored penance under my seat, just like Fred T. A man in Baucau had taught me to skin mammals by cutting a slit in the back of their necks and blowing them up like a balloon. I was doing things for recreation that I am not ready to confess.

"Fuck you!" I yelled.

I stepped behind a gate pillar and laughed at the rocks, which were harmless as long as I stayed hidden. I started waving my fists like a madman, violence an uncontrollable swell. That seemed to stun them, because it all went silent again, a slow-rolling shimmer of light. And in that moment, I stepped out from behind the pillar into this surreal calm where everybody started thinking maybe the *ema halo* thing had merit.

Out of nowhere, this little man came running at me with a shovel raised above his head, looking to brain me. I cocked my arm, and I was just about to unload when he stopped, a shovel's length away. He looked confused, and I was swollen with pharmaceutical-grade courage, the child alone in winter. I heard my old trainer Mr. Henry say, "Turn it over, turn that bitch over," and I sucked a hitch breath and sat down on my back foot, like you do.

The little man with the shovel just stood there. He stared at me. I stared at him. The thugs on the porch stared at the crowd; the crowd stared at each other. And we had this beautifully intimate moment I have experienced only among men who know that one of them is about to die in the time-proven manner, by hand, with malice. That is what I saw at the bottom of the ocean, trapped in the empty boil of my blindingly fucked-up life. That moment. It is what I most remember about Timor.

The silence and the light.

18

The Ozarks

[JUNE 2013]

I moved back to the United States on a Sunday. It was hot. I had been drinking.

"Dad's home, Dad's home!" would have been nice, but those days were over. I had been gone almost seven years. Things had changed.

The first thing I remember is clearing customs at LAX. I have never slept well on planes, so I had dropped a Xanax climbing out of Hong Kong and chased it with Dewars all the way across the Date Line. I was lucky enough to fly first class in those days, but even lying flat in Emirates pajamas, I tossed and turned all thirteen hours.

By the time I got off the plane at international arrivals, I was a hungover, sleep-deprived mess. I had the usual ten thousand dollars in my sock, because that's the limit for cash declaration, and a carry-on bag containing two T-shirts and a pair of jeans. I had a worn-out copy of *Blood Meridian,* my favorite novel; some trinkets for the kids.

The woman at passport control looked long and hard at me before saying, "Welcome home," and I walked out to the taxi stand thinking I had dodged a bullet. I bought a ride to Joe's house in Venice, but he wasn't there, because I had not warned him, so I climbed the fence, picked his lock, and crashed until noon the next day. There was a woman in the kitchen when I woke up, and I did not know her, but I told her my name, and she said, "That's what I figured."

And I'd love to call my return triumphant, but there were no banners or balloons waiting when I arrived in the heartland. Jake picked me up at the airport, but all I could think about was how everyone was driving on the wrong side of the road. Then we pulled up the driveway of a house I had never seen, only to realize Collin and Chelsea were not kids anymore. I remember some awkward hugs, wondering what was for dinner, then getting handed the keys to my old Chevy Silverado, finding myself posted up in Room 603 at the Lamplighter Motel, staring at a microwave oven and a dorm-size fridge.

This is not my beautiful house, I was thinking, because I love the Talking Heads, and when you front a band, lyrics pop up to explain things. *Let the water hold me down.*

The Lamplighter Motel had no room service, but they offered free HBO, and you could go downstairs to Ziggie's Cafe for a Starship burger and a strawberry shake. There was a Kum and Go a couple of blocks away, so I grabbed a twelve-pack of Coors, a pint of Tito's, and a toothbrush. I had a real bad feeling about the future, but if anything, I am resilient, so I plopped myself down on one of two queen-size beds and started watching *Platoon* on a twenty-eight-inch screen.

There is this part in the movie where Charlie Sheen's character says, "Hell is the impossibility of reason. That's what this place feels like. Hell."

And jet lag was always worse flying east, so I was thinking about everything I had left behind, because my family had moved to Missouri while I was gone, but as you might have guessed, I'd built a life in Asia, too. I was feeling a little bit hopeless, because I'd spent decades in denied areas, but there were no blood chits for this kind of train wreck, no numbers to call for exfil. It didn't matter that I had a suntan and could buy the Lamplighter with the money in my checking account. I was on my ass. There was no surf in Missouri. Money had no value.

I remember lying there, chasing Tito's with beer, watching that scene in *Platoon* where Chris Taylor is hiding in the jungle with the towel over his head, and he's kinda nodding off when, all of a sudden, the Cong come sneaking up the trail. Shadows in the rain. And I'll admit I'm prone to flashbacks, so I barely noticed when the jungle sidled up with the jet lag and the Kum and Go liquor to trigger misgivings that I had fled, though not forgotten, in Asia.

Before I attempt to explain my return to forever, it is important to remember that mushrooms were legal in Bali. Any day of the week, you could walk into the Galaxy Bar and order a two-bag shake. And before we add illegal drugs to my list of failures, I will note, as John Fowles wrote, that my sleep had become dreamless like all the slumbers of the damned. Micro-dosing hadn't been invented, so I embraced full-blown hallucination as a way to dig deeper into whatever I called myself. We have not yet discussed religion, but I have always believed in God, so I went looking for the Holy Ghost, thinking he might intervene against ghosts that ailed me.

My first hallucination started when I was sitting by the pool at the Kamala Pantai on one of my visa runs from Timor. I remember feeling a little apprehensive at first, because of that guy who had worked for my dad jumping out a window while on acid. But I was a risk-taker, so just before dark one Friday night, I ate a bag of jagged blue morsels, and about twenty minutes later, I felt gamelan tunes creeping across my skin, whispering poems by Rumi. It was this awesome body rush of hope, a realization that though darkness had seized me, I still remembered light.

That first revelation involved sniping, not the bisection of terrorist brain stems, but the movement of mass through space as a function of time. I remembered how, as a boy, I had worked shagging range balls at the Sunset Hill House for a pro named Phil Martignetti.

"See that young man over there?" Mr. Martignetti would ask his clients. He had a Titleist 5 iron that he called "the Truth," and he would point it right at me. "That's your target."

Tuesdays and Thursdays, I would follow him outside the tee box, where he would break the ice with a couple of jokes before outlining the basics of the draw, the fade. I would be standing next to a granite boulder in the middle of the ninth fairway, 161 yards from the tee box facing the Kinsman, which rose east, a back azimuth of 202 and a magnetic declination of 9.36 degrees. And because I loved maths, I would calculate all those numbers using made-up equations. It was a nine-hole links, opened in 1897, at 1,900 yards with a slope of 94. A Second Empire resort of 350 rooms, 150 staff, one bowling alley, and zero hope of surviving the 1970s.

I remember standing out there as clients arced shots across the sky. Most times, I could get close to where the balls landed, but sometimes I would lose shots in the clouds or the glare of the sun, and one time, a retired banker from Montreal tagged me just above the knee. I had not yet heard of that man Leibniz nor his calculations involving continuous rates of change, but my dad was fond of saying, "What goes up must come down," so I had learned calculus to protect myself in the space beneath curves. By the end of the summer, I could move to within inches of impact and shag balls with an efficiency Mr. Martignetti would brag over.

Despite those early revelations, I did not eat mushrooms again until I moved to Bali. It was during the celebration of Nyepi, which is the Balinese Day of Silence, a time for fasting and meditation. By law, everybody must stay indoors during Nyepi, hiding from the flyover demons, and there are no lights or fires allowed, lest the spirits see them and become angry. There is no travel, no recreation. The beaches are empty, the clubs dark, the whole island sheltered in place, hiding from ghosts and the *pecalang,* security officers who patrol the streets in traditional garb, looking for offenders.

Bali honors invisible things, so locals bang pots and burn coconut leaves to warn off spirits; find dark places to celebrate Omed-omedan, "the Kissing Ritual," choosing love, not for pleasure but out of faith. People read poems between raptures but feel no guilt, because Nyepi is about salvation, which has always been linked to sin.

I remember the Goddess of the Moon breathing for me, that first hallucination, the spirit of all women, the rains a cave of gardens.

I heard my mother saying, "Thursday's child has far to go," and I wondered if she was Balinese, because the Balinese celebrate a path of endlessly looping beauty. They live nourished in the belief that Sanatana Dharma will guide our missteps to someplace better, because we fail, though not forever.

God's grace is unconditional, lent freely to heal man's inherent flaws. I saw the power of love, the futility of hatred.

Which proved helpful, because faith has often confused me. I grew up Catholic, an altar boy fed fish on Fridays, believing the word of God was written in sandalwood smoke and wine-slurred Latin. When that failed me, I talked atheism with Chris Hitchens while sipping whiskey at the Frick; considered the works of Aleister Crowley, only to be washed in the blood of the murky Rappahannock.

I have read the Book of Mormon, tucked prayer notes into the wall of the Second Temple, walked barefoot with Muhammad through the Dome of the Rock, washed a pilgrim's feet in Somalia. I have breathed the moldy air of the Sistine Chapel, smoked reefer at Stonehenge, prayed the Stations of the Cross along the Via Dolorosa, paid extortion to a Hindu holy man who surveyed my surf shop with a tape measure so he could determine how much to charge for the blessing.

I have played guitar at a Baptist wedding, evoked the Old Testament God in a gunfight, sworn oaths of matrimony, pissed on an animist totem in a cemetery outside Tutuala. I have ushered spirits bloody into death, held them fresh-born as they emerged anew.

And you may ask yourself, "Well, how did I get here?"

I remember lying there in the Lamplighter Motel, watching Charlie Sheen in the jungle, thinking about the noise of the world, the price of solace, how our lives pass trajectories of their own. Then a gunfight broke out, and I said fuck it, chugged the last of the Tito's, turned off the TV. I lay on the bed pretending I was walking alone in breezes, my mind sore for comfort and Ogoh-ogoh telling me it is all right to look back on what used to be.

I held up my hand and used my fingers to count the places where I had not died. Then I closed my eyes and walked through fields of constellations, swinging wildly at those white star clusters until my arms cramped for classified reasons, because there will always be war, and God has arranged the heavens to prove it.

I was shitfaced.

I thought about my old house in Bali, the mists gathering low to the stepped terraces of rice, little cloth flags meant to scare off cobras. I felt the Moon Goddess shed me, laughing, flitting away. And then everything changed, because that's what happens in flashbacks. The light shifted from dim to blinding, and I felt myself falling, weightless and then heavy until I was back inside the man in the Lamplighter Motel, all my former selves mortal, a pilgrim lost in doubt.

In that damask moment, I felt the profound loss of a wife and four wonderful kids, a family that had once believed me noble. I thought about friends I had abandoned, abused, failed; people who would wonder why I'd gone away; parents who used to be proud.

And I was just about to ask the Moon Goddess to explain the role of free will in a life fully formed when my phone rang, and I realized it was time to get up, because Jake was calling about meeting me for coffee.

They say the first step toward sanity is acceptance of a higher power. It can be anything: a doorknob, a pierced ear, Saskatchewan. Mine was that mongrel prick Bucky Corliss. He taught me that we are all born a jungle—twisted, tangled, and raw; green with envy; crawling with hidden things, an itch. That the world lurks primitive within us, wan, a rheumy light. That man is ruled by fear, though not always his own. That we are learners.

If I ever dream again, I will be walking through mountains with the Goddess of the Moon. She will lay her hand upon my heart, and we will share a song about eternity. She will point to my reflection in a sky of lakes, and she will ask the question I got from my parents when I was a child, from the CIA when I was not.

What is your name?

I will stare up at her, trying to make sense of arcs and trajectories, the paths of golf balls over New Hampshire, arrows through jungles, bullets across savannahs. In that moment, I will admit that it is not a name I have lost along the way. It is the concept itself. Identity.

People can ask all they want. I have no idea.

The second time someone assumed I was crazy, it was a three-part diagnosis. The first part involved a professional referral from Rose, who had earned her doctorate in psychology and hung out a shingle. The second part involved some poor son of a bitch who probably needed therapy himself after a couple of sessions with me. The third was the most difficult: It came from a guy in a mirror trying to be honest with himself. The ego confronting the id.

My return to America was not an easy transition, not by any measure. There was the whole matter of logistics, trying to repatriate money and possessions. The jet lag didn't help; nor did my early attempts at swearing off booze.

It took me only a couple of weeks to move out of Room 603 and into a two-bedroom apartment with a single bed and a couple of guitars. The boys found me a building in need of renovation, so I bought it, along with a Harley and a nine-pound sledgehammer. I decided that I would spend one calendar year living sober. I promised to have no interaction with the outside world except Home Depot, building inspectors, my family, and a homeless guy I hired because he claimed to have been a bass player for David Allan Coe.

It worked well enough for about three months, and I really felt I was making progress. But then Rose sat me down over scones one morning, kindly told me that if I had any hope of finding my way back to health I should seek help. I agreed, of course, because I loved her, and that was the whole point in giving up surfing.

She referred me to a reputable therapist, who ultimately corroborated what I imagined her diagnosis would be. I scheduled the appointment myself, but it took several cancellations before I finally worked up the nerve to show. It was late summer when I rode my Harley to a strip mall across the street from where I had started, all those years ago, at the FBI's Springfield resident agency.

"Hi. What is your name?" the receptionist asked.

"My name?" I shrugged. "I thought that kind of stuff was confidential."

"Pretty much, but how else can I bill your insurance?"

I looked around the office, saw that it was empty, a safe space decorated with silk ferns, vinyl chairs, and a bowl full of lollipops.

"Jon," I told her. "My name is Jon."

She gave me a clipboard with some forms to fill out, and when I was done, I asked if it would be okay for me to record things. I thought "Dr. Rosie" might want to review the session later.

"It's your fifty-five minutes, Jon. Record all you want."

I transcribed the session. I will print it here:

cw: Hi.

drm: Hi. Chris, right?

cw: Sure.

drm: This says Jon Christopher, but . . .

cw: Chris, yeah. That's fine. Call me Chris.

drm: All right, Chris. Nice to meet you. How can I help? What brings you in today?

cw: You're a shrink, right? My wife picked you.

DRM: Your wife picked me?

CW: She's a psychologist, works for the railroad. I think it's mostly addictions, conductors who deal with people driving through crossings, getting hurt on the job, suicides, stuff like that.

DRM: Stuff like what?

CW: She knows you somehow, knows about you, said you come recommended.

DRM: I mean, how may I help you?

CW: I don't know. This was her idea. She told me there are things I need to resolve if I have any chance of getting back on track.

DRM: Issues to resolve?

CW: Alcohol, anger, cognition. You got a *DSM*-IV, right? Pick a chapter.

DRM: Do you think you have mental health issues?

CW: You're the professional, brother. Figure it out.

DRM: Figure it out?

CW: They teach you that in shrink school? Repeat everything I say? It drives me nuts.

DRM: Do you think you're nuts?

CW: What are you people called? Therapists? Counselors? What do I call you?

DRM: I'm a psychologist. Please call me Daniel.

CW: Master's?

DRM: I have a master's and a PhD. Those are my diplomas, licenses, credentials.

CW: Just so you know, I don't believe in any of this.

DRM: You don't believe in what?

CW: Therapy. Talking to a guy like you is not going to help a guy like me.

DRM: What is a guy like you?

CW: We've only got an hour.

DRM: Tell me a little bit about yourself. You said you've been away. Been away where?

CW: Asia, mostly. Before that it was Africa, Middle East, Kosovo—is Kosovo part of Europe? Yemen, Pakistan, Israel, Vietnam, Afghanistan, I don't keep track; all over.

DRM: Are you from Springfield?

CW: No.

DRM: Where did you grow up?

CW: New Hampshire.

DRM: What do you do for a living?

CW: Lots of things. I like to write.

DRM: Anything I would know?

CW: Probably not. My last book was years ago. Some poems.

DRM: But you live here now.

CW: Apparently.

DRM: You said you have children?

CW: Four.

DRM: Do you live with them?

CW: No.

DRM: Do you live alone?

CW: Yes.

DRM: Job?

CW: I don't need a job.

DRM: Why not?

CW: I made a lot of money in Asia.

DRM: Hobbies? What do you like to do for fun?

CW: I like rodeo, guitar. But all I do is work, manual labor. I haven't had a drink in three months. I don't go out, not even once. I try to spend time with Rose and the kids. Manual labor. I just work. I get up and put my boots on and go up to my building and work.

DRM: All right. What about your parents? Brothers, sisters? Any issues there? Substance abuse? Depression? Tell me about growing up in New Hampshire.

CW: My dad never drank, but his dad died from it. Cirrhosis of the liver. My mother took what she called nerve pills. We didn't always get along.

DRM: Didn't get along?

CW: You're doing it again.

DRM: I'll tell you what. I'm just going to listen. You seem a bit angry, and I don't want to make you uncomfortable, so talk if you want, or we can sit here and have a nice quiet think for the next forty-five minutes. I have nowhere else I need to be.

CW: Everybody says that. You know? That I'm angry. I'm not angry. I'm just telling you it does not help, turning everything I say into a question.

Protracted silence.

CW: All right. Fuck it. In January 2006, I was the most famous FBI agent in the world.

DRM: The most famous FBI agent in the world?

CW: It started on 9/11, with *Larry King*. Then I got hired by NBC to do all their programs, *Meet the Press*, the *Today* show, *Hardball*, *CheckPoint CNBC*. I was a regular on *Imus in the Morning*, did *Politically Incorrect; Howard Stern*, in studio with

Robin, what else . . . *Arsenio Hall. The Daily Show; Coast to Coast* with Art Bell, remember that lunatic? I got a prime-time game show with Penn Gillette, called *Identity,* which is ironic as hell, because I've had a lot of them.

DRM: A lot of what?

CW: Identities. Work stuff. Shit I made up on my own because it was fun. I did a BBC show once with Don King, which was weird. I did *Breakfast with Frost;* had a book signing in London at Harrods with a life-size cardboard cutout, and it was half a block from where I lived junior year in college. *Breakfast with Frost* was big. Ever heard of it?

DRM: No, sorry.

CW: I almost got to sit in with Warren Haynes one time, on *Jimmy Kimmel Live!* I had an op-ed contract with *The New York Times,* masthead at *GQ,* spreads in *FHM, Men's Health,* the Sunday *Magazine.* I started out writing speeches in D.C., used to ride down to the White House in a GTO convertible for meetings in the Oval Office. I met Prince Charles one time at Windsor Castle, a polo match, and he almost ran me over with his pony.

DRM: "Sit in"? Sit in how?

CW: Playing guitar. Warren Haynes is the shit, but it didn't work out.

DRM: Prince Charles, the future king of England?

CW: I toured with a speakers' bureau, corporate events, university debates against Nadine Strossen, president of the ACLU. I spoke to Parliament, drank at the Soho House in New York, Hal's in Venice, Claridge's in London. Private jets, parties at Sub Mercer, movie premieres, box seats, parties at the Chateau Marmont. Hell of a run.

DRM: The ACLU?

CW: It was great. All these fascinating people I got to hang out with. All the best restaurants, front row at *Saturday Night Live,*

first-class travel, awesome hotels. I rode in the pace car at the
Talladega 500. I was a volunteer fireman. I drank out of the
Stanley Cup at Luc Robitaille's house in 2002 with the Red
Wings. His wife, Stacia, was a singer. They had this big plexi-
glass stage over their pool. I had a wife and four kids, kind
parents, generous friends. But then, one day, I bought a ticket
to Nairobi and dropped off the face of the earth.

DRM: Chris, are you all right?

CW: I was working side projects with David Mamet, Michael
Schiffer, Peter Berg, Freddy Forsyth; chamber concerts at the
Morgan; exhibitions at the Frick. I rented the penthouse
mansion across from the Met for the release of my second
novel, with an introduction by Ron Insana. It was a beautiful
night, the Philharmonic playing in Central Park. It was a spy
thriller called *White,* the most realistic treatment of classified
operations ever published, from continuity-of-government
infrastructure at Mount Weather to secure communications
networks in the White House. Everyone thought it a bunch of
fiction except for people who knew what I was divulging, and
they were pissed. That was probably the end of my writing
career, because you do not screw with those people; they made
me an example. Then back up to New Hampshire on the
weekends to hang with Rosie, watch the kids play soccer, mow
the lawn.

DRM: Chris.

CW: I had these special skills, right?

DRW: Mr. Whitcomb.

CW: Shooting, interrogation, disguise. And I figured out this
great gig working the line between what governments can
legally do and what corporations can't otherwise accomplish.
Money and tradecraft, sources and methods. Knowledge is
power, brother, but power involves money, and I went deep
down that hole, I'll tell you that for free.

DRM: Can I get you something? Would you like some water?

CW: It all seemed so intriguing, secret this and secret that. I could be anybody I wanted. I had famous friends, friends in governments, too; it's all connected. So, I'd flit between them, the FBI guy when it served me, drinking Pimm's with a fake accent when I needed a thrill.

DRM: I can call your wife.

CW: I would go way the hell out there where no one was going to find me. Then I'd go home and be "Dad" to the kids, "sweetheart" to Rosie. I ran that motherfucker for twenty-five years, ran it into the ground. Now it's Missouri; a single bed; an old saddle; and a pair of steel-toe boots.

DRM: Chris, I think I'm going to pause this here, for a minute. I'm going to get you a bottle of water. Let's rest a bit and then we can schedule another appointment when you're feeling better.

CW: When I lived in Timor, the locals said I had *ema halo,* which roughly translated to "making people forget." "Forget to live." Over time I realized that I wanted to forget myself.

DRM: Mr. Whitcomb.

CW: That darkness. That's why I'm here.

19

Bogotá, Colombia

[JANUARY 2014]

I found my higher power during a bluegrass gospel performance at the SAC River Cowboy Church. The congregation didn't have a building of their own at the time, so we met at a stockyard used for auctioning cattle. I could waste your time explaining, but you may remember I once called myself "Team Rope Header" and I liked wearing a cowboy hat. Jesus re-entered my life as a bull rider named Sidd—which works just fine, because God has a whole bunch of six-pack names. The important thing is that I traded faith in three-letter agencies for one that seemed kinder.

And I don't want to brag, but by the end of my first year, things were looking up.

I had just lived 371 consecutive days of sobriety, had been declared stable by a psychologist named Daniel, had moved into the third-floor loft of a stunning six-thousand-square-foot Victorian mercantile building I had worked hard to renovate in a hip part of town. I had helped Mick and his wife, Paige, open a store called Nomad, where they sold things we shipped back from Asia. And most important, I had convinced Rosie that it was now safe for me to attend Collin's high school basketball games and clap along as Chelsea and the cheer team worked the sidelines. I believed my dark days at the Lamplighter were behind me.

Chrisameechie.

As it turned out, my old buddy L. Bellagio had been busy, too. He had worked his way onto Hollywood's A-list as a director of movies you most certainly have seen. He knew every producer in town and sounded confident when he called me with the idea of pitching a television series called *Police and Thieves.* The premise was simple: that men who fight monsters sometimes become monsters themselves. I had been to the hard parts of the world, he told producers, bloodied myself in the battle between good and evil, lost my bearings somewhere between those assignations. L. Bellagio thought viewers might find it interesting to ride along as I retraced my path from the flames of Mount Carmel to warrens full of lesser angels. It was okay that I had broken; I was healing at the broken places.

The show sold quickly to HBO. We filmed the pilot in Colombia.

"Como estas," the series starts, with a man called Sombra. It was my first on-camera interview since Guantánamo Bay. Sombra is carrying a fighting cock and an M4 carbine with an infrared laser and a suppressor. He's wearing white Crocs, a flat-top haircut, and a T-shirt that reminds me of Noriega.

"Bien, mi amigo. Gracias," I tell him.

Then he says, "Dicen que estuviste aquí durante la guerra contra las drogas. FBI."

But I don't speak Spanish, so I say, "Sorry. Hablo poco español."

He nods because he doesn't speak my language, either, but he is a sniper like I used to be, and there is a special bond in certain professions that requires no translation.

"'Sombra' means 'shade,'" our interpreter tells me, though nothing in this part of Latin America ever fully makes sense. Colombia is a beautiful country marred by decades of violence, the murky interactions of drug cartels, FARC and ELN guerrillas, paramilitary enforcers, and three-letter agencies throwing Just Say No dollars at a war nobody will ever win. Sombra is a member of a secretive forty-man special reconnaissance team, one of those shadow warriors you read about, a bugbear who hides in the jungle until you least expect him. Then one night, your coke lab explodes, and your ears end up on a string around his neck.

These guys are heroes, professionally sound in vilified ways.

"Can you believe this place?" Joe asks me at one point. Joe the photographer. "It's a frat house for killers, Whit. You see that guy with the grenades?"

And I should block the scene a bit, because the *Police and Thieves* concept was simple, but everything else requires some explaining. Though I had just spent one calendar year renovating a building, I was still not at the top of my game. I had grown my hair to my shoulders, added a second full sleeve of tattoos, stopped shaving for a year. I tried to dye the gray brown, because I hated the face I saw in the mirror, but the brown faded ochre, then orange, reminding me of Sufi Muhammad, which did not help my self-esteem. My driver's license photo would scare you.

"So, what are you thinking?" Michael had asked L. Bellagio during that first pitch meeting in L.A. I'm talking about Michael Lombardo, of course, the president of HBO. His mind was rapier sharp, his office impressive.

"I'm thinking Whit knows evil," L. Bellagio told him. "Let's dig up some of those old boots he buried doing spy stuff in jungles. Maybe meet some secret units fighting well-known offenders."

"Cops and robbers?"

"Police and thieves."

Michael Lombardo kept looking at me like he wanted to call Security. But I was thinking, this is the guy who built *Game of Thrones, Boardwalk Empire, True Detective,* so he was probably cool with complex characters.

"You were in the FBI?" he asked me. "Seriously?"

"Yut."

"Interesting." Then he turned to L. Bellagio. "All right. How much do you need?"

"We'll work it out. Call Ari."

A couple of months later, I found myself standing on the terrace of a confiscated villa in Bogotá, looking down on the ghettos of Uzme. Our HBO crew consisted of a producer named Brandon; a director named Serge; the sound guy, who will remain nameless because sound guys always remain nameless; and Joe, because Joe is a line item on every budget.

"Let's go, Whit," he told me. "Quit dicking around. We're going to lose the light."

The light, I should note, was gorgeous. Bogotá is a sprawling metroscape built low into mountains, the old and the new and the barrios, which are hard to describe. Poverty looks different from a confiscated villa full of killers when you are from Hollywood and trying to dig up boots wielding egos and cameras.

"Vive usted aquí?" I asked Sombra once we were inside.

Serge had set up a two-shot in the living room, where there was a huge fireplace and three leather couches. It was a large, open room with vaulted ceilings and lots of glass. I was thinking it must have been beautiful when the drug dealers owned it.

"They live here between missions," our handler said. Every agency has a flack, but Sombra's team was Colombian, and this guy was American, which seemed odd but not really.

"Como estas?" Sombra nodded to Serge. "Aquí?"

"*Aquí,* yes." Serge pointed to one of the couches. "That's good."

Then a second member of Sombra's unit walked in to see what was going on. "Hola, hola." He laughed a little bit. "Hollywood Sombra."

The guys called the new guy "El Diablo" because he had this fiery look, but I called him "bro" because I once worked with his boss. He was wearing Diesel jeans with sky-blue Timberland boots, had a big yoked-up pit bull on one of those choke-chain collars with a harness-leather muzzle. I was sitting on the other couch, and the dog started growling, tried to come my way.

"Sorry," El Diablo said, but he wasn't. Guys are guys, always pissing on each other's legs.

"No problem." I smiled. "Dogs bark at me."

Joe said, "Who's a good boy?" He liked dogs. "Who's a good boy? Look at that fucking thing, Whit. Let's put him in the shot."

Then the sound man said, "Can we do anything about the weights?"

Serge said he'd get the dog on B-roll, later, then pointed to Brandon, who walked into an adjacent room that had been converted into a gym. He said something to one of the guys working out on a squat rack, and things quieted down.

"What about his pistol?" I asked. "Should we turn him, so it shows?"

Serge said, "Nah. It's just a head shot; you'll never see it."

"Head shot?" Diablo prickled.

"It's a term of art, bro," I told him. "*Relajarse.*"

And that brings us to the point in the story. Once Serge set the shot, and the sound guy positioned his boom, Sombra and I talked for a bit, a typical back-and-forth, questions and answers. I had done a lot of interviews during my years on TV, conducted FBI investigations, taught interrogation to the CIA. Most times, things stay formal, both parties clinging to roles, the good cop/bad cop sort of thing.

But there was a moment, about an hour into our talk, when Sombra got very quiet, and the villa got quiet, and the rest of the people in the room got quiet, even the dog. Sombra told me a story about an op they had done, a big job with his entire unit going after a high-value target somewhere in the mountains. There had been a helo ride and a hot landing, with door gunners raking shit down, and it was really heavy for a long time, so long that it started to get dark, and they all realized they were going to be pinned down for the night.

Sombra looked at me in that familiar way, nodded, then told me about how he ended up in a mortar crater with two of the men he had killed. It was a small hole, and he couldn't get out of it, and nobody was coming in, because it was a classified mission, so he lay there between two men he had gutted. The sun went down, and the moon came up, and killing the two men had been easy, but he was Catholic and had been raised an altar boy, proud of the sacraments, including confession. And it was hot in the jungle, even at night, but the bodies lying against him got cold, they got stiff; they had nothing to say.

Sometime in the middle of the night, he had a dream that his father was there in the hole with him, though his father had passed. And his father didn't say anything in the dream, but when he was little, Sombra remembered, his father had told him that an enemy soul could not haunt him if he touched the body humbly. So, in the dream, he placed one hand on each man, and in that moment, his father was gone. The fear was gone, the night eventually ended, he got away.

And I didn't say anything after we were through, because the interview was for HBO, just theater. But Sombra's team invited me to stay the night, so after Joe and the others went back to the city, Sombra and I had dinner and shot some guns. Then we went down to the team room, which was in the cellar, painted camouflage with netting on the ceiling. They had a shitload of beer in fridges, and we drank it all.

About midnight, Sombra and I had a nice chat, where language did not seem to be a problem. When we were finished, I went up to a roomful of bunk beds, where everyone was snoring. I lay there, safe among soldiers who knew the human cost of inhuman acts. I thought about being trapped in a hole with death, wishing my dad had come in dreams to explain things. I thought about how Rosie was not from that world and could never understand, but that she wore a shine coat of love and patience, forgiveness that felt unconditional even at the Lamplighter Motel. I thought about kids, our kids, how they had chosen goodness, despite me, the optimism of youth. I remembered the Farm, the Clear Day Farm, where I had started out optimistic.

In the morning, I got up, took a shower, and put on clothes the Jungla had given me. The DEA-backed group of commandos featured in *Police and Thieves*. I shaved in a mirror steamy from the showers, wiped away the fog, and saw a clean-cut man, felt hopeful that my image was changing.

When Mick and Jake were small, we would take them to a playground near Lunga Reservoir, a recreation area for Marine Corps families living TDY at the Basic School in Quantico. The FBI Academy was just down the road, and the HRT compound was part of that campus. In those days, there was no base security at all, just a single Stop sign between our house and what we referred to as the back gate in Stafford. Lunga had a little beach and a merry-go-round, swings, and one of those stilt houses with a slide and a pole.

Weekends when I was in town, Rosie would pack a cooler, and we'd drive the kids over for a swim. Sometimes we'd walk the Yellow Brick Road, which is famous among military and law enforcement types, a lovely trail through the woods. Occasionally, the boys would want to shoot guns or sit in helicopters, so we'd drive over to the office and have a look around. This one day, I decided fourth grade was old enough to learn full automatic, so I loaded up an MP5, and we walked out to the ranges.

Rosie said, "You two pay attention to Dad. This stuff is serious."

I said, "Listen to your mom. She saw a guy get shot to death outside a liquor store when we lived in D.C. Guns are dangerous, but they can be your friends, too."

Mick said, "What?"

Jake said, "Hurry up, Dad. I gotta pee."

I showed them the basics: how to keep the muzzle pointed downrange, the Weaver stance, sight alignment, trigger pull, follow-through. Then I made sure everybody was wearing eyes and ears and took the boys under my arm one shooter at a time. Jake went first, a couple of single-fire rounds of 9 mm, which are loud but no problem for a grade-schooler, very little recoil.

"Make it go faster," he told me.

So, I switched from single fire to full auto and told him to hang on as we rolled a magazine into the berm. Both boys stood quiet for a minute, because it was a lot of action, and neither of them really knew when the shooting was over.

"It sounds like a train," Jake said.

I showed them how to drop the magazine, put the thing on Safe, and do a tactical reload. Then Mick stepped up, and we did it all over again.

"Well, what do you think?" Rosie asked when we were done.

Mick said, "Cool. But I got one question. Why do the bullets come out sideways?"

Rosie laughed, and I laughed, then the boys laughed, because kids want to be like their parents. I never got that out of my head, how everything seems so literal when you're a child.

"That's not bullets, bud," I told him. "It's the spent casings. They're not going to hurt you. The bullets come out the barrel, but they are going too fast to see and they will hurt you."

"Yeah, right, Dad. Nothing goes too fast to see."

Mick and Jake were a year apart but best friends, Irish twins, so much alike. They were curious and kind, athletic, and they paid attention in school. There were no video games in those days, so they would play outside, dreaming up adventures while I was in places like Chiang Mai.

After a while, we walked over to the hangar, and I showed them the helicopters. They were hungry, so we went across the street to the cafeteria for lunch with the new agent trainees, who seemed happy because they had not seen their own kids for months. Later, we went home, and Rosie gave the kids a bath, and it was still wonderful that third year on HRT.

I would tuck them into bed, twin beds in the first room at the top of the stairs. I had written them a fanciful story about growing up in the White Mountains with the Hackyerhairoff Indians, a brave yet notorious tribe who had helped Rogers Rangers find their way home from a battle near Lake Champlain. Sometimes I would bring in my guitar and sing them a song I had written with their names in it. If they'd been really good, I would tell them stories about the Lost Boys, how there were trapdoors beneath their beds that would mysteriously open when they were older to reveal great treasures, but only when the treasures were ready to be found.

Then, that one night after the trip to Lunga, Jake had a nightmare. I was in a mood to slay dragons, so I scooped him up in my arms.

"Easy, bud," I whispered. "It's just a dream."

"I know, Dad," he told me, trembling. "But I was out in the woods, and there were some people with guns, and they were hunting Jakes, and I was scared because I was a Jake."

I sat there on his bed until he fell back asleep. I was thinking about when I was his age, trapped in dreams, confused about process. I remembered how I would lie in bed after Saturday night Mass, the altar boy trying to make sense of angels. How some had wings, others had fangs, Vantablack spears ready to slaughter the willing. I thought about the seraphim throne guards of God, those lesser angels, too, whether or not I still knew the difference.

And we went to Mass every Sunday in those years, a Catholic church in Aquia Harbour. Rose and the kids. It was a big church with a T-shaped nave, an altar in the middle. The church was always full of military and law enforcement families living straight and narrow, the best of humankind. I remembered standing in church for the Lord's Prayer one time, everyone looking reverently down with their eyes closed, but I had mine open, composing a five-paragraph order, trying to decide how I would fight my way through them. I started with the men I knew: HRT, the strongest first; then the marines; the fat, the weak, the elderly sporting O_2 tanks and walkers.

"They're just kids," Rosie told me that night, after Jake's dream, when we were alone. "Kids have dreams. It's not your fault."

I don't remember what I said, because my mind was spinning. All I could think of was how I had been a child once myself, asleep in the room at the top of the stairs, scared without a brother beside me, because we slept alone. Boogeyman under the bed.

"I love you, Spooch," I told her. I called her Spooch.

"I love you, too," she said. "It will all be great in the morning."

Things were simpler then.

.   .   .

We spent about three weeks in Colombia shooting *Police and Thieves.* We started with the commandos known as the Jungla, traveled to their training center in El Espinal in the back of troop trucks under canvas tops. We hired fixers who walked us into the barrios, where the police were not allowed to go. I met the man we called "El Diablo" there. He had been shot through the arm when rival gangs were having a party and it was too loud for his daughter to sleep. He introduced me to a man who had been gutted in prison, showed me where they had sewn him back together, cried explaining that humans try to be good, but it's hard.

After about three weeks mapping the line between good and evil, we went up to the roof of the hotel, where they had a bar looking out over the city. We had filmed signs of the war on drugs, the bullet holes in buildings; had toured places tourists were not allowed to go, the darkest parts of the favelas. One of the crew bought pure cocaine from a local plantation, and I almost tried it, thinking it was just a plant, not the root of all evils.

I didn't.

The next morning, Serge told everyone that we had not yet filmed the true face of thieves, at least not a face worthy of HBO. So, without telling anyone, he had found a former death squad commander who would talk to us on camera. The man claimed the rank of general and went by a nickname I didn't understand. He lived about three hours away and had agreed to meet us for a coffee. I should have asked questions, but I didn't, because I had set aside sobriety and was hungover; it was our last day trip, and we were ready to go home.

We left the hotel after breakfast. Brandon, Joe, the sound man, and I climbed into a van with a driver, called "El Gato." It was all smoking and joking on our way out of town, Brandon checking in with Serge riding in a separate car with the primary fixer. We stopped a couple of times to piss and shoot B-roll. Then, after four hours of driving, we crossed a bridge over a broad band of light brown waters.

I said, "Wait a minute. Is that the Catatumbo River?"

Joe said, "The what?"

I said, "Brandon?"

He said, "El Gato?"

El Gato just nodded his head.

"Are we going into Catatumbo?" I asked.

No answer.

So, I asked Brandon to call Serge in the car behind ours, and he admitted that he had not told me, but I had not asked, either. And by the time I had finished calling him a stupid motherfucker, we were already across the bridge and in one of the most dangerous places on earth. There is no law in Catatumbo, no police or military presence. The Jungla did not know we were there, because no one had told them. We could not call Sombra or anyone else, because there was no cell service.

I will admit that I have done some stupid shit in my life, but this ranked with the worst. As it turned out, Serge had made secret arrangements to pay ten thousand dollars in cash for an interview with HBO to a general who was most famous for taking forty Colombian soldiers captive, hanging them from trees, and sodomizing them with broomsticks as they died. He had not bothered to research the general. He had not checked travel times, comms, the veracity of his fixers. To be fair, I should have been paying attention, but I had not.

I could tell you how it was a miracle we escaped being kidnapped and held for ransom by a general famous for atrocities; that we raced through villages and jungle trails for hours, flanked by men on motorcycles with AK-47s, trying to hunt us down. But I have already told enough stories about death, and we obviously survived, so whatever. The whole debacle was recorded on camera, with sound, so maybe it will turn up on TV someday.

The point to the story is that once we got back across the river, we stopped in a dirt lot outside a bodega. Our fixer got a call from a cousin of his who worked for the general, and the cousin was crying, begging us to come back, because they had a gun to his head, and they were going to kill him if we did not comply.

I took the phone and said, "Is he listening? The general?"

The cousin said, "Yes."

I said, "Fuck yourself, General. We're not coming back. Kill that crying prick."

Joe and I went to a local bar later that night for beers, and I ordered a burger. We talked about all the times we had gotten lucky, that cinder block room at the Wesh–Chaman crossing where we knew we were going to die.

How just when everything seemed darkest, those louvered doors had burst open and Raziq the warlord had stormed into the room wearing a North Face parka, yelling, "Mr. Chris! Mr. Chris! You are late!"

How Cat Stevens on Crack and the others were Raziq's men. How it's difficult to tell the good guys from the bad, because it's all really just a matter of opinion.

Joe said, "Think the general killed him? The fixer?"

I said, "Better him than us. Please pass the ketchup."

The next day, I got ahold of Sombra, and we went to a tattoo shop where we both got inked. We talked about death and forgiveness. When we were done, I looked down at my right arm and saw a banner with large red letters spelling out "NOITPMEDER."

It was "REDEMPTION" spelled backward, so I could read it in a mirror.

That is when I realized *Police and Thieves* would never be picked up as a series, because not even HBO can explain certain things. And that was where I made the turn.

20

Zimbabwe, Africa

[OCTOBER 2018]

Zimbabwe is the only country I entered walking.

Meaning I have no immigration stamp in any passport, though I did take a bunch of pictures. One of those photos depicts four men on a railroad trestle, two in nicely tailored suits, two dressed for leisure. We are all wearing shades, none of us has a gun, everyone is smiling.

I mention this scene for two reasons. The first is to prove that not all trips to Africa involve war, kidnapping, or famine. The second is to claim this photo as the single most important evidence of my return from shadows to the visible world. Bogotá had revealed parts of me that might be worth saving, but closure is more than a tattoo you can read in a mirror.

And though a picture is worth a thousand words, this is a book with no illustrations, so allow me to introduce the characters. The first man in the photo is Michael Lee, a sales executive—tall, smart, and handsome with a full head of hair. He lives in Texas, writes novels about big-game hunting, and claims to have killed more things than I have. A bald-faced lie.

The second man in the photograph is Big Jim Davis, a six-foot-ten former special agent in charge of the FBI's Denver Field Office, longtime chief of the National Press Office, number one man in Baghdad during the war. I have a mug shot of him in the shower with Saddam Hussein, shortly after the capture, administering *habeas grabus* to the world's most wanted fugitive. Jim got a kick out of telling people that when Delta pulled Saddam out of the hole, he had four hundred thousand dollars in cash, a .45-caliber pistol, and a case of Butterfinger candy bars. He said Saddam was a nice guy for a monster, a proud leader, even during delousing.

The third character in the photograph was a quiet geneticist called Niles. Fourth was me, of course, and the man behind the lens was an elegant Dutchman we will call Mies de Cravat. Mies spent most of his career as an executive for luxury brands, most recently Estée Lauder. He spoke all the Romance languages, dressed impeccably in exotic locations.

Now that you know the players, I will block the scene.

By the end of 2015, I had decided to try my hand, again, at being a team rope header. Bogotá was great, but HBO passed on the series, so after several months following the Professional Bull Riders tour, I settled on a stunning stretch of mountains outside Livingston, Montana. I know this is a long way from Zimbabwe, but bear with me. I have no simple stories.

"What are you doing?" I heard a man ask. It was Big Jim Davis. "Are you in Montana?"

"I'm freezing my nuts off," I told him. "Trying to rope this bull."

"What bull?"

It was snowing hard, three degrees below zero. My birthday.

"Are you on the goddamned phone?" my other buddy yelled.

His name is Kent Hanawalt, and he is one of the great cowboys of his generation, a philosopher fan of Thomas Sowell and Wild Turkey; nimble in the saddle, fun around campfires. It was Kent's bull we were roping on his wife, Kathy's, family homestead, the Lazy H. If you have ever seen the movie *A River Runs Through It,* you have seen their place, that wide shot of mountains where Brad Pitt talks about youth in voice-over narration.

Michael Keaton lives there on the West Boulder River, near Tom McGuane, whom I mention only because both are artists who cherish the spiritual beauty of the place. Poets live there, too, like my buddy Brian Trisler and the spiritualist chef Phil Minsky. Songwriter Katherine Taylor Davis sings its rhythms, fiction writer Callan Wink fly-fishes there dreaming up stories, as did Jim Harrison, a favorite. The brilliant American artist Ellie Lukens throws stones in pools and paints hope-disguised ripples en plein air. If you ever go there, call out the name

"Senior," and the falling waters will remind you of a beautiful man named Michael who has passed on, but remains. I think of him often.

"What do you need, Big Man?" I hollered into my cell, over the wind.

"I've got a job for you."

"Doing what?"

"Who cares? I need help."

"Where?"

"Denver. I'll see you in the morning."

Then Kent yelled, "Whit, you're as worthless as tits on a Chevy."

"Sorry, boss. It was my buddy Jim."

"Sorry won't cut it, Whit. Pull that slack, goddammit!"

And I know what you're thinking: that Zimbabwe is a long way from the Lazy H, but that's the way it works in a life fully formed. You can't get hung up on maps, or reason. As it turns out, Big Jim Davis had retired from the FBI and thrown in with an entrepreneur named George, who is best known for creating America's 911 emergency call system. George is brilliant, a humanist, keenly focused on saving the world. He sure as hell helped save me.

Which brings us back to Africa, because that job Big Jim mentioned was helping George build a Rapid DNA company that could ID bad guys like bin Laden using a man-portable box that fit inside the trunk of a car. My job was to sell technology to spy agencies around the world, from Mossad and MI6 to lesser-known entities in places like Ukraine and Mozambique.

"Holy shit. Look at those hippos," I remember Michael Lee saying as we circled Victoria Falls in a King Air 500 on our way from Beira to Lusaka. "Wish I had my rifle."

The great thing about flying private across Africa is that from three thousand feet, the beauty is vast but manageable. There is so much to gawk at: the plains where Hemingway hunted impalas; famous lakes; the Zambezi. I remember imagining what Livingstone had encountered trading beads with Subiya-Kololo chief Sekeletu in search of diamonds. I thought about Robert Redford and Meryl Streep in a biplane acting out Karen Blixen's memoirs of colonial times.

Then we landed at the Livingstone airport, the cabin door opened, and we looked out to see the tarmac completely deserted except for a marching band in full military regalia playing "Auld Lang Syne."

"A party?" Big Jim said, that Bill Murray line from *Stripes.* "For me?"

After lunch at the Royal Livingstone, we wandered across the bridge into Zimbabwe, then flew back to dinner near Melrose Arch, in Johannesburg, with a small white man in a red Ferrari. His name was Dr. Smith, and if every government has a financial shaman, he was the snake rattler for the African National Congress. I have had few man crushes in my day, but this guy was brilliant, rich in obvious ways: Einstein hair, mustard stains on his single-stitch suit.

I realize that I sometimes work back and forth through plot lines, but that's the way it works in the intelligence community. You start out roping a bull on the West Boulder, sneak into Zimbabwe for selfies, end up at Melrose Arch having dinner with a white guy in a Ferrari.

"Look at that sign," Niles said, pointing at the wall of an esplanade as we dined on grilled springbok. It was a billboard for Courvoisier: "One Life. Live Them."

We all laughed, sorting spoons at that lovely dinner. Then Dr. Smith said, "I think we will take eight. Eight units at first, with tech support. What is that, four million dollars?"

Big Jim, the FBI man through and through, said, "What about customs?"

The intelligence officer at our table said, "We do not have to worry about customs."

Of course not, I thought. *Spies never stoop to logistics.*

There are some things I have not told you. I feel bad, considering all the time we've spent together, but my truths have always been guarded.

I have not told you that my brother's name is Michael; that he is seven years my junior, a cook turned cop turned fireman, the youngest. I have not told you that my sister, Kerry, was captain of the cheerleading squad in high school, born February 29, a leap year baby, that she married a skier named John, raised two lovely daughters. I have not told you that my favorite number is seven; that my mother is a fire sign, Aries; that I once got in a study hall fist-up with my buddy Gary Braun over a girl named Kathy Aldrich. He won.

I have mentioned Uncle Harold and a man with three watches, but have not explained the Christmas party at Meg Ryan's house. I have not told you that my uncle Mike's real first name was "Michel," which he hated. I have introduced Sue, but not other poolside conversations I may or may not have had in Chiang Mai. I have not said that I used to spar with Jon Voight at Wild Card West, that he has a wicked left hook.

I have disguised sources and methods, leaning on legally prescribed omissions because there are rules about publishing secrets in books. Maybe you understand.

And quite frankly, we're down to our last pages, so you're probably wondering about other things, too, some big reveal exposing hidden truths of the world. You want to know how a good man could have gone so bad, chasing a slant of light up a broad, gray river in search of a snail crawling the edge of a razor. Fair enough. I can boil it down to a single recent adventure.

Our last story starts in a courtyard at 50 Vladimirskaya, in front of the National Opera of Ukraine, in Kiev. It was one of my favorite buildings in the world, prior to the war, maybe still is.

"Jack! Jack!"

"You hear that?" my American associate asks me.

"Jack, yak spravy?"

It's a sunny morning. Spring, tulips cheerful in gardens. I see a man on a bicycle.

"Mr. Mayor!" Jack hollers. "How you been?"

The man on the bike is Vitali Klitschko, mayor of Kiev. I know him as Dr. Ironfist, the six-foot-seven PhD who lost to Lennox Lewis on his way to becoming WBC and WBO heavyweight champion of the world. I'm thinking, *Wow, Klitschko? Maybe Jack will introduce me, because we have so much in common. I'll tell him about fighting Big Bob at Finley's, hanging with Chuck Liddell in a greenroom, some late-night show.*

"Come to the office!" the mayor yells. "Come see me!"

"Yes, sir! Keep up the good work!"

I want to tell the champ about the time I saw Bob Dylan in a fluorescent-orange jumpsuit, sparring with L. Bellagio in the basement of a synagogue in Santa Monica. It was a pretty-boy gym with couches and a leopard skin rug, and David Paul was working the focus mitts when this small man walked out, shuffling. I knew it was him, but what do you say in a situation like that? It was wilder than that time I ended up eating radish sprouts at Moon Zappa's restaurant, Lumpy Gravy, with Madonna in a boiled wool cowl.

"Jesus Christ, Jack." I laughed. "Is there a human being on this planet you do not know?"

We were in town for meetings because George's Rapid DNA instruments were really catching on. Ukraine needed our technology, fighting Russians in the Crimea, and Jack knew all the buyers. Michael Lee called Kiev a greenfield opportunity; I went there often.

"What time is your flight tomorrow?" Jack asked me.

"I leave at nine for Dubai; you leave at three for Tbilisi. We meet Saturday in Bahrain. I booked us into the Metropole, our first meeting is a hookah bar called Isis Café."

"Isis Café?"

"Is what it is."

Jack. How the hell do I describe Jack? He grew up in Montana, on a barren ranch, so poor he walked to school hungry. He worked his way up through the army to the state legislature before moving to D.C. as chief of staff for a U.S. senator. He wrote well, raised millions, fixed scandals, married the highest-ranking African American member of the Trump administration, made a name for himself in the Republican Party. He was a businessman who once got knocked cold by a descendant of a Mongol prince while drinking homemade vodka in a goatskin yurt. When he got up, he told the guy he hit like a girl; they were friends for life.

Jack was six foot four, 285 pounds with a caveman beard. He drank gin neat for breakfast from juice tumblers, quoted Reagan, was descended from Brahmas. The guy could take a punch.

"Walk faster," he told me. "I refuse to be late."

Our first meeting was with a colonel in a group called White Wolves, a little-known paramilitary unit within the Security Service of Ukraine, formerly KGB, now called SBU. When not fighting Russians in the Donbas, this colonel ran a medical supply business, and our technology dovetailed with his plans to identify Putin's insurgents who were creeping in as locals.

"White Wolves are Cossacks," he explained the first time we met. "From the Caspian Steppe, Ukrainians, not Russians. We are a warrior race; did they teach you that in school?"

"No, Colonel, not that I remember."

He told me how he had served in the Red Army but had moved home to Kiev so he could do his part fighting imperialist aggression.

Then, later, after we were friends, he presented me with this crazy-cool sniper rifle with a high-dollar scope. He said it was a gift of good faith regarding future interactions. Then we got into his van and drove several hours south, to where his men were running live-fire training exercises in a gravel pit. I found the White Wolves to be some of the most courageous fighters I had ever met, and though I can't offer details, I can say I'm not surprised that almost all of them are now dead.

Russians are brutal. But I digress.

After our meeting, Jack and I met a forty-two-year-old expat named Phillip for drinks at a rooftop bar. I remember looking out over the city, wondering why Soviets painted everything pastel colors, only to let them fade streaky gray over time. Phillip invited us to dinner with his wife, a stunning finance executive. Then, after dinner, we met two middle-aged men in suits who took us to a strip club. The first thing they asked me was if I knew Hunter Biden.

I said I had never heard of the man. They nodded.

"You like this woman?" he asked, referring to the entertainment, about three drinks into our acquaintance.

"Sure," I answered. "She's very flexible."

"I have cash for private dances," he told me. "But for sex, you are on your own."

And it was all about business, of course, but that is how you know you're dealing with an intelligence agency; they have lots of cash and weird rules about spending it.

I got up the next morning feeling pretty good about things, and made a couple of calls, including to Knackers, who wanted me to meet him in Tel Aviv if I had time. He had hot leads, he said, and I had met his connections there, so I told him I would try. Big Jim was back in Johannesburg, so I called him for updates, had a nice coffee, went to my barber.

Later that day, I flew from Kiev to Tbilisi, where my contact in the State Security Service of Georgia liked to talk about the Golden State Warriors while drinking absinthe near my favorite rug shop on the Kura River. Then to Bahrain to share hookahs with men wearing dishdasha at the Isis Café. After that, Jack and I went to Erbil, the oldest city in the world, a perfect circle of light in the dark Iraqi desert. Then back to Istanbul, on our way to Ankara, where we met to sip tea in the second-floor office of a former Turkish general.

"Proximity fuses?" I asked.

"Don't worry. It's all legal," Jack told me. "Your phone is off, right?"

The office looked out over Ankara, which looks like Santa Monica, French doors open to the street. There was a water bubbler and a tea service of dainty glass cups on the table, two visitors in overstuffed chairs, the general at a desk, me and Jack on a red vinyl couch.

"Mark Forty-eight, model zero?" he asked, reading from a long shopping list of weapons.

"We need the sixteen-inch barrels. Can you get the sixteen-inch barrels?"

"Yes."

"Not Chinese."

"I did not say Chinese."

It was a gorgeous day, and we were there to sell Rapid DNA, but Jack was a complex man, and we lived complex lives in a complex world, which is one of the reasons we got along.

"Grenades. We need grenades, but they have to be M67."

"Shouldn't be a problem. Lemme make a call."

One of the two buyers, tall and skinny, was wearing a polyester suit with a disco collar open so you could see gold chains in his chest hair. He had a walleye and a five o'clock shadow at ten in the morning. The other guy was fat with two prominent scars. He stank.

"COO? EAR-Ninety-Nine?" the skinny man asked.

"We cover end user certificates to Basarabi," Jack said. "It is your move to Sudan."

And, yes, it was a full-on arms deal going down on the second floor of a general's house in Ankara, Turkey. You learn to roll with things, and this was not my gig, so I sat there until we finished our tea. Then the general drove us to a building ten minutes away. There was a large table with eight chairs, two Turks seated, one standing at the window. He did not turn around.

Everyone shook hands and exchanged cards except for the guy at the window, and I laughed a little under my breath, because tradecraft involves acting, but this guy was a goof. He waited silently staring out the window until I had finished my presentation. Then he walked across the room and stood close enough that I could smell Baharat on his breath.

"Tell me, please," he said in unaccented English. "How does an FBI agent interview CIA director James Woolsey on CNBC and think he can fly here to sell me biometric devices?"

"My life is transparent." I shrugged.

You have to think on your feet in situations like that, because Erdogan fields one of the most ruthless organizations in NATO, and tradecraft also occasionally involves blindfolds and watersports in windowless rooms.

"Your enemies have our technology. So should you."

Thirty-six hours later, I was back in London having a vodka drink at the Chiltern Firehouse in Marylebone with associates who may or may not have included a member of DEVGRU Black Squadron, two men from MI5, a constable with the Metropolitan Police.

"They have a Krispy Kreme donut stand at the Istanbul airport," one of them said.

"Two." I nodded. "Constantine must be rolling over in his grave."

For those who have not stayed at the Chiltern Firehouse, there is a key at the front desk that unlocks a special door to the parapet, which in the nineteenth century was the second-tallest promontory in the United Kingdom, behind St. Paul's. The view at night is spectacular.

"Want to hear something crazy?" I asked the guys. It was a beautiful evening; you could see the Millennium Wheel glimmering over the soft glow of the Tate. "I was living in South Kensington in 1980 when the 22nd stormed Princess Gate during the Iran hostage siege. We heard the breaches; I watched the whole deal go down."

"To men in the fight," the SEAL said.

We toasted.

Then back to D.C. for a change of clothes, up to Montana for the weekend, a short flight to our offices in a large Midwest city. After work, I dropped my bag at the Holiday Inn Express and walked across the parking lot to TGI Fridays to meet a former Task Force Orange Arabist who had taken a lateral to the CIA. We ordered calamari.

"What do you know, brother?"

"Same old."

The place was filling up, so we moved to a booth, and one beer turned to three. My friend used his true name in our associations, but you can call him Paco. Paco Rabanne.

"What did he look like?" he asked me. "The guy standing by the window."

I told him, then described the other two thugs, provided a long list of names, dates, travel times, license plate numbers, GPS coordinates, food preferences, scars, marks, and tattoos, everything I could think of that might help the CIA's National Resources Division keep Americans safe, because I am a patriot, and the intelligence community is not always what you think.

"How did it go in Tbilisi?"

I told him.

"Any news from Erbil?"

I filled him in.

"Copy that."

When we were done, Paco Rabanne drove me to a nearby strip joint, where we found a two-top near the corner stage. And lest you think me even less a role model, I will note that briefings are most confidential where the music is loud, the lighting is dim, and the women are naked, with no place to hide recorders. Best of all, it's easy to spot interlopers in a gentlemen's club because if a dude is paying attention to you, he ain't there for the dancing.

"You know, I'm thinking about checking out," Paco confided, after we had completed all our official interactions. "Got any tips for retirement?"

"Retirement? You?"

He was a true hero of the shadow wars, but he had been at war a long, long time.

"Tell you what, brother," I said. "Play golf, go fishing, buy a dog, take a nap. After about a week of that shit, you're going to call me, and we'll meet up in Mombasa. I know a place."

And here is where I make my revelation. My grand confession.

"It never goes away, brother," I told him. "Not for guys like us. Once you've been behind the curtains, there's no life but the stage. You will never, ever truly give it up."

He thought about this for a while; so did I. Then he pointed to one of the dancers. "What about her?" he asked me.

"Sure," I answered. "She's very flexible."

"Cool, because I have cash for dances. But for sex, you are on your own."

21

The Heartland

[TODAY]

Thursday nights, I front the house band at a bar called Lindbergh's. The stage looks down one of those perfect shotgun-straight rooms you just love to play. It's the oldest place in town, an 1880s back bar carved out of mahogany with beveled mirrors, chandeliers hanging from ceilings made of tin. It has wood floors worn black from dancing, framed photos of bands that have played there since the seventies, a full light show, an awesome PA. The walls are covered with large oil portraits of legendary talents: Bob Dylan and Hank Williams, Johnny Cash, Tom Waits.

There's a surfboard mounted vertically on the west wall, one of those classic seven-foot-four Gerry Lopez Bolts that I shipped back from Bali and gave the owners. There's a huge family-style table made of ironwood from an old Indonesian fishing boat that I designed myself, hoping to place it in a castle. The castle hasn't worked out, but tonight it is surrounded by a dozen members of my family and assorted friends who have come out to jam.

The band is called Stone Pages, mostly classic rock covers, Allman Brothers to Zeppelin. It's me and my buddy Jeff Reikoff up front, with Cara Villapiano and the legendary Tom Wittrock on guitar. My buddy Mo and I started the band in 2015, and we have played everywhere from Memphis and Nashville to London and New York, but he's out of town at the moment, so we're doing our best to cover his parts. Fortunately, we have Dan Penovich on drums, Sean Clavin,

John Merrifield on keys, Ray Bridges on bass. All consummate pros.

And it's one of those magical nights that musicians dream about, everybody dancing and smiling, that special feeling you get when the whole night is tuned to concert pitch, the players and their patrons.

Jesse is holding down the bar with a star named Ayce, Cory working the door, which is cool, because he is also a talented realist who painted the portraits on the walls, now paying rent between commissions. And you know I love the Talking Heads, so we're balls deep in "Once in a Lifetime," my favorite song. Sometimes I think I waste my time jotting prose because music is the language of the world, and David Byrne is its prophet. He wrote my arc in three chorused verses.

And you may ask yourself, "Well, how did I get here?"

It's the oddest feeling when you're up there onstage, trying to peer out through the Rosco gels, down into the crowd, surfing the rhythms that hold us all together, the vibrations of the cosmos pulsing in identifiable patterns. Notes and rests, just notes and rests.

And if you have performed a song enough times, there is this special comfort you drift off into, allowing yourself deeper understanding of time, its movements. It's a Zen kinda thing, like I remember drinking Basque wine in Torremolinos while the feral cats howled, sea breezes wafting north from Morocco, salty warm through open windows. Reading *Siddhartha*.

You may ask yourself, "Where does that highway go to?"

Sometimes, in those moments, I think about other stages I have played, like that belly dancer gig in Yemen; Arlene's Grocery; the flatbed trailer in Oxford, Maine, where Uncle Mike busted out that man's teeth with a revolver. I think about venues on my wish list: the Budokan, Red Rocks, the Beacon. If I could go back in time, I would play the Fillmore, the Royal Albert Hall, Whisky a Go Go, the Golden Bear, backing Bonnie Raitt. I never dreamed about playing Woodstock because it happened only once and it is sacred, but sometimes I think about the stage at 315 Bowery Street, which is sacred, too, but for some reason, I got to play there.

CBGB, the birthplace of punk. It was the reunion of White Thunder, one night only.

"I can't believe this, Whit," Joe's girlfriend, Lindsey, was saying. CBGB. She was crying. "We all thought you would be the first one to die."

And I'm done talking about death, but you may remember the card game with Brad Pitt and my mentioning a guy named Steve Scher, whose name is tattooed on my arm. I cannot wrap up a story about my life without mentioning his. Scher was the first in our New York crew to turn fifty, and he was a restaurateur who knew absolutely everyone, so he threw a big party at a place called Rain. I flew all the way from Bali to wish him well.

L. Bellagio said, "We need a drummer!"

Then DJ Abby Klein walked in and sat down in the front row with Claudia Vick and Connie Britton and some famous but less talented performers. Most everyone was drunk and crying. Joe stood off to the side, wearing a Bowery Hotel bathrobe over his James Perse T-shirt with turndown slippers. He was necking a bottle of some Gran Cru. Mo was there; and Baru, Baldi, Richie, and Tobes, a whole mob of friends and family, because everyone loved Stevie.

I remember the lights dimming, the room growing quiet, and Joyce Varvatos walked up to introduce the band, because her husband, John, had turned CBGB into a store selling vintage stereos and thousand-dollar jeans.

"I am pleased to welcome a legendary band to the stage tonight," she said. "This is their only U.S. appearance, and we are so fortunate to have them. Let's give it up for White Thunder!"

Everybody clapped, and I turned to L. Bellagio, who hugged Joyce and took the mic.

"This is for Stevie," he said.

L. Bellagio couldn't sing for shit, but he was a damned good actor, so we launched into "Sweet Home Alabama," which made no sense, because Scher loved the Grateful Dead. I was playing a Les Paul with a Marshall half stack; I think it was a Plexi.

"Big wheels keep on burning," L. Bellagio started singing. "Carry my bone when I am."

I looked over at the bass player, a twenty-two-year-old stock clerk.

He was hanging deep in the pocket like it was the Grammys. I don't think the drummer actually knew how to play drums; I don't even know where he came from. Might have been the doorman.

"Singing songs about the . . . something, something . . . Alabamy miss my friend."

L. Bellagio was getting kinda pitchy, but White Thunder was loud and proud, and nobody cared about getting the words right, because everyone was sobbing. The girls were crying, the guys were crying, people walking down the street might have been crying, just because it was so fucking sad. Even thinking about it now is tough, but I had sworn (in writing) when Ralph Payette broke my thumb, that I would never cry again, so I was choking it back.

I have gotten ahead of myself again, so let me remind you that Steve Scher is the guy from the Brad Pitt card game at the Mercer Hotel, the name tattooed on my arm, the famous restaurateur who is still dead as of this writing.

"Fucking Scher," I could see Joe mumbling. "Always gotta be the center of attention."

I bring this up because I was supposed to be the first one to die. Everybody knew it, including me. It was not until Steve Scher passed away that I started to understand the childishness of my morbid games. He had been a lawyer, a gambler, a lover of music and golf and women and kids. He had loved his wife, Aimee; and his son, Hudson; and his friends and his mother and father and his brother, Bobby. He had loved me. I loved him.

Death never crossed his mind; it just stole him.

I always thought I would end up a writer. Prior to my time in Somalia, I wrote every day. But something changed deep within me while I was gone, and when I got back, I felt blocked. I wrote nothing at all for fifteen years. Not a word. No poems or prose, not a song.

Falling off the face of the earth had been easy. When Little, Brown killed my last novel, for valid reasons, I just went faster and faster, running from all the demons I thought were trying to hunt me down. And that worked in Africa and Asia, because both are giant expanses of nobody-gives-a-fuck. It helped that I was a child alone in winter, born to deprivation, able to go days without water, weeks without food. I was accomplished at sleeping standing up, nourishing myself on dreams long after the dreams had ended.

But then one day, during Covid, when no one was traveling, Rosie walked me into a windowless room with nothing but a desk and a chair. She said people who live unusual lives have an obligation to record them, that any man who wrote poems on napkins while cleaning behind the Fry-o-Lator at Bilbo Baggins could always make a comeback.

She said beach girls from Orange County do not normally marry ski racers from New Hampshire, especially when they show up on a Greyhound bus with thirty-seven dollars in their pocket and paddle into the Wedge wearing chinos. Good people still loved me, she said, despite my failures. Life is not a zero-sum game.

I called L. Bellagio, who is a great writer himself and knew me well. I asked him how I should go about writing a memoir where there were no heroes, no stories of inspiration.

He said, "Whit, nobody cares about you running around the world shooting people in the head. They want to know what it's like to go down that hole, come out stronger. That's your story right there."

Rosie started digging up boxes full of things I had tucked away, important parts of myself in albums and journals. I found that picture of the kid in the snow, the one with Uncle Mike and the sled and all that business about some spry winter jay. I wanted to know what happened to that boy, so I went back to Franconia, where I had grown up, and I climbed Mount Lafayette, as I had so many times. I stood on that summit, in the cellar hole of an old hotel, looked down through popcorn clouds while remembering that first flight in the Grumman Goose, shadows drifting over glacier-rounded hills. I counted rivers with Indian names like Pemigewasset and Merrimack wandering off in no particular direction, only to stall and pool in valleys lined by granite cliffs faded gray. Birch forests spilling out of talus slopes, a lumpy quilt of Dartmouth green and logger burn, second-cut hay dotted with heifers and calves.

I looked over to the Cannon cliffs where my dad rescued climbers, the blank slab where the Old Man of the Mountain had stood watch since the beginning of time, only to fall one day without notice, because that's what symbols do. I remember where I was when my dad called to give me the news.

In that moment, I thought about mortals and gods, realized that life is a glimmer of pixie dust we were never meant to understand. A white star cluster.

To be honest, it never occurred to me that I would grow old, or that others would pass young—like Big Jim, who arrested Saddam Hussein, only to keel over walking his dog. Jack died poolside in Bahrain, selling grenades while drinking gin. My brother Mike died a hero. Uncle Harold died rich but alone; Uncle Mike drank himself to death surrounded by mobs who loved him.

We shot his ashes out of a cannon.

Eventually, I came to realize that I have made too much of secrets. Secrets are silly things humans conjure and cling to because they make us feel special in a mundane world. In my experience, the only secret is God. God is love. We fail, though not forever.

In the end, I am a kid who saw the world from a hilltop in New Hampshire, kneeling at the hearth with a bunch of *New York Times* articles about wealth, the power of dreams, and the CIA.

I'm a romantic who leaned on Emily Dickinson for advice on love, Hemingway for perspectives on war, Conrad for guidance on what lies at the end of the river. Poor advice, in my opinion.

One of the great things about "Once in a Lifetime" is that it ends in crescendo.

It's a blast if you are playing in the band, one of those songs that explains it all, the mysteries of the world, the human condition. You can feel life throbbing through the floor, the weight of lives suspended in time, gravity just a tether that keeps everyone from shooting up to the heavens, because the sky is already full of stars. I thought about earth, fire, water, and air; human beings connected in joy via melody and shots of tequila.

Then my buddy Dan started tapping glissades down the ring toms, with BJ Rossi sitting in on congas. Mick and Paige were up getting some rug, with Chelsea and Collin and their friends doing young people dances, bobbing their heads with their hands in the air as my grandson, Brody, tried not to look embarrassed. I saw Jake sitting at the ironwood table with Rosie, who has always been the heart of the party but not much of a dancer.

Jeff cranked up his Telecaster, and Tom stepped into his Les Paul, and I was singing like it was the anthem Jesus would have chosen if he'd owned a guitar.

Once in a lifetime . . .

And then, of course, it ended, because all songs end, but it was the last song of the set, so the lights dimmed and I put my amp on standby, and all the dancers went back to their tables. The guys in the band passed around some high-fives and toweled down, and the house music came up, playing Gary Clark, Jr. I stepped off the stage and said hi to people, as you do, then went over to the family, and we hugged it out.

But you get thirsty playing a big night in a crowded room, so after a while, I went over to the bar and ordered a drink: Vodka-soda-hold-the-vodka.

I should have been enjoying the magic of that moment, the span of my life played out in a song. But for some reason, I was thinking about twelve-year-old Macallan, neat, in a Solo Cup by a pool in Chiang Mai. I was thinking about all those otherworld layovers where I had stepped back from the thrill of live performance to stare at myself in some backbar mirror, pretending my name was whatever the mission required.

I sat there for the longest time, trying to find meaning in that reflection, some sense that the child alone in winter could have found his way from the Granite State to places that don't exist on a map.

And just when I was about to let go of those old adventures and return to my crew, a beautiful girl sidled up and sat down beside me. She said her name was Emma, that she hated cats and planned to have a layover for a couple of days because there was so much to do in Missouri. She thought it might be nice to check out Bass Pro Shops, do some sightseeing, balance her chi.

I told her my name was Caesar, that I would be flying out the next day, that I didn't like cats, either. I told her I had never heard of Bass Pro Shops; asked about her family, where she'd gone to school, life's most embarrassing moments, whether she understood cricket. She smiled once or twice, dodging my attempts at humor.

"Could you help me out a little bit," I asked her, after a while. "I'm dying over here."

"All right," she said. "Try again, Two Truths and a Lie."

"What?"

"Two Truths and a Lie. The game. You tell me two truths and one lie; I try to figure out which is which. Then vice versa. You go first."

I looked at her for a long minute, attempting to size her up. The basics were obvious, because these gigs always went pretty much the same way.

"I have been to seventy-three countries," I told her. "My grandmother's name was Mildred. I once got eaten by a grizzly."

"A grizzly? You never got eaten by a grizzly."

"Fair enough. Your turn."

"I can ride a bike no hands, I'm the tallest girl in my class . . . my favorite singer is Miley Cyrus."

"Wow, that's a tough one," I told her. "Miley Cyrus, huh? Is that a six-pack name?"

"Six-pack name?" she said. "Come on, Grampa, what the heck is that?"

In that moment, I heard a voice call *Chrisameechie.*

It was like he was standing next to me, Uncle Mike, my youth and its resolution connected to his through time. I felt the weight of lies and bullets, things the government had taught me to bear but never explained. I heard the whisper of currents, deep beneath the ocean, the loneliness of a life among spies, a truth that hides in drowning. I smelled the smoke of fires that had scarred then cleansed me. I tasted great gulps of life few would swallow.

Chrisameechie . . .

And then Rose waved from the table, and I turned away from the mirror. I threw Emma over my shoulder and tickled her and walked back to where I belonged, as she yelled "Grampa!"

In that moment it all made sense, the beginning and the end and all those hard, hard places in between. We are all born into this world anonymous, free to make decisions but bound to what those decisions make us.

I will always be that child alone in winter. But I now have a name, and that name sustains me. I am no longer anonymous, not to myself.

Acknowledgments

I would like to thank my friend David Vigliano for taking a chance on an out-of-print writer. I want to thank the brilliant Andrea Walker for her insights, patience, and grace. Thank you Mark Warren for all you have done to make this book possible; all the wonderful people at Random House who have brought it to print.

From one anonymous male to another, I want to thank my friend GSL, a great patron of the arts, without whom this book might never have been finished.

I want to thank the legions of people who have shaped my life without ever understanding how. I'm grateful to you individually, though I cannot name one soul without overlooking another. I believe you feel me.

Finally, I want to thank my family for unconditional love in the face of insurmountable odds. We fail, though not forever.

ABOUT THE AUTHOR

CHRISTOPHER WHITCOMB is a writer, entrepreneur, and former FBI Hostage Rescue Team sniper with operational experience in more than thirty countries. He is the bestselling author of *Cold Zero: Inside the FBI Hostage Rescue Team* and the novels *Black* and *White*. He has written for numerous outlets including *The New York Times, GQ,* Netflix, CBS Films, and HBO. He has a BA from Hamilton College and an MA from the University of Virginia.

ABOUT THE TYPE

This book was set in Bembo, a typeface based on an old-style Roman face that was used for Cardinal Pietro Bembo's tract *De Aetna* in 1495. Bembo was cut by Francesco Griffo (1450–1518) in the early sixteenth century for Italian Renaissance printer and publisher Aldus Manutius (1449–1515). The Lanston Monotype Company of Philadelphia brought the well-proportioned letterforms of Bembo to the United States in the 1930s.